Dr. Brook Taylor's Method of Perspective Made Easy

Frontispiece.

W. Hogarth inv. et delin. — L. Sullivan sculp.

Whoever makes a DESIGN *without the Knowledge of* PERSPECTIVE *will be liable to such Absurdities as are shewn in this* Frontispiece.

Thomas Barnard

Dr. *BROOK TAYLOR*'s METHOD of PERSPECTIVE Made Eaſy,

Both in THEORY and PRACTICE.

In TWO BOOKS.

BEING

An Attempt to make the ART of PERSPECTIVE eaſy and familiar;

TO

Adapt it intirely to the ARTS of DESIGN;

AND

To make it an entertaining STUDY to any GENTLEMAN who ſhall chuſe ſo polite an Amuſement.

By JOSHUA KIRBY, PAINTER.

Illuſtrated with Fifty COPPER PLATES; moſt of which are Engrav'd by the AUTHOR.

The Practice [of Painting] *ought always to be built on a rational Theory, of which* PERSPECTIVE *is both the Guide and the Gate, and, without which, it is impoſſible to ſucceed, either in Deſigning, or in any of the Arts depending thereon.*

Leonardo da Vinci upon Painting, p. 36.

The SECOND EDITION.

IPSWICH: Printed by W. CRAIGHTON, for the AUTHOR.

Sold by the AUTHOR, at the *Golden Eagle* in *Great Queen's-Street, Lincoln's-Inn Fields, London*; and alſo by J. and P. KNAPTON, on *Ludgate Hill*; T. OSBORN and Co. in *Gray's-Inn*; T. and T. LONGMAN, in *Pater-noſter Row*; R. and J. DODSLEY, in *Pall-Mall*; W. MEADOWS, in *Cornhill*; W. OWEN, at *Temple-Bar*; J. SWAN, near *Northumberland-Houſe* in the *Strand*; F. NOBLE, in *King's-Street, Covent-Garden*; and J. NOBLE, in St. *Martin's Court*. At CAMBRIDGE, by W. THURLBOURN; at OXFORD, by J. GREEN, Engraver; at NORWICH, by J. GLEED; and at IPSWICH, by W. CRAIGHTON.

MDCCLV.

TO

Mr. HOGARTH.

SIR,

IF your extensive Knowledge and Genius in the Art of Painting did not entitle you to a Dedication of the following THEORY of PERSPECTIVE, the great Obligations which I am under for your Friendship and Favour, would claim not only this, but every other Token of my Gratitude and Affection. But this Work in a peculiar Manner has a Right to your Patronage and Protection, as it was YOU who first encouraged me to write upon the Subject: And if it has any Merit, the Publick, in a great Measure, are obliged to you for it.

I shall not follow the common Method of Dedicators, by attempting a Panegyrick upon your

your amiable Qualifications; which might appear like Flattery, and offend your Modeſty: I ſhall only beg Leave to ſay, that your own inimitable Performances are greater Inſtances of your Genius in the Arts of Deſign, your Knowledge of the Human Paſſions, and your Contempt of Vice and Folly, than it is in my Power to expreſs; and that,

I am, SIR,

With the greateſt Eſteem and Gratitude,

Your moſt obliged,

And obedient Servant,

JOSHUA KIRBY.

A LIST *of* SUBSCRIBERS.

N. B. *Those whose Names are mark'd thus* * *are* Members *of the Academy of* Painting, Sculpture, Architecture, *&c. in* London.

A

SIR Thomas Allen, Bart.
Nathaniel Acton, Esq;
Mr. George Adams, Mathematical-Instrument-Maker
Mr. David Adkinson
Mr. William Aldrich
*Mr. Allen, Painter
Mr. Richard Allick, Painter
Mr. Henry Anderson
Mr. Thomas Ailing
Mr. H. Atkinson
Mr. James Audley.

B

Right Hon. Earl of Bute
John Bagnall, Esq;
William Baintun, Esq;
Mr. Andrew Baldrey, Painter
Mr. John Banks
Mr. T. Bardwell, Painter
Miles Barne, Esq;
Mr. John Barnard, Ship-Builder
Mr. Christopher Barry
*Mr. James Basire, Engraver
Mr. R. Bateman, Painter
Mr. W. Bathurst
John Battie, Esq;
Mr. John Bayley, Engraver
The Rev. Mr. Charles Beaumont
Mr. James Bencraft
Mr. John Bennet, Mathematical-Instrument-Maker
The Rev. Mr. Ralph Blois
Mr. William Blois
*Mr. Jacob Bonneau, Drawing-Master, 6 Books.
Botesdale Book-Club.
Mr. Thomas Bowell
Mr. George Bowling, Mason
Mr. Edward Bowman
The Rev. P. Bracebridge, D. D.
Mr. Bernard Broadbelt
Mr. Richard Brompton, Painter
Philip Broke, Esq;
Rev. Mr. John Broke
Mr. Wm. Browne, Architect
Mr. John Browne
Mr. Joseph Browne
Mr. Daniel Browne
Mr. Nathaniel Bucke
Mr. John Burrel
James Burrough, Esq; F. R. S.
Mr. William Butcher, Engraver
Robert Butler, Esq;
The Rev. Mr. Robert Buxton
Mrs. Ann Buxton

C

Turner Calvert, Esq;
Rev. Mr. Richard Canning
Mr. William Castleton
The Rev. Mr. Philip Carter
The Rev. Mr. Samuel Carter
*Mr. Thomas Carter, Statuary
*Mr. Charles Catton, Painter
*Mr. Wm. Cazal, Drawing-Master
Richard Charlton, Esq;
*Mr. Charles Cheere
The Rev. Mr. Christian
The Rev. Mr. Church
Mr. George Church, Bricklayer
John Clarke, Esq;
Mr. William Clarke
Mr. William Clarke
Mr. Samuel Cleverly
The Rev. Mr. Henry Close
Mr. Robert Clowes
Mr. Butler Clowes, Engraver
The Rev. Mr. John Clubb
*Mr. Francis Coates, Painter
Thomas Coggeshall, Esq;
*Mr. William Collins, Statuary
Mr. William Collingwood
Mr. John Cooke
Mr. Joseph Cooper, jun. Painter
Mr. John Cooper, jun.
Mr. T. Coopley
The Rev. Mr. Daniel Copland
Mr. Henry Copland, Engraver

Mr. John Cornish, Painter
Mr. William Craighton
Mr. Edward Crane, Painter
Mr. Richard Crawley
Philip Crespigny, Esq;

D

The Right Hon. Earl of Dysart
John Dade, Esq;
Dr. William Dade
*Mr. Richard Dalton, Painter
Sir Francis Dashwood, Bart.
Mr. Eleazer Davy
James Dawkins, Esq;
Henry Dawson, L. L. D.
Mr. Richard Dawson, Painter
Mr. R. Deard
Peter Delme, Esq;
Robert Delton, Esq;
Mr. Arthur Devis, Painter
Mr Robert Dingley
Mr. P Dixon
*Mr. John Donowell, Architect
Mr. F. Drummond

E

Theodore Ecclestone, Esq;
*Mr. John Eccardt, Painter
Mileson Edgar, Esq;
Robert Edgar, Esq;
Mr. G. L. Edwards
Mr. George Elliott
Mr. Robert Ellison
Mr. William Elsden, Carver
Mr. J. Etty
Mr. T. Evans.

F

Sir Cordel Firebrace, Bart.
Mr. Andrew Ferguson
Mr. Joseph Finley
Mr. Thomas Finley, Architect
Mr. Zachariah Fiske, Painter
Mr. William Fokard
Mr. Ingham Foster
The Rev. Mr. Richard Fowller
Mr. George Fowley
Mr. Richard Francklin
Mr. J. Francklin
Mr. William Franks
Mr. M. Freake
Cha. Frederick, Esq; Surveyor General of his Majesty's Board of Ordnance.

G

Sir Thomas Gooch, Bart.
*Mr. Thomas Gainsborough, Painter
Mr. Thomas Gardner
Mr. James Gillingham
Mr. G. Glynn
Mr. John Gorham
Mr. John Gravenor
The Hon. Col. Gray
Mr. James Green, Engraver
*Mr. Charles Grignion, Engraver
Joseph Grove, Esq;
*Mr. John Gwyn, Architect.

H

Mr. Hailstone
Mr. Gavin Hamilton, Painter
Mr. Hamilton, Architect
Mr. William Hammond
Mr. William Hammond
Mr. Hammond, Painter
Mr. John Hammond
Mr. Hannan, Painter
Robert Harland, Esq;
Mr. Josiah Harris
Mr. Canham Hart
Mr. William Havard
*Mr. Francis Hayman, Painter
*Mr. Richard Hayward, Statuary
Mr. Nathaniel Hedges
Mr. Thomas Henderly
The Hon. Nicholas Herbert, Esq;
The Rev. Mr. Thomas Hewett
Mr. Joshua Highmore, Painter
Mr. Edward Highmoor
Mr. John Hingeston
The Rev. Mr. Robert Hingeston
The Rev. Mr. Peter Hingeston
Benjamin Hoadley, M. D.
Mr. William Hoare, Painter
*Mr. Hogarth, Painter, 6 Books
Rowland Holt, Esq;
*Mr. Nathaniel Hone, Painter
Mr. Peter Houltum, Painter
The Rev. Mr. Henry Hubbard, Fellow of Emmanuel College, Cambridge.
Mr. Thomas Hudson, Painter
Mr. Hunt.

J

Mr. Samuel Jacomb
Mr. Jeffreys
Mr. R. Ingham
Mr. Thomas Jolly
Mr. Owen Jones
Henry Iſaacs, Eſq;
Mr. Richard Jupp, jun.
Mr. Bartholomew Juſtinier

K

Sir John Kemp, Bart.
*Mr. Wm. Keable, Painter, 3 Books
Samuel Kent, Eſq;
Mr. Samuel Kilderbee
Mr. Dover Kilderbee
Mr. William Kirby
Mr. Knapton, Painter.

L

Sir James Lowther, Bart.
Sir Richard Lloyd, Knt.
Mr. George Lambert, Painter
Mr. J. P. Lamborn
Mrs. Lancaſter
Mr. Robert Lane
Mr. Robert Larwood
Robert Leman, Eſq;
Offley Lewis, Eſq;
Mr. William Leſlie
Library of Catherine Hall, Cambridge
——— CorpusChriſti College, ditto
——— Emmanuel College, ditto
——— Jeſus College, ditto
——— St. Peter's College, ditto
——— Trinity College, ditto
Mr. Littleton
Richard Savage Lloyd, Eſq;
The Rev. Roger Long, D. D. Maſter of Pembroke Hall, Camb. Lowndes's Profeſſor of Aſtronomy, and F.R.S.
Mr. J. Lovatt
William Lynch, Eſq;

M

Right Hon. Lord Viſcount Middleton
*Mr. Robert Maberly, Painter
*Mr. James M'Ardell, Engraver, 2 Books
*Mr. Thomas Major, 2 Books
Mr. Jonathan Mallet
Mr. G. Manning
Mr. John Manning
Mr. Marquand, Architect
Mr. Marquois
Mr. Marſden
Mr. Thomas Martin, F. R. S.
Mr. Joſeph Martyr
The Rev. Charles Maſon, D.D. Senior Fellow of Trinity Coll. and Woodwardian Lecturer of the Univerſity of Cambridge
The Rev. Mr. Maſterman
Mr. John Meadowe
John Middlemore, Eſq;
Mr. Charles Middleton, Chaſer
*Mr. J. S. Müller, Engraver
Mr. T. Miller
Robert Milner, Eſq;
——— Montague, Eſq;
Mr. T. Moore.
Mr. James Morris
Mr. Benjamin Morris
*Mr. G. M. Moſer, Chaſer, 2 Books
Mr. Thomas Mulliner
Hutchenſon Mure, Eſq;

N

Right Rev. Lord Biſhop of Norwich
Hon. Richard Savage Naſſau, Eſq;
*Mr. F. M. Newton, Painter
Mr. Nichols
Mr. Edward Nickſon
Mr. Robert Stiles Norman

O

Robert Onebye, Eſq;
Mr. John Oldfield, Writing-Maſter
Mr. Thomas Oſborne, Bookſeller.

P

Mr. Thomas Paddington
*Mr. James Paine, Architect
Mr. John Palgrave
Mr. Thomas Palmer, Plaiſterer
Mr. John Parſons
Mr. Robert Parſons, Carver
Mr. Francis Patton, Engraver
Mr. Thomas Patty, Carver
Mr. Pennie, Painter
Mr. R. Penniſon
Mr. Francis Perry
Mr. F. Peters
Mr. A. Pond, F. R. S.

Mr. Peter Pullyn
Mr. Robert Pyle, Painter

Q

His Grace the Duke of Queensbury

R

His Grace the Duke of Rutland
Sir John Rous, Bart.
*Mr. Benjamin Radcliffe
Humphry Rant, Esq;
Mr. John Redgrave, Architect
The Rev. Mr. William Reeve
Mr. E. Reeves, Carver
*Mr. Joshua Renolds, Painter
Mr. Nicholas Revett
Mr. William Richards
Mr. Richards, Painter
*Mr. Peter Roberts, Chaser
*Mr. Edward Rooker, Engraver
Mr J. Rose, Plaisterer
*Mr. F. L. Roubiliac, Statuary
Capt. Robert Rowning
The Rev. Mr. Tobias Rustat.

S

Mr. Thomas Sanby, Draughtsman to his Royal Highness the Duke of Cumberland
Mr. P. Sanby
*Mr. Samuel Scott, Painter
Mr. Scullard
Mr. Seldon
Mr. Seton, Engraver
*Mr. Seton, jun.
*John Shackelton, Esq; Principal Painter to his Majesty
John Sheppard, Esq;
Mr. Robert Sherman
Mr. George Silverside
Mr. John Simmons, Painter
Mr. John Simpson
Mr. Thomas Singleton, Carver
Mr. John Slarke, Painter
Mr. Henry Smart
The Rev. Mr. Justice Smith
Robert Sparrow, Esq;
Thomas Staunton, Esq;
Mr. Stuart, Painter
Mr. Stevens
Mr. Stevens
Mr. Luke Sullivan, Engraver, 4 Books
Mr. John Swan, Bookseller, 6 Books.

T

The Right Hon. Lord Talbot
Major Taylor
The Hon. Horace Townshend
Philip Thickness, Esq;
Michael Thirkle, Esq;
Mr. R. Trevor
Mr. Samuel Trew
Mr. N. Tucker, Painter

V

The Right Hon. Lord Villieres
The Hon. Edward Vernon, Esq;
E. Venn, M. D.
The Rev. Mr. Edward Ventris
Mrs. Sarah Unett
Mr. Urell
Mr. T. Urling

W

*Mr. Sam. Wale, Painter, 4 Books
Mr. Charles Walford
Mr. William Walford
*Mr. A. Walker, Engraver
John Warburton, Esq; Somerset Herald and F. R. S.
Mr. Francis Warden, Plaisterer
Justly Watson, Esq; Engineer
Mr. Weecks
——— Western, Esq;
Mr. Wieland, Chaser
*Mr. Benjamin Wilson, Painter, and F. R. S. 4 Books
Robert Wilson, Esq; Gray's-Inn
Mr. R. Wilson
*The Rev. Mr. James Wills
Mr. Wolfe, Architect
Mr. Joseph Wood, Engraver
Mr. John Woods
Mr. James Worsdale, Master Painter to his Majesty's Board of Ordnance
Mr. Thomas Wright
William Wyndham, Esq;

Y

*Mr. Yeo, Engraver, 2 Books
Mr. R. Young.

PREFACE.

THE many Treatises already published upon PERSPECTIVE, *may make it appear needless to augment the Number; it is therefore necessary to give the Reasons that induced me to undertake such a Work.*

The Design of the following Treatise, is, by exhibiting a NEW SYSTEM OF PRACTICAL PERSPECTIVE, *to make this hitherto intricate, but useful Art, easy and familiar to every Capacity: And to dress it in the most simple Garb; that its Parts may be clearly seen, and its whole Design (so far as it relates to Painting, &c.) easily understood. For certain it is, that no Subject hath been treated in a worse Manner than this, notwithstanding the many Volumes which have been wrote upon it; some purely Mathematical, and therefore unfit for the generality of Persons who are concerned in the Arts of Design; and others wholly Mechanical, made up of incoherent Schemes, unapplicable Examples, and such a Confusion of unnecessary Lines, as tend only to puzzle and discourage the Learner. My Intention, therefore, is, to steer between the abstruse mathematical Reasoning of some, and the tedious and false Explications of others; and from thence to produce a System of Perspective upon certain and simple Principles, easy to be understood and applied to Practice.*

This is a general Account of the following Work; which is the Product of several Years Study and Application: And how I have succeeded in the Attempt, is submitted to the Candour of every ingenuous Reader. But that such an Undertaking was necessary, is sufficiently testified by the many eminent Painters, and other curious Artists, who persuaded me to prosecute my Design, and have generously encouraged the Publication of this Work.

I have intitled this Treatise DR. BROOK TAYLOR'S PERSPECTIVE, &c. *out of Gratitude to that ingenious Author, for furnishing me with Principles to build upon; and because his, though a very small Pamphlet,*

phlet, is thought the most correct, concise, and comprehensive Book upon the Subject. I have not proceeded exactly in his Method; for that was not agreeable to my Plan: Nor have I explained his Propositions, Theorems, &c. in a regular Manner; since that also was inconsistent with the Order of my Work: But I have had Regard to his Principles in general, so as to make his Meaning more intelligible, and that kind of Perspective of more universal Use. This Book of Dr. TAYLOR's *was first published in the Year* 1715, *and was intitled* LINEAR PERSPECTIVE; *and in the Year* 1719 *he published another small Tract, which he called,* NEW PRINCIPLES OF LINEAR PERSPECTIVE; *and which he intended as an Explanation of his first Treatise. But, notwithstanding both these Treatises are so curious and useful, few have been able to understand his Schemes; and when they have understood them, have been as much puzzled in applying them to Practice. And in the Year* 1738, *Mr.* Hamilton *favoured the World with two Volumes in Folio, intitled* STEREOGRAPHY, *which he has explained in the Manner of Dr.* Taylor, *and which, though a very curious Work, and worthy the Perusal of every good Mathematician, yet, I may venture to affirm, that but very few of those Persons who are Students in the Arts of Design can comprehend it; and were they qualified with a sufficient Stock of Mathematical Knowledge, it would take up more Time than they either could, or would chuse to spare. However, I must frankly acknowledge, that I think it the best System of* Mathematical Projection * *that ever was, or, perhaps, ever will be, made public; and I should be very ungenerous in not confessing that it has been of great Service to me in several Parts of my Work; and that I am indebted to it for some Things which I should never have thought of, had not that ingenious Gentleman pointed them out to me; and I hope, that this publick Acknowledgment will prevent the Imputation of Plagiarism, and be a sufficient Satisfaction for the Liberties which I have taken with his Work.*

* MATHEMATICAL PROJECTION comprehends all kinds of Projection whatsoever; such as the Projection of the Sphere, the Cylinder and its Sections, Conic Sections and the like.

The

The Plan which I have proceeded upon in the Prosecution of my Design, is this: I have divided the whole Work into two Books; the first I have called A COMPLEAT SYSTEM OF PERSPECTIVE, *which contains the Theory and its Application to Practice; and the second,* THE PRACTICE OF PERSPECTIVE, *which contains the practical Part only. This Method of treating the Subject seemed to me the most eligible; because there are some who do not like to take Things for granted, but choose to be convinced by Demonstration, and to have the Reason of Things explained upon certain Principles. For such, I intend the first Book; and for others, who either want Time or Capacity to go regularly through the theoretical Part, I have wrote the second Book; that such Persons may be enabled to determine the Appearance of all Kinds of Objects upon the Picture with the greatest Ease and Expedition: So that the whole together (if I am so happy as to have succeeded in my Attempt) may be called a compleat System of Perspective, so far as it relates to the Art of Painting, &c.*

In the first and second Chapters of the first Book, I suppose my Reader a mere Novice, not only in Perspective, but in every Thing which it is necessary he should know as previous thereto; and therefore I have begun with an Explanation of Mathematical Instruments, and have shewn their different Uses; after which I have explained a few Geometrical Definitions and Propositions, and from thence I have proceeded to shew how to describe (in a mechanical Manner) such Geometrical Figures as may occur in the following Work. And because Perspective is an optical Science, I have given some short Abstracts from the most eminent Writers upon Opticks; by which Means the unlearned Reader will have a general Notion of the Eye and the Nature of Vision, the Reflection and Refraction of the Rays of Light, and of the Cause of Colours. I say the unlearned Reader, because I do not presume to give Instructions to Persons who are well acquainted with the Mathematicks or Philosophy, but only to such as are ignorant in these Matters, but are nevertheless desirous of seeing the Foundations upon which Perspective is built; and therefore, all that hath been hitherto advanced, may be omitted by the learned Part of my Readers, as an imperfect Abstract of what they are infinitely better acquainted with than myself.

The Third Chapter of the ſame Book begins with an Introduction to Perſpective, which I have endeavoured to explain in a familiar Manner, by ſuch Objects as we are every Day converſant with; and then I have proceeded to the Theory, which I have ranged under the following Heads, viz, 1. Of Objects which are in Planes perpendicular to the Picture; 2. Of Objects which are in Planes perpendicular to the Ground; *And* 3. Of Objects which are in Planes inclined to the Ground; *becauſe there are no other Situations in which Objects can be diſpoſed; that is, they muſt be either perpendicular, parallel, or inclined: And every Example, which I have produced, is immediately applied to Practice; and by that means the Theory and Practice are ſo cloſely connected, that they ſerve to explain each other, and to fix both very ſtrongly in the Memory.*

And thus having explained the Theory and general Practice of Perſpective, I have in the fourth Chapter of the ſame Book, conſidered the different Kinds of Perſpective, viz. when the Picture is either perpendicular, parallel, or inclined. The perpendicular Picture is what is commonly made uſe of, and is placed perpendicular to the Ground; the parallel Picture is placed parallel to the Ground, (ſuch as Ceilings, and the like ;) and the inclined Picture, is ſuppoſed to be inclined to the Ground, and is rather more curious than uſeful. I have next given an eaſy Method of determining the Repreſentation of any Objects upon Domes, vaulted Roofs, and other uneven Surfaces, by means of Reticulation or Net-Work; which is all that is contained in this Chapter. The fifth Chapter of the ſame Book contains the Perſpective of Shadows, both in Theory and Practice; and this I have treated in the very ſame Manner as I have done the Perſpective of Objects: So that what is contained in this Chapter, is deducible from what hath been already advanced in the third Chapter, and follows like ſo many Corollaries from thoſe general Propoſitions. The ſixth Chapter of the ſame Book contains ſome general Inſtructions for chooſing a proper Diſtance for the Eye, &c. and the bad Effects of viewing a Picture from any other than the true Point of Sight; and the ſeventh and laſt Chapter, is principally copied from Mr. Hamilton, *and contains an Explanation of Aerial Perſpective, the* Chiara Oſcura, *and Keeping in Pictures.--And thus having gone through the Theoretical*

oretical Part, I have proceeded to the ſecond Book, which contains the practical Part only; in which I have obſerved much the ſame Order and Method as in the Theory, and therefore that needs no farther Explanation.

The Figures I have made choice of, to demonſtrate and explain this Syſtem of Perſpective, are not ſet off with Ornaments, to attract the Eye, but are done with Simplicity, to inform the Underſtanding; and are ſuch as every common Mechanick has clear and determinate Ideas of, and conſequently of the moſt univerſal Uſe: For the SQUARE, *the* TRIANGLE, *and the* CIRCLE, *are not only the Foundation of moſt geometrical Figures, but are alſo the ſimple Materials of Shapes in general, and of which regular Buildings, in particular, are always compoſed. And I may, without the leaſt Arrogance, affirm, that, had the ſeveral Writers upon Perſpective ſhewn how to find the Repreſentations of thoſe three Figures only, upon different Planes, and in various Situations, their Works would have been more intelligible, and of much more Service, than they now are with ſuch a Multiplicity of ornamental Schemes and unapplicable Examples. In ſhort, the Principles of Perſpective are few and ſimple, and therefore to explain them by a vaſt Number of ornamental Figures, would ſerve only to divert the Eye and miſlead the Judgment, and to make that appear obſcure and difficult, which in its own Nature is extremely clear and eaſy.*

And here it may not be improper to obſerve, that the Learner is deſired to draw out every Figure as he proceeds, which will ſerve to fix them in his Memory, and to make their Explanations more eaſy and familiar to him. It is a Method I have always practiſed myſelf, with Succeſs; and therefore think it may be of Service to others: However, thoſe who by an extraordinary Capacity can carry on a long Train of Ideas together, and can recollect, compare, and combine them as they pleaſe, need not give themſelves this Trouble.

This is a general Account of the following Work: But before I quit the Subject, I ſhall beg leave to ſay ſomething upon the Uſefulneſs of Perſpective to every Perſon that is any ways concerned in the Arts of Deſign, and to recommend the Study of it in particular to every TYRO *in the Art of Painting; which I could wiſh might put a Stop to that Ridicule and Con-*

Contempt with which it has been treated by a sort of People, who are too ready to condemn a Branch of Science, which they have neglected to gain a sufficient Knowledge of. These Persons bring to my Mind a Story of Leonardo *da* Vinci, *a famous Italian Painter who flourished in the latter End of the fourteenth Century* *. *He tells us, that a Friend of his, named* Boticello, *had a peculiar Pique against Landskips, thought them much beneath his Application, and looked upon them in a most contemptible Light: But, says* Leonardo, *the Reason was, because he was a very sorry Landskip Painter: And our Author adds, that for this Reason his Merit in other Matters was the less regarded.*

That Perspective is an essential Requisite in a good Painter, is attested by all our most eminent Artists, and is moreover confirmed by almost every Author † *who has wrote upon Painting; nay, the very Term Painting implies Perspective. For to draw a good Picture is to draw the Representation of Nature, as it appears to the Eye; and to draw the Perspective Representation of any Object, is to draw the Representation of that Object as it appears to the Eye: Therefore the Terms Painting and Perspective seem to be synonymous, though I know there is a critical Difference between the Words. Yet this will serve at least to shew the near Alliance between Painting and Perspective; that if the one doth not comprehend the other, Perspective, however, may be said to be the Basis upon which Painting is built; and therefore he who attempts to paint a Picture without having a general Knowledge of it, will always wander in the Mazes of Uncertainty, be subject to the greatest Errors, and his Works, like those of* Boticello, *will be the less regarded. And what is said of the Usefulness of Perspective to Painters in particular, may be applied to Artists in general; such as Engravers, Architects, Statuaries, Chasers, Carvers, &c. It will also be an entertaining Study to any Gentleman, who has either a Taste for Drawing, or is a Lover of Painting; as it will enable him to draw out the Representation of any Building or Prospect, and to form a tolerable Judgment of a Picture without any other Assistance. I would not be understood to mean, that a*

* Vid. *Leonardo da Vinci* upon Painting, p. 31.
† Ibid. p. 29. *Fresnoy's* Poem upon Painting, p. 19, v. 115. And *Du Piles* upon Painting, Chap. 18.

Person

Perſon is always to follow the rigid Rules of Perſpective, for there are ſome Caſes in which it may be neceſſary to deviate from them; but then he muſt do it with Modeſty, and for ſome good Reaſon, as we have ſhewn in ſome Parts of this Work. Nor would I be thought to deſire the Artiſt to make Uſe of Scales or Compaſſes upon all Occaſions, and to draw out every Line and Point to a Mathematical Exactneſs; no, the Deſign of this Work is quite the Reverſe; it is to teach the general Rules of Perſpective, and to enforce the Practice of it by eaſy and ſelf-evident Principles; *to aſſiſt the Judgment, and to direct the Hand, and not to perplex, either by unneceſſary Lines or dry Theorems. Upon the whole: He that has a true Genius, and will take Pains to learn the Principles delivered in this Treatiſe, will be taught to* SEE *Objects with ſuch Exactneſs, and his Judgment will be founded upon ſuch ſolid Principles, that he will be enabled to draw out any Repreſentation with more Eaſe, and with much more Correctneſs, than the greateſt Genius who is ignorant of Perſpective, or he who deſpiſes the Rules of ſuch a neceſſary Art.*

CONTENTS.

Compleat SYSTEM of PERSPECTIVE.
BOOK I.

CHAP. I.
Containing Matters previous to Perspective.

CHAP. II.
Some Optical Observations.

CHAP. III.

The Theory of Perſpective.

CHAP. IV.

Of parallel inclined Pictures.

CHAP. V.

The Perspective of SHADOWS.

CHAP. VI.

Containing several essential Requisites.

CHAP. VII.

BOOK II.

The PRACTICE of PERSPECTIVE.

CHAP. I.

CHAP. II.

SECT. I.

To PREPARE *the* PICTURE, *&c.*

SECT. II.

To find the Repreſentation of Objects which lie flat upon the Ground, ſuch as the SQUARE, *the* TRIANGLE, *and the* CIRCLE, *&c,*

SECT. III.

To find the Representation of objects that are perpendicular *to the* Ground.

SECT. IV.

To determine the Representation of Objects that are inclined *to the* Ground.

CHAP. III.

The Practice of Perspective abbreviated.

SECT. I.

2. *To*

SECT. II.

The foregoing Rules more particularly applied to common Practice.

CHAP. IV.

Horizontal Perspective.

CHAP. V.

The Perspective of Shadows.

SECT. I.

SECT. II.

CHAP. VI.

Chap. VII.

Several Methods of Perſpective, by the moſt eminent Authors.

APPENDIX.

A Com-

A Compleat SYSTEM of PERSPECTIVE.

BOOK I. CHAP. I.

Of Instruments used in Drawing, Geometrical Definitions and Propositions, and Practical Geometry.

SECT. I.

Of INSTRUMENTS *used in* DRAWING.

THE Instruments necessary in Drawing are as follows, *viz.*

1. A Tee-Square. Fig. 1.
2. A Parallel Ruler. Fig. 2.
3. A Drawing-Board; which is a smooth Board made exactly square at the Corners.
4. A Sector. Fig. 3.
5. A Pair of Compasses and a Drawing-Pen.
6. A Semi-Circle, or Protractor. Fig. 4. This Instrument is half a Circle, divided into 180 equal Parts, which are called Degrees.

These are all the necessary Instruments in Drawing, and may be had at any Mathematical-Instrument Maker's *.

In regard to their different Uses: They are almost universal; but I shall only consider them as applied to particular Purposes; and first, of the TEE-SQUARE and DRAWING-BOARD.

1. Let it be required to draw one Line CD, perpendicular to another Line AB. Fig. 5.

After having fixed a Piece of Paper upon the Drawing-Board, apply the square Arm ED of the Tee-Square to the Side of the Board, and draw the Line AB; then lay it in the same Manner against the Top or Bottom of the Board, and draw a Line touching the other Line in the given Point. Thus, let D be the given

* Mr. *John Bennet*, at the *Globe* in *Crown Court*, between St. *Ann's* and *Golden Square*, *London*, has had particular Directions from the Author, for making a very simple and useful Case of Instruments, fit for the above Purpose.

Point; then draw CD, and the Line CD will be perpendicular to the Line AB.---And if an oblique Line AC is wanted; lay the Arm AB of the Square, which turns upon a Screw C, against the Edge of the Board, and move the Ruler backwards and forwards, 'till you have got it to the Inclination you want.

Fig. 2. 2. The PARALLEL RULER is to be used when we would work upon a loose Paper, without using a Drawing-Board: Thus, let it be required to draw one Line CD, Fig. 8, parallel to a given Line AB; and let C, or D, be the Distance it is to be from AB: Lay the Edge AB of the Ruler, to the given Line AB, and keep the Limb a b, fixed; then move the other Limb cd, to the Distance proposed, and draw a Line, as CD, which will be parallel to AB. So that having given only one Line, and erected a Perpendicular thereon, we may draw any Number of parallel Lines, or Perpendiculars to them; only observing to set off the exact Distance of every Line by a Prick of the Compasses, like C or D.

Fig. 3. 3. The SECTOR is made of two brass Rulers, AB, AC, artificially fixed upon a Center A: This Instrument is usually filled with a great Number of different Scales, which, tho' very useful in many Parts of the Mathematicks, are nevertheless foreign to our Purpose; and therefore, I shall consider it only as having what is called a Line of Lines on one Side, and a Line of Polygons on the other; which different Scales are expressed upon the Sector, by the Letters LL and PP, as in the Figure; LL stands for the Line of Lines, and PP for that of Polygons. The Line of Lines serves as an universal Scale for dividing any Line into equal Parts, or into any given Proportion; for instance, divide
Fig 24. the Line AB into six equal Parts: Take the Length of the Line in your Compasses, and set one Leg of them in the Point 6, upon the Line of Lines; then open the Sector 'till the other Leg of the Compasses coincides with the Point 6, which is on the Line of Lines upon the other Limb of the Instrument; in this Position keep the Sector fixed, 'till you have taken the Distance from 1 to 1; which Distance will be one sixth Part of the Line given. And in the same Manner, a Line may be divided into any Number of equal Parts, even though they should exceed the Numbers upon the Sector; suppose, for instance, it was required to divide a Line into 24 equal Parts; then set the Length of the Line from 12 to 12 and divide the 1-12th Part into two Parts, which will answer the Purpose.

The

The Line of Polygons is called so from its Use; which is, to divide a Circle into any Number of Parts, as in Fig. 27. which Figures are called by the general Name of Polygons; and the Method of using this Scale is extremely easy. For having first described a Circle, take the Radius (that is half its Diameter) and set it upon these Lines from 6 to 6; in this Position keep the Sector fixed, and you will have a Scale for dividing any Circle of that Radius into any Number of equal Parts; for if you want a seven-sided Figure, (or Heptagon) take the Distance from 7 to 7; if an eight-sided Figure, (or Octagon) take the Distance from 8 to 8, and so on.

4. The last Instrument is the SEMI-CIRCLE or PROTRACTOR, Fig. 4. which is used in drawing all kinds of given Angles, and in the following Manner.

Let it be required to make a right Angle * CAB, from the Fig. 7. Point A, upon the given right Line AB.----Lay the lower Side BC of the Instrument, exactly even with the Line AB, and in such a manner, that the Point, or Center A, will coincide exactly with the Point A upon the Line AB; then make a prick at 90, and draw AC, and the thing proposed is done.---And after the same Manner any other given Angle may be drawn, which a little Experience will make much more easy than Words can do.

SECT. II.

GEOMETRICAL DEFINITIONS *and* PROPOSITIONS, *principally from* Simpson's *and* Pardie's Geometry.

1. AN Angle is the Inclination of two right, or straight Lines, Fig. 5. AD, CD, meeting each other in a Point, as D; and the middle Letter D always denotes the Angle.

2. When one right Line CD, falling upon another AB, makes the Angles on both Sides equal, those Angles are called right Angles, and the Line CD is said to be perpendicular to AB; and if any Line AC be drawn from a Point A in one Line, to any Point C in the other, the Line so drawn is called the Hypothenuse.

3. An acute Angle BDE, is less than a right Angle BDC.

4. An obtuse Angle ADE is that which is greater than a right Angle ADC.

5. Parallel Lines are such as are equally distant from each Fig. 6. other, as AB, CD.

* For right Angle, see Geometrical Definitions in the next Section.

6. A plane Figure is that which lies evenly between its Bounds or Extremes; thus any ſmooth Surface is a plane Surface, and is therefore called a Plane.

Fig. 9, 10. 7. All plane Figures bounded by three right Lines, AB, AC, BC, are called Triangles.

Fig. 10. 8. An equilateral Triangle ABC, is that whoſe Bounds or Sides are all equal.

Fig. 11. 9. Every plane Figure ABCD, bounded by four right Lines, is called a Quadrilateral; and if its Sides and Angles are equal, it is called a Square.

10. Any quadrilateral Figure, whoſe oppoſite Sides are parallel, but not equal, is called a Parallelogram.

Fig. 12. 11. A right Line is ſaid to be perpendicular to a Plane when it ſtands on it at right Angles; thus the right Line EF, is perpendicular to the Plane ABCD, when it ſtands like a Pillar upon the Ground, and is inclined no more to any one Side of the Plane than to the other.

Fig. 13. 12. One Plane ABCD, is right and perpendicular to another EF, when, like a well-made Wall, it inclines and leans on one Side no more than it does on the other.

Fig. 9, 10. 13. Two right Lines, if they meet ſo as to cut or croſs each other, are in the ſame Plane; wherefore all the Angles, A, B, C, and Sides AB, BC, CA, of every Triangle, are in the ſame Plane.

Fig. 14. 14. If two Planes ABC, EFGH, cut or interſect one another, they ſhall do it in a right Line EF, which Line is called their Common Section.

15. If a right Line FG, be perpendicular to two right Lines FD, FE, which are in the ſame Plane ABC, that Line is alſo perpendicular to that Plane.

16. If a right Line FG be perpendicular to three right Lines, FI, FE, and FD, thoſe three Lines are all in the ſame Plane, ABC.

17. If two Lines FG, EH, are perpendicular to the ſame Plane ABC, they will be parallel to one another.

Fig. 15. 18. Two Lines EG, FH, perpendicular to the ſame Plane ABCD, cannot be drawn through the ſame Point G.

Fig. 16. 19. If two parallel Planes ABCD, EFGH, are cut by a third Plane IKLM, the common Sections, OP, QR, are parallel.

Fig. 17. 20. If the Lines GM and HN, are divided by parallel Planes, then GI will have the ſame Proportion to IM, as HL has to LN; and the Section MN, IK, of any plane Triangle MGN, by two parallel Planes, is always in a given Ratio; that is, IK is in the ſame Proportion to IG, as MN is to MG.

21. A

21. A ſolid Angle E, is made by the meeting of three or more Planes, and there joining in a Point; like the Point of a Diamond, or the Corner of a Die, or Cube. Fig. 18.

22. If we imagine a Line, as EB, fixt above in the Point E, to be moved along the Sides of any regular Figure, ABCD, that Line, by its Motion, will deſcribe a Figure that is called a Pyramid.

23. If a Line faſtned as before, move round a Circle, AB, it will deſcribe a Figure that is call'd a Cone; and the Circle is its Baſe, and a Line drawn from the Vertex C, to D, is called its Axis. Fig. 19.

24. If a Line AD, move uniformly about two angular Figures, ABC, DEF, which are every Way equal, having their Sides and Angles mutually parallel and correſponding exactly to one another, as DF to AB, DE to AC, &c. then that Line by its Motion ſhall deſcribe, if it hath three Sides, a Priſm; if four, a Cube or Parallelopiped. Fig. 20.

25. If a Line move uniformly round two equal and parallel Circles, it ſhall deſcribe or generate a Cylinder; and the Line joining the Centers AB, in the two Baſes, is called its Axis. Fig. 21.

26. If any ſolid Body is laid with one Face upon another Plane, the Space which that Face takes up is called its Seat; thus the Cube CG, reſts with its Face CDEH, upon the Plane IK; therefore, CDEH is the Seat of the Cube on that Plane; and thus the Points C and D, are the Seats of the Lines CA, DB; as are alſo CD, DE, the Seats of the Lines AB and BF; and ſo likewiſe, the Seat of the oblique Line DF, is the Line DE. Fig. 22.

SECT. III.

Of PRACTICAL GEOMETRY.

To erect a Perpendicular CD, *from* D, *near the Middle of a right Line* AB. Fig. 5.

FROM D, ſet off on the Line AB, any Diſtance DA, DB, equal to each other; then from A, deſcribe at Pleaſure the Arc cd, and with the ſame Diſtance from B, deſcribe the Arc ab; and then from the Point C, where they cut each other, draw CD; ſo will CD be perpendicular to AB.

To let fall a Perpendicular CD *upon a Line* AB, *from a Point* C, *without the Line.* Fig. 6.

From the given Point C, deſcribe the Arc AEB at pleaſure, and from the Points A and B, deſcribe two other Arcs cutting each other in F; draw CF, then are CD and FD perpendicular to AB.

To

Fig. 7. *To erect a Perpendicular* AC, *upon the Extremity* A, *of a Line* AB.

With any Diſtance, deſcribe the Arc e f g from the given Point A, and ſet off the ſame Diſtance upon the Arc from e to f, and from f to g; then from the Points g, f, deſcribe the Arcs a b, c d; and from their Section C, draw CA, which will be perpendicular to AB.

Fig. 8. *To draw one Line* CD, *from a given Point* D, *parallel to a given Line* AB.

Draw, as you think proper, the oblique Line AD from the given Point D, cutting AB in A; and from the Point A, with the Diſtance AD, deſcribe the Arc DB, cutting AB in B; then from D, with the Diſtance DA, deſcribe the Arc AC; and make AC equal to BD; and then draw the Line CD, which is parallel to AB.

Or it may be done yet eaſier, by deſcribing two Arcs C, D, with the ſame Radius as in the other Figure, and drawing the Line CD to touch them both.

Fig. 9. *To make any Triangle, as* ABC, *from three given Lines*, AF, BE, CD.

Draw a Line AB at Pleaſure, and make AB equal to the given Line AF; then from the Point B, with the Radius BE, deſcribe an Arc c d; with the Radius CD, from the Point A, deſcribe another Arc a b, cutting the former Arc in C; then from C draw Lines to A and B; and then will ABC be a Triangle whoſe Sides are reſpectively equal to the given Lines AF, BE, and CD.

Fig. 10. *To make an equilateral Triangle upon a Line given*, AB.

Take the Length of AB in your Compaſſes, and from the Points A and B, deſcribe two Arcs cutting each other in C; then from C, draw CA, CB; and then is ABC an equilateral Triangle.

Fig. 11. *To make a Geometrical Square* ABCD, *on the given Line* AB.

From the Point B erect the Perpendicular BC; from B, with the Radius AB, deſcribe the Arc AC, cutting the ſaid Perpendicular in C; from A and C, (with the ſame Radius) deſcribe two more Arcs cutting each other in D; then draw DA, DC, and the Figure propoſed is compleated.

Fig. 23. *To make an Angle, with the Line* AB, *equal to a given Angle* X.

From the Point A, with any Radius, deſcribe the Arc cd; from D, with the ſame Radius, deſcribe the Arc a b; take the Length of

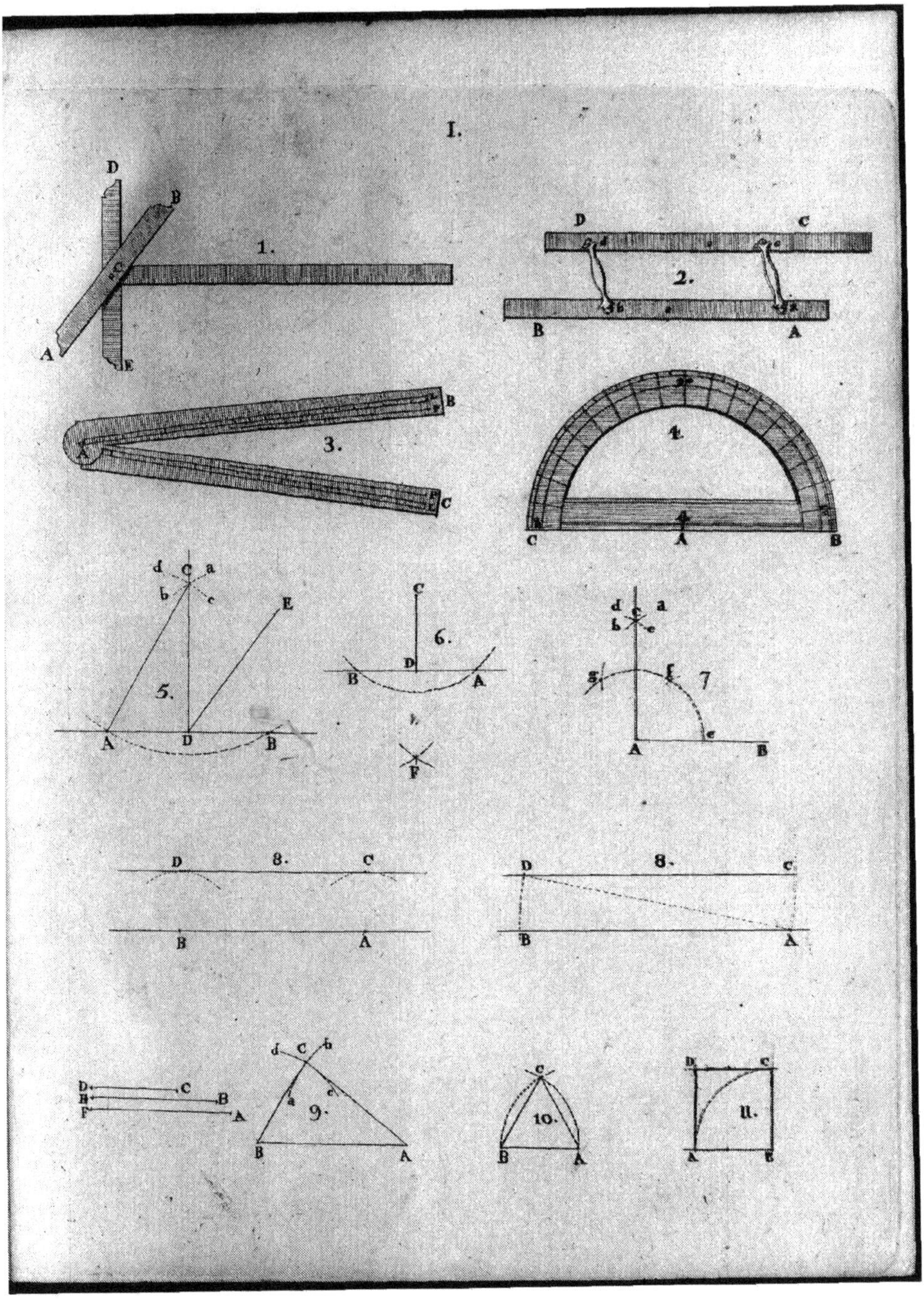
I.
1.
2.
3.
4.
5.
6.
7
8.
8.
9.
10.
11.

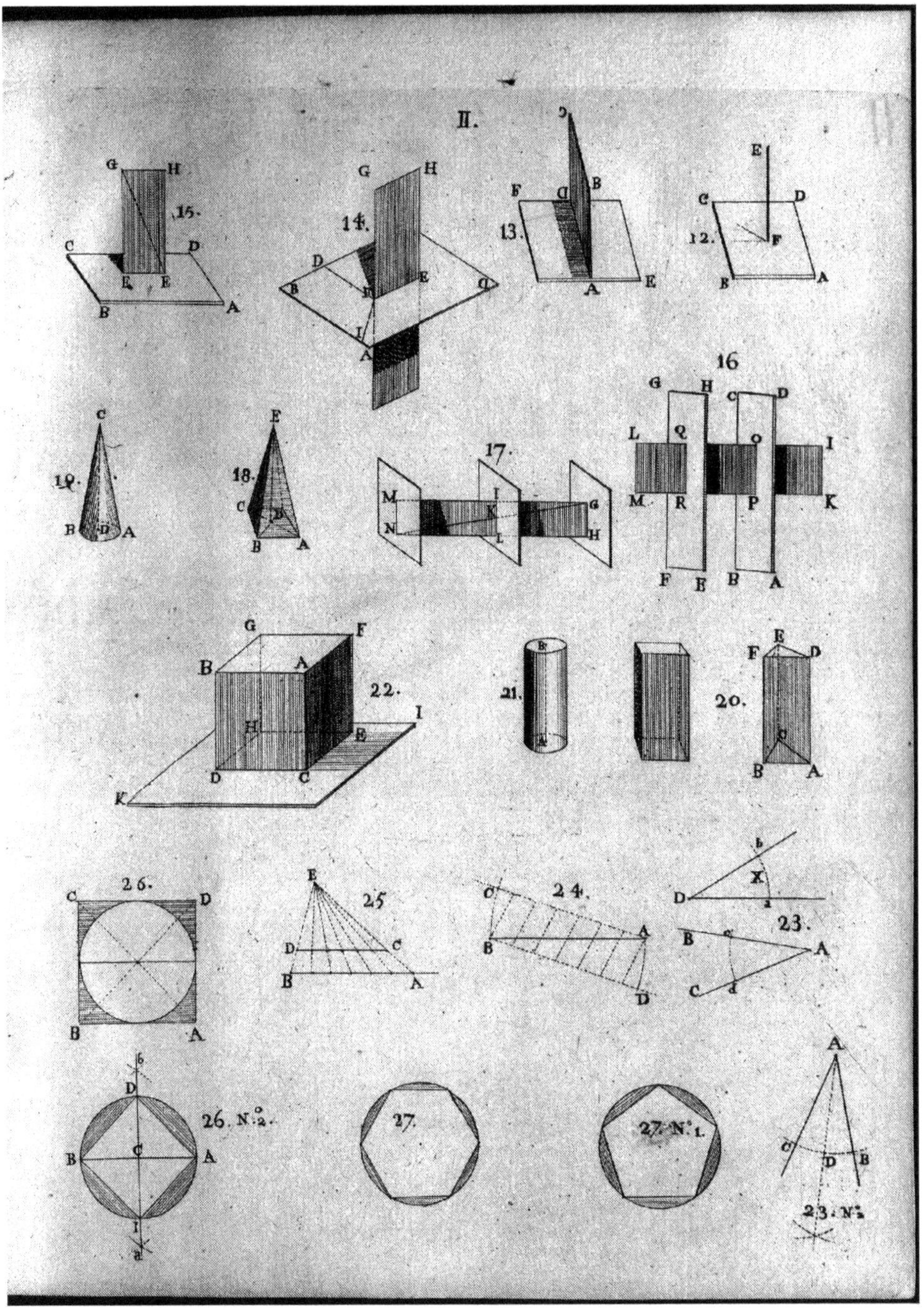
II.
15.
14.
13.
12.
16
19.
18.
17.
22.
21.
20.
26.
25
24.
23.
26. N.° 2.
27.
27. N.° 1.
23. N.° 2.

of ab, and transfer it from c to d, and through d draw a Line to A; then is the Angle BAC equal to the given Angle aDb.

To bisect, or divide an Angle A *into two equal Parts.* Fig. 23. No. 2.

From the Point A, with any Radius, describe the Arc BC; divide BC into two equal Parts, and draw AD.

To divide a right Line AB *into any Number of equal Parts.* Fig. 24.

From the Point A draw at pleasure the Line AC, and make BD parallel thereto; then carry as many equal Parts along the Line AC, from the Point A, and along the Line BD, from B, as you would divide the Line AB into (for instance, six Parts) and draw the transverse Lines, which will divide the proposed Line as was required.

Or, it may be done by drawing a Line AB, parallel to a given Line CD; then by setting as many equal Parts upon the Line AB as CD should be divided into, and by drawing Lines from thence to a Point, as E, from every Division, and in such a Manner, that the outward Lines AE, BE, shall touch the Ends of the Line CD, as in the Figure. I say then, the Line CD will be divided into six equal Parts. Fig. 25.

To inscribe a Circle within a Square ABCD. Fig. 26.

Draw the Diagonals AD, BC, and where they cross each other will be the Center of the Square, which consequently is the Center of the Circle also.

To inscribe a Square in a given Circle. Fig. 26. No. 2.

Draw the Diameter AB, from A and B describe the Arcs a, b, and draw DE; from A, D, B, E, draw Lines as in the Figure, which will be the Square required.

As to the Geometrical Construction of Polygons, I shall not take up the Reader's Time about them; for they may be described very easily by Means of the Scale upon the Sector for that Purpose, as has been observed before, under the Word SECTOR. Fig. 27.

CHAP.

CHAP. II.

Of the Eye and the Nature of Viſion, the Reflection and Refraction of the Rays of Light, and the Cauſe of Colours.

SECT. I.

Of the Eye *and the* Nature *of* Vision.

THE Deſign of this Chapter is, to explain to the unlearned Reader the Conſtruction of the Human Eye, and to give him a general Idea of the Nature and Cauſe of Viſion; and not to proceed in a regular Manner upon Opticks, but only to take Notice of ſome particular Parts of it, by which he will be enabled to ſee more clearly the Nature of Perſpective. In order to which, I ſhall take Quotations from the moſt eminent Writers upon that Subject, and not preſume to give him much of my own, as nothing which I can offer will be new, or ſo much to the Purpoſe.

" Every viſible Body emits or reflects inconceivably ſmall Particles of Matter from each Point of its Surface, which iſſue from it continually (not unlike Sparks from a Coal) in ſtrait Lines and in all Directions. Theſe Particles entering the Eye, and ſtriking upon the Retina (a Nerve expanded on the back Part of the Eye to receive their Impulſes) excite in our Minds the Idea of Light, and as they differ in Magnitude, they produce in us the Ideas of different Colours.

" That the Particles which conſtitute Light, are exceedingly ſmall, appears from hence, *viz.* that if a Hole be made through a Piece of Paper with a Needle, all the Rays of Light which proceed at the ſame Time from all the Objects on one Side of it, are capable of paſſing through it at once without the leaſt Confuſion; for any one of thoſe Objects may as clearly be ſeen through it, as if no Rays paſſed through it from any of the reſt. Further, if a Candle is lighted, and there be no Obſtacle in the Way to obſtruct the Progreſs of its Rays, it will fill all the Space within two Miles of it every Way with luminous Particles, before it has loſt the leaſt ſenſible Part of its Subſtance thereby.

" That

" That these Particles proceed from every Point of the Surface " of a visible Body, and in all Directions, is clear from hence, " *viz.* because where-ever a Spectator is placed with regard to the " Body, every Point of that Part of the Surface which is turned " towards him, is visible to him. That they proceed from the " Body in right Lines, we are assured, because just so many and " no more will be intercepted in their Passage to any Place, by an " interposed Object, as that Object ought to intercept, supposing " them to come in such Lines. The Velocity (or Swiftness) with " which they proceed from the Surface of the visible Body, is no " less surprising than their Minuteness: For by the Calculation " of the most accurate Philosophers, they are no more than about " seven Minutes in passing over a Space equal to the Distance be- " tween the Sun and us, which is about eighty-one Millions of " Miles, and is considerably more than a Million Times greater " than the Velocity of a Cannon Ball.

" A Stream of these Particles issuing from the Surface of a " visible Body in one and the same Direction, is called a Ray of " Light.

" As Rays proceed from a visible Body in all Directions, they " necessarily become thinner and thinner, continually spreading " themselves as they pass along, into a larger Space, and that in " proportion to the Squares of their Distances from the Body; " that is, at the Distance of two Spaces, they are four Times " thinner than they are at one; at the Distance of three Spaces, " nine Times thinner, and so on: The Reason of which is, be- " cause they spread themselves in a twofold Manner, *viz.* upwards " and downwards, as well as side-ways." *----This may be the Fig. 33. more clearly comprehended by the following Experiment.

" Let the Light which flows from a Point A, and passes through " a square Hole bcde, be received upon a Plane, BCDE, parallel " to the Plane of the Hole; or, if you please, let the Figure BD, " be the Shadow of the Plane bd; and when the Distance AB is " double of Ab, the Length and Breadth of the Shadow BD will " each be double the Length and Breadth of the Plane ab; and " treble, when AB is treble of Ab, and so on; which may be " easily examined by the Light of a Candle placed at A.

" Therefore the Surface of the Shadow BD, at the Distance " AB double of Ab, is divisible into four Squares, and at a treble

* Vide Rowning's Opt. Part 3, p. 4.

"Distance into nine Squares, severally equal to the Square bd, as "represented in the Figure. The Light then which falls upon "the Plane bd, being suffered to pass to a double Distance, will "be uniformly spread over four times the Space, and consequently "will be four times thinner in every Part of that Space, and at "a treble Distance will be nine times thinner, and at a quadruple "Distance sixteen times thinner than it was at first; and so on "according to the Increase of the square Surfaces bcde, BCDE, "*&c.* or of the square Surfaces Abfg, ABFG, *&c.* built upon "the Distance Ab, AB, *&c.* Consequently the Quantities of this "rarified Light, received upon a Surface of any given Size or "Shape whatever, removed successively to those several Distances, "will be but one quarter, one ninth, one sixteenth, of the whole "Quantity received by it at the first Distance Ab. Or in general "Words, the Densities or Quantities of Light, received upon any "given Plane, are diminished in the same Proportion as the "Squares of the Distances of that Plane from the luminous Body "are increased; and on the contrary, are increased in the same "Proportion as those Squares are diminished. For the Lights of "the several Points of the Body, which severally follow this Rule, "will compose a Light which will still follow the same Rule."*

Having thus far explained what we are to understand by the Rays of Light, we will now proceed to a Description of the Human Eye, and consider the Nature of Vision.

Fig. 28. "ATYC is the Representation of an Human Eye, dissected "through its Axis †, all the Parts being twice as big as the Life.

"Here the transparent Coat, called the Cornea, is ABC; the "Remainder ATYC being opake, and a Portion of a larger "Sphere. Within this outward Coat Anatomists distinguish two "others; the innermost of which is called the Retina, being like "a fine Net, composed of the Fibres of the Optick Nerve YVT "woven together, and is white about the Parts p, q, r, at the "Bottom of the Eye. The Cavity of the Eye is not filled with "one Liquor, but with three different Sorts. That contained in "the outward Space ABCOEGFD is called the Aqueous Hu-"mour, being perfectly fluid, like Water; the other, contained

* Vide Smith's Opt. P. 17, Art. 57, 58.

† The Axis of the Eye is a Line drawn through the Middle of the Pupil and of the Crystalline Humour, and consequently falls upon the Middle of the Retina. And the Axes of both Eyes produced, are called the Optick Axes; which will be better understood after the Description of the Eye.

" in the inward Space E p q r D F G is a little thicker than the " White of an Egg, and is called the Vitreous Humour; the third " Humour, FG, is shaped like a Lens* of unequal Convexities, " lying between the two former, and fixed to the side Coats by " Filaments or Threads extended all round it, and is called the " Crystalline Humour, being hard like the White of an Egg " boiled, but as clear as the other two, and differs from them in " a greater Degree of Refractive† Power; whereby the Rays that " came from the Points P, Q, R, having received a Degree of " Convergence ‡ by the Refraction of the Cornea ABC, are " made to converge a little more by other Refractions at the Sur- " faces of the Crystalline FG; so that uniting in as many Points " p, q, r, upon the Retina, they represent the Points of the Ob- " ject P, Q, R, from whence they came." ‖

The Picture of an Object upon the Retina being produced much in the same Manner as a Picture by a Lens, *viz.* in both Cases by Means of the Refraction of the Rays of Light, we will therefore, first shew how by the Passage of those Rays through a Lens, a Picture may be produced; as this will be one considerable Step towards explaining the Nature of Vision: For which Purpose I shall quote an Experiment from the incomparable Sir *Isaac Newton*. §

" Let PR represent an Object without-doors, and AB a Lens Fig. 29. " placed at a Hole in the Window-shutter of a dark Chamber, " whereby the Rays that come from any Point Q of that Object, " are made to converge and meet again in the Point q; and if a " Sheet of white Paper be held at q, for the Light there to fall " upon it, the Picture of that Object PR will appear upon the " Paper in its proper Shape and Colours. For, as the Light " which comes from the Point Q, goes to the Point q, so the " Light which comes from other Points P and R of the Object, " will go to so many other correspondent Points p and r; so " that every Point of the Object shall illuminate a correspondent " Point of the Picture, and thereby make a Picture like the Object

* By a Lens in this Place is meant a Glass which collects the Rays of Light into a Point, like a common Burning-Glass.

† When a Ray of Light passes out of one Medium into another of a different Density, it will be bent near the Surfaces of those Mediums, which bending is called Refraction.

‡ If several Rays approach each other so as to meet in a Point, they are said to converge; and if they proceed from a Point and go further off continually, they are then said to diverge.

‖ Vide Smith's Opt. p. 26.

§ Vide Newton's Opt. p. 11.

“ in Shape and Colour, this only excepted, that the Picture shall be inverted. And this is the Reason of that vulgar Experiment of casting the Species of Objects from abroad upon a Wall, or Sheet of white Paper in a dark Room.*

Fig. 28. “ In like Manner, when a Man views any Object PQR, the Light which comes from the several Points of the Object is so refracted by the transparent Skins and Humours of the Eye, (that is, by the Cornea ABC, and by the Crystalline Humour FG) as to converge and meet again in so many Points in the Bottom of the Eye, and there to paint the Picture of the Object upon the Retina. And these Pictures, propagated by Motion along the Fibres of the Optick Nerves into the Brain, are the Cause of Vision. For accordingly as these Pictures are perfect or imperfect, the Object is seen perfectly or imperfectly. If the Eye be tinged with any Colour (as in the Disease of the Jaundice) so as to tinge the Pictures in the Bottom of the Eye with that Colour, then all Objects appear tinged with the same Colour. If the Humours of the Eye by old Age decay, so as by shrinking to make the Cornea and Coat of the Crystalline Humour grow flatter than before, the Light will not be refracted enough, and for want of a sufficient Refraction will not converge to the Bottom of the Eye, but to some Place beyond it, and by consequence paint in the Bottom of the Eye a confused Picture.—This is the Reason of the Decay of Sight in old Men, and shews why their Sight is mended by Spectacles. For these Convex Glasses (or Lenses) supply the Defect of Plumpness in the Eye, and by increasing the Refraction make the Rays converge sooner, so as to convene distinctly at the Bottom of the Eye, if the Glass has a due Degree of Convexity. And the Contrary happens in short-sighted Men, whose Eyes are too plump. For the Refraction being now too great, the Rays converge and convene in the Eyes before they come at the Bottom; and therefore the Picture made in the Bottom, and the Vision caused thereby, will not be distinct, unless the Object be brought so near the Eye as that the Place where the converging Rays convene may be removed to the Bottom, or that the Plumpness of the Eye be taken off, and the Refractions dimi-

* A Person may easily satisfy himself of the Truth of this, by only taking a common Burning-Glass in one Hand, and a Piece of white Paper in the other, and let him hold the Glass before any Object, and the Paper on the opposite Side of the Glass; then by moving the Glass or Paper backwards and forwards 'till he gets the Rays to their proper Focus, he will see the Picture of the Object upon the Paper, but it will not be so distinct as in the dark Chamber.

“ nish'd

" niſhed by a Concave-Glaſs of a due Degree of Concavity; or " laſtly, that by Age the Eye grows flatter, 'till it comes to a due " Figure: For ſhort-ſighted Men ſee remote Objects beſt in Old " Age; and therefore they are accounted to have the moſt laſt- " ing Eyes." *

" As to the Diſtinctneſs of Viſion in a perfect Eye, that evi- " dently depends upon the Refraction of the Rays; and it is then " as diſtinct as poſſible, when the Refraction is ſo made, as that " all the Rays which come from one and the ſame Point of the " Object, meet together exactly in one and the ſame Point of the " Bottom of the Eye: But this is never preciſely ſo, but in thoſe " Rays which come from that Point of the Object which is at the " Extremity of the optick Axis Q q; for it is evident, that thoſe " Rays which come from the other Points, are reunited ſo much " the leſs exactly one than the other, as they are more diſtant " from this Axis; wherefore we cannot have at the ſame time, " the moſt diſtinct Senſation but in this Place alone, and the reſt " will be more confuſed." † Fig. 28.

The farther diſtant the Eye is from an Object, ſo much leſs will the Picture of that Object be upon the Retina: For let E be an Eye viewing the ſeveral Objects AB, CD, EF, at the Diſtance OQ, OR, OS.---Having drawn the ſeveral Rays A a, B b, C c, D g, E e, F f, through the Pupil O, it will be manifeſt, that the Picture of the neareſt Object AB, will be painted at the Bottom of the Eye in the Space ab, the Object CD in the Space cg, and the fartheſt Object, EF, in the Space e f; therefore, as the Space a b, is larger than the other two, c g or ef, the Picture of AB will be larger than the Picture of the other two Objects CD or EF, which are at a greater Diſtance from the Eye; and theſe Pic- tures will be to each other, as the ſeveral Diſtances OQ, OR, OS, are to each other. ‡ From hence then we may eaſily con- ceive, that *the Eye* may be ſo far removed from *the Object*, that at laſt the Image of that Object will totally diſappear. || Fig. 30.

" But the Degree of Brightneſs of the Picture of an Object " painted upon the Retina continues the ſame, at all Diſtances be- " tween the Eye and the Object, provided none of the Rays be

* Vide Newton's Opt. p. 12.
† Vide Clarke's Rohault, vol. 1. p. 249.
‡ Ibid,———————— p. 243.
|| The Rays of Light O A and O B, which come from the extreme Points of the Object to the Eye O, form an Angle A O B, which is called the Optick or Viſual Angle; and the Rays O A and O B are called Viſual Rays.

" ſtopt

" ſtopt by the Way, and that the Pupil does not alter its Aperture.
" For inſtance, when the Eye approaches as near again to the
" Object, the Picture upon the Retina becomes double in Length
" and double in Breadth, and conſequently quadruple in Surface;
" for the Surface would be double, if its Length alone or Breadth
" alone was double. The Quantity of Rays received through the
" ſame Aperture of the Pupil, at half the Diſtance from the Object,
" is alſo quadruple, and being equally ſpread over four times the
" Quantity of Surface of the Retina, they are juſt as denſe as
" before, when the Object was at twice that Diſtance.

" It follows then that the faint Appearance of remote Objects,
" is owing to the Opacity of the Atmoſphere, which hinders Part of
" their Light from coming to the Eye. Accordingly we find that
" the Sun, Moon, and Stars, appear very faint when near the
" Horizon, and brighter continually as they riſe higher; becauſe
" the Tract of Vapours which lies in the Way of the Rays, is
" longeſt and thickeſt near the Horizon; and becomes thinner and
" ſhorter as the Objects riſe higher, and conſequently does leſs
" obſtruct the Paſſage of the Rays.*

Fig. 31. " Parallel Lines ſeen obliquely, as ABC, DEF, appear to con-
" verge more and more as they are farther extended from the Eye.
" Becauſe the apparent Magnitudes† of their perpendicular Inter-
" vals AD, BE, CF, *&c.* are perpetually diminiſhed. And for
" the ſame Reaſon they appear to converge towards an imaginary
" Line, OG, drawn from the Eye parallel to them.

" This is the Reaſon that the remoter Parts of a Walk or Floor
" appear to aſcend gradually, and the Ceiling to deſcend towards
" the Horizontal Line OG: And that the Surface of the Sea, ſeen
" from an Eminence, appears to aſcend gradually in going from
" the Shore; and that the upper Parts of very high Buildings ſeem
" to lean forward over the Eye below, becauſe they ſeem to ap-
" proach towards a vertical Line OG.

Fig. 32. " The apparent Magnitude of a given Line, AB, ſeen very ob-
" liquely at a given Diſtance, OA, increaſes and decreaſes in pro-
" portion to the Increaſe and Decreaſe of OP, the perpendicular
" Diſtance of the Eye, from the Line AB produced; provided
" the Line AO be very large in compariſon to AB. For let the
" Ray BO cut a Line AC perpendicular to AB in C; and while

* Vide Smith's Opt. p. 29.

† By apparent Magnitude is here meant the Bigneſs of the Picture upon the Retina.

" the

III.

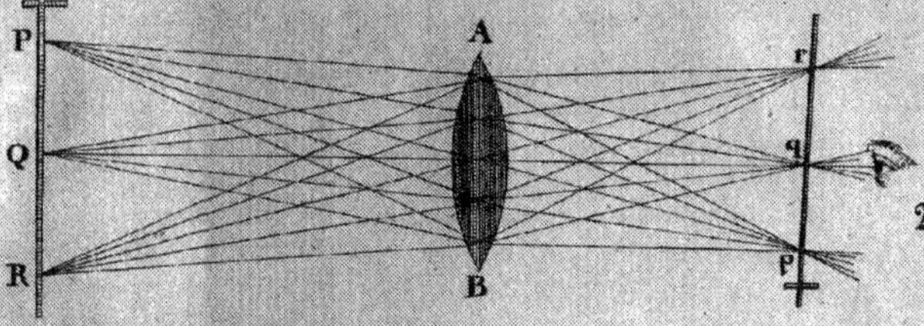

29.

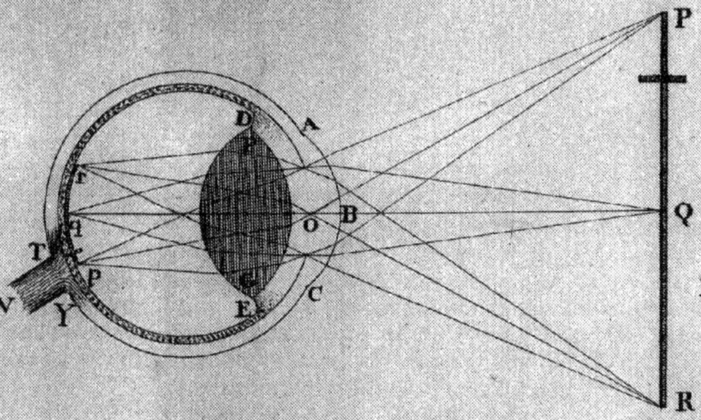

28.

30.

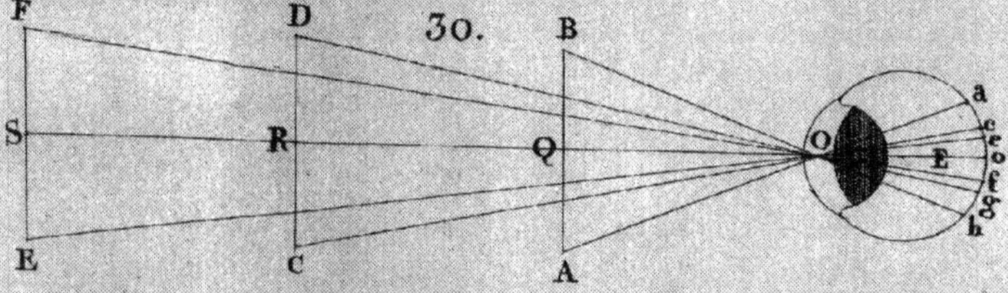

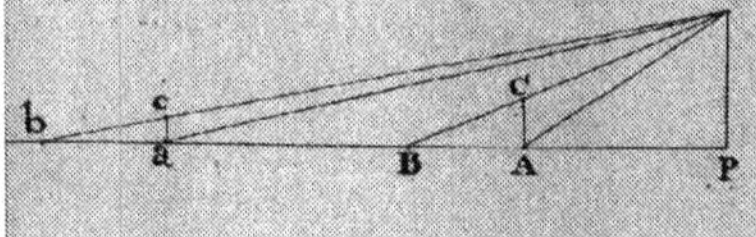

32.

31.

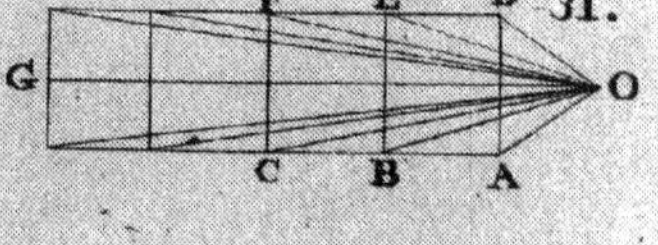

" the Eye is raiſed or depreſſed in the Perpendicular OP, the Line " AC will increaſe and decreaſe as OP does, and ſo will the " Angle AOC ſubtended by AC, and this Angle meaſures the " apparent Magnitude of AB.

" Hence the apparent Magnitudes of equal Parts AB, ab, of " a Line PAb, ſeen very obliquely at great Diſtances from the " Eye, are reciprocally in a duplicate Proportion of thoſe Diſ- " tances. For Example, let Ob be double of OB, and the " Angle OBP will be double of ObP, and accordingly ſince AB, " ab, are equal, the Perpendicular AC will be double of ac, and " being ſeen twice as near as ac, will appear four times bigger " than ac. Again, if Ob be treble of OB, the Line AC will be " treble of ac, and being ſeen three times nearer than ac, will " appear nine times bigger than ac, and ſo on.

" Hence the apparent Magnitude between a Row of Columns " are diminiſhed in a greater Proportion than their Heights.

" The quick Diminution of the apparent Magnitudes of the " remoter Parts of long Lines or Diſtances, is the Cauſe of great " Difficulty and Uncertainty in our Eſtimate of their Quantities. " For be the Differences of ſeveral Diſtances or Heights never ſo " great in themſelves, they will become inviſible at laſt by reaſon " of the Smallneſs of the Angles they ſubtend at the Eye, occa- " ſioned by their Obliquity; and then thoſe unequal Heights and " Diſtances will appear equal." *

SECT. II.

Of the REFLECTION *and* REFRACTION *of the Rays of* LIGHT.

" WHEN a Ray of Light falls obliquely upon a ſmooth po- " liſhed Surface, it is turn'd out of its Way either by Re- " flection or Refraction in the following Manner. Imagine the " Paper upon which this Figure is drawn to be perpendicular to " the Surface of ſtagnating Water, and to cut it in the Line RS, " and that a Ray of Light, coming in the Air along the Line " AC, falls upon RS at the Point C. Then ſuppoſing the Line " PCQ to be perpendicular to the Surface of the Water, if the " Ray be reflected, or turn'd back at C into the Air again, it will Fig. 34.

* Vide Smith's Opt p. 58.

" deſcribe

" describe a straight Line CB, inclin'd to the perpendicular CP " at an Angle PCB exactly equal to the Angle PCA, and there- " fore the Angle of Reflection is always equal to the Angle of " Incidence.

Fig. 35. " But if the Ray that came along AC goes into the Water at " C, it will not proceed straight forward, but being refracted or " bent at C, it will describe another strait Line CE, inclined to " the Perpendicular CQ, at a lesser Angle ECQ, than the " Angle ACP; and the Line CE, will always be so situated, " that when any Circle, described about the Center C, cuts the " Line CA in A, and CE in E, the Perpendiculars AD, and " EF, drawn from A and E to the Line PQ, shall always bear " the same Proportion to each other, whatever be the Magnitude " of the Angle ACP. In Water the Line EF is always three- " quarters of AD.

" In both these Cases the Line AC is called the incident Ray, " CB the reflected Ray, CE the refracted Ray, C the Point of " Incidence, PCQ the Perpendicular (at the Point) of Incidence, " the Angle ACP the Angle of Incidence, BCP the Angle of " Reflection, ECQ the Angle of Refraction; the Line AD the " Sine of Incidence, that is, of the Angle of Incidence; and " EF the Sine of Refraction, that is, of the Angle of Refraction.

" As Rays of Light are incessantly thrown out and dis- " persed in all possible Directions from every Point of a luminous " Body; so when they illuminate other Bodies, on which they " fall, they are also incessantly thrown back from every Point of " those Bodies. For the Points of opake Bodies so enlightened, " are visible to the Eye at any Point of Space and in any Point of " Time, as well as the Points of the luminous Body that en- " lightened them. The numberless Rays which flow from all " visible Bodies, called Objects, may be methodically distributed " in this Manner. The Surface of the Object is considered as " consisting of Physical Lines, and these Lines as consisting of " Physical Points, and these Points are conceived to radiate all " manner of Ways. It is usual to make use of nothing else for " an Object but a Physical Line. For by how much that Line is " increased or diminished in apparent Magnitude, or Brightness, " or Distinctness, so much the Diameter, or Length, of any Ob- " ject, in its Place, would be increased or diminished.

Fig. 36. " The Point Q, from which Rays diverge, or towards which " they converge (being made to go back towards the same Point,

" though

" though they may never meet at it) is called their Focus. And " in both Cases any Parcel of these Rays, as QBC, or QBA, " considered apart from the rest, is called a Pencil of Rays. " This Figure represents the Manner in which the Rays of a Pen- " cil, QAB, diverging from any Point of an Object Q, and " falling upon a strait Line ABC, or upon a polished Plane re- " presented by it, do all diverge after Reflection as if they came " from another Point q. The Ray QC, which falls perpendicu- " larly upon the Plane AB, is reflected back again along the " same Line CQ; but all the rest falling upon it with greater " and greater Degrees of Obliquity, as the Points of Incidence lye " farther and farther from C, are also reflected with Degrees of " Obliquity respectively greater. It will seem reasonable therefore, " especially by attending to the Figure, that the reflected Rays, " produced backwards, should meet the Perpendicular QC, pro- " duced in a Point q, situated as far from the reflecting Plane on " one Side, as Q is on the other: And consequently that all the " Rays flowing from a single Point Q, will after Reflection di- " verge from a single Point q, at an equal Distance on the other " Side of the reflecting Plane.

" On the contrary, if q be a Focus to which the incident Rays " are made to converge, the Point Q will be their Focus after " Reflection from the Surface ACB.

" What has been said of the Point Q, is applicable to every " other Point of an Object PQR; namely, that as the Focuses " Q, q, lie at equal Distances on each Side of the reflecting Plane, " so the Focuses P, p lye on each Side at other equal Distances, " and R, r at other equal Distances, in Lines Pp, Rr, drawn " perpendicularly through the Plane AB. Hence it is easy to " understand by Inspection of the Figures, that these Focuses " p, q, r, with innumerable others, lying all in the same Order as " the corresponding Points P, Q, R, compose an imaginary Line of " the same Length and Shape as the Line PQR; and that the " Situation of the Line pqr, with respect to the back side of the " reflecting Plane, is the very same as that of PQR with respect " to the fore side of it. This Line pqr is called an Image or " Picture of the Object PQR."* Fig. 37 38, 39

This may suffice to shew the Nature of the reflected Images of Objects from polish'd Planes; the Knowledge of which is abso-

* Vide Smith's Opt. p. 7.

lutely neceſſary in ſeveral Parts of Painting, eſpecially in Landſkips, where Water is often introduced; the Tranſparency of which, depends upon giving the Repreſentation of that Fluid its true or local Colour, and in giving the Reflections their proper Depths and Appearances.---Proceed we now to a farther Conſideration of the Refraction of the Rays of Light, as introductory to the Cauſe of Colours.

In the 35th Figure we obſerved, that if a Ray of Light went out of Air into Water, it would not proceed ſtrait forward, but be bent and turned out of its direct Courſe at the Point of Incidence C; and that the Reaſon of this Refraction, or bending of the Ray, was owing to its paſſing out of a rarer or thinner, into a denſer or thicker Medium; and in Proportion as this Medium into which the Light enters, is more or leſs denſe, the Ray will be more or leſs refracted. Now what is ſaid of one Ray, will hold equally true as to any Number of Rays: But ſince the Rays of Light are not alike, but diſſimilar, ſome greater and others leſs, they will be differently refracted at their Exit out of one Medium into another Medium; and being thus ſeparated, each Species of Rays will exhibit a Colour peculiar to itſelf; which is the Subject of the next Section.

SECT. III.

Of the Cause *of* Colours.

" THE Sun's Rays are not homogeneous (that is alike) but of
" different Kinds, and each Sort has a different Degree of
" Refrangibility; that is, in paſſing through a denſe Medium they
" are differently diſpoſed to be refracted, being bent or turn'd
" out of their firſt Courſe to different Diſtances from the Perpen-
" dicular; and theſe ſeveral Sorts of Rays have each a peculiar
" Colour, *viz.* thoſe which are leaſt refrangible, are Red; the
" ſecond Sort, Orange; the third Sort, Yellow; the fourth Sort,
" Green; the fifth Sort, Blue; the ſixth Sort, Indigo; and the ſe-
" venth Sort, Violet, which laſt are moſt refrangible, or refracted
" to the greateſt Diſtance from the Perpendicular.

Fig. 40. " To illuſtrate this Matter, let GF repreſent a Parcel of the
" Solar Rays entering through the Hole H of a Window-Shutter,
" into a darkened Room, and there let them fall on the Priſm
" ABC, in the Point F: In paſſing through the Priſm they will be
" ſeverally refracted in a different Degree, and thus ſeparated from
" each

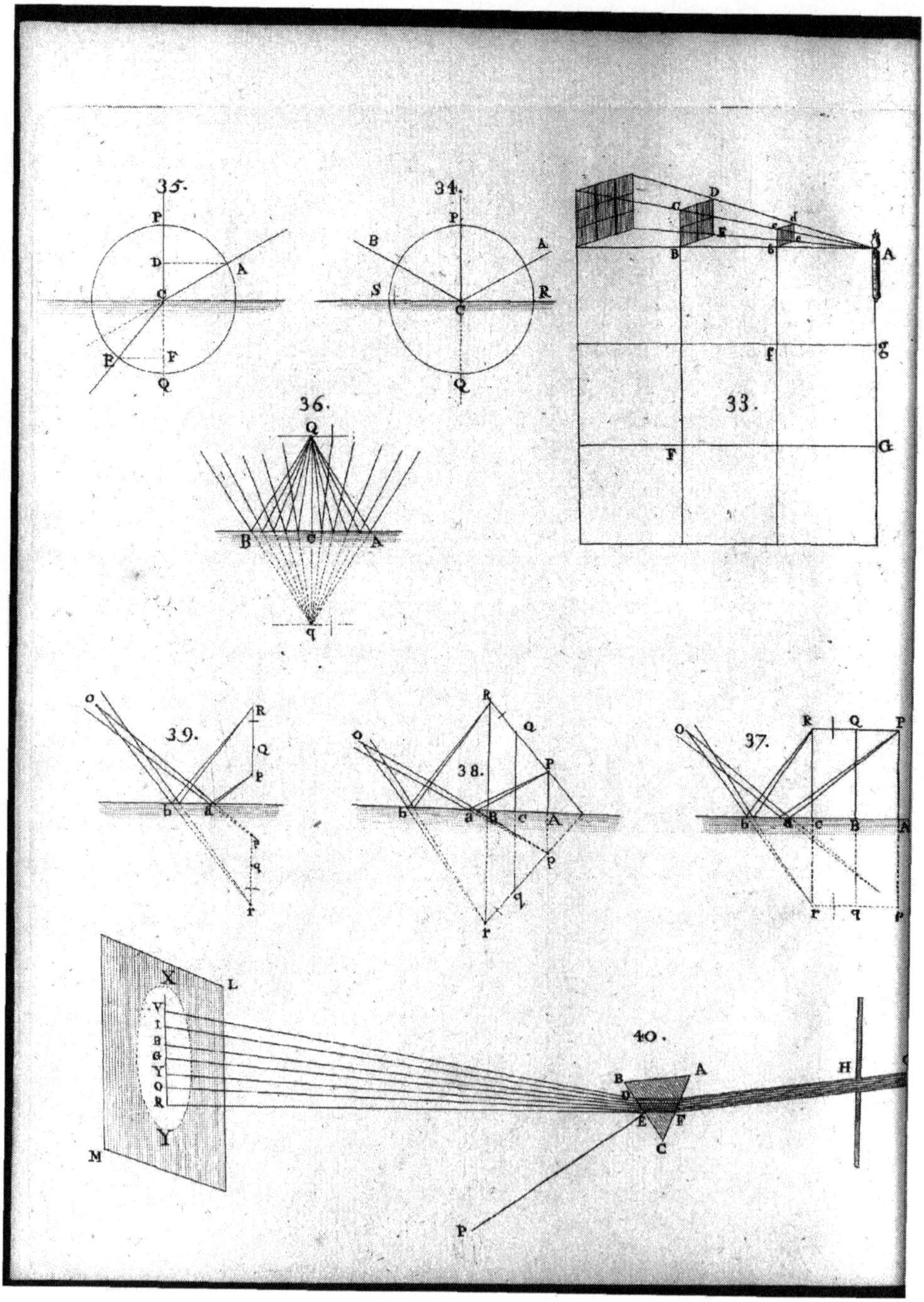
35.
34.
33.
36.
39.
38.
37.
40.

" each other, so that at their Exit on the other Side at E, they " will proceed at different Distances from the Perpendicular EP " to the other Side of the Room, where they will make a long " and various-coloured Image of the Sun XY; which is, perhaps, " one of the most surprizing and agreeable Spectacles in Nature.

" The several Sorts of Rays, after they are refracted, appear in " their own proper Colours, in Order as follows, *viz.* Those " which are least refracted, or fall nearest the Perpendicular EP, " are Red, and make the red Part of the Spectrum at R; the " next are the Orange at O, the Yellow at Y, the Green at G, " the Blue at B, the Indigo at I, and the Violet at V: And these " seven are all the original simple Colours in Nature; and of " which, by various Mixtures, all others are compounded, in the " common Refractions and Reflections from natural Bodies.*

" From hence then we may conceive, that Colour is a Sensation " produced in the Mind, by the Impression made in the Eye, by " certain Kinds or Sorts of Rays of Light, separated from others " by means of their different Refrangibility and Reflexibility, " whereby they are divided into several Parcels, each endowed with " its own distinct colour-making Power. And Bodies, whose Sur- " faces are disposed to reflect one kind of these Rays more copiously " than any others, exhibit, and are said to be of that Colour " which is peculiar to the Rays they most copiously reflect; and " the infinite Diversity of Bodies, and the different Mixtures and " Modifications of different colour-making Rays thereby occa- " sioned, must therefore produce that infinite Variety of Colours " which beautifies the Face of Nature." †

* The Truth of all this any Person may convince himself of by making the Experiment, or by only holding a Prism between his Eyes and the Sun; then by turning it round, he will see the several Colours in their proper Order, as above described.

† Martin's Philos. vol. II. p. 156.——Hamilton's Pers. p. 1.

CHAP. III.

The THEORY *of* PERSPECTIVE.

SECT. I.

An Explanatory Part, by Way of INTRODUCTION.

PERSPECTIVE is the Art of drawing upon any Surface the Representation of Objects as they appear to the Eye: In order to which, it is necessary to suppose the Light should come from every Part of the Representation in the very same Manner, and with the very same Strength of Colour, as it would do from the real Objects themselves, were they put in the Place of the Picture; because then, the Eye will not be able to judge, whether what it sees be a few Colours artificially laid upon a Canvas, or the real Objects themselves in the same Situation.

This is a general Definition of that kind of Perspective I am going to explain; which, is only what relates to the Arts of Painting and Designing; but not to any of the Mathematical Arts, which are too abstruse for my Speculations, and would be of no real Service to those for whose Use this Work is chiefly intended: And although Perspective Representations may be drawn upon any Surfaces, be they ever so irregular, yet I shall first confine myself to smooth even Planes, such as a Canvas, Wall, Cieling, or the like.---This being premised,

Fig. 41. Let E be the Eye, HE its Height from the Ground OP, and TOSX a square Object laid flat upon the Ground. Now it is evident, from what was said in the last Chapter, Sect. 1. that the Eye will see the Object TOSX, by means of the Rays of Light which come from every Part of the Object to the Eye. Let us therefore suppose a transparent Plane GLPP, like a Glass-Window, to be fixed perpendicularly upon the Ground OP, between the Spectator HE, and the Object TOSX; and it will be as evident, that the Rays TE, OE, SE, and XE, will be cut by the transparent Plane GLPP, in the Points tosx; which Points are called the Projection, or in other Words, the Perspective Representation of the corresponding Points TOSX, of the original Object.* And if Lines are drawn from the several Points tosx, so as to join each other, the Figure so described, will be the Projection, or Perspec-

* See Definition 6, Sect. II. of this Chapter.

tive

tive Reprefentation, of the whole original Figure TOSX, upon the Picture.

In like Manner, fuppofe TOSX to be raifed perpendicular to the Ground OP, and parallel to the Picture, but every thing elfe remaining in the fame Situation as in the former Figure; then will tosx be the Reprefentation of TOSX: For it is the Section of the Picture with the Rays TE, OE, SE, and XE, which come from the original Object to the Eye. And here let us obferve, that when the original Object is parallel to the Picture, its Reprefentation, tosx, will not only be parallel to the Original, but exactly like it, though fmaller in Proportion as the original Object is farther from the Picture; and if the Original be brought to G, fo as to coincide, or touch the Picture, then the Reprefentation will be equal to the Original: But on the contrary, the Original may be fuppofed fo far removed from the Picture, that the Angles, which the Rays fubtend at the Eye, growing fmaller and fmaller continually, it will at laft totally difappear, and confequently its Reprefentation upon the Picture will difappear alfo. Again, when the Original is brought to coincide with the Picture, the Reprefentation of TX will not only be equal to the Bottom of the Original, but will be at the Bottom of the Picture, in the Line GL, which is its Section with the Ground Plane OP: But as the Original is removed farther and farther from the Picture, the Reprefentation will rife higher and higher, 'till at laft, the Original being fuppofed at an infinite Diftance, its Reprefentation will vanifh into an imaginary Point C, exactly as high above the Bottom of the Picture as the Eye is above the Ground, or original Plane OP, upon which the Spectator, the Picture, and the original Object are now fuppofed to ftand. And fo alfo in regard to Objects that lie flat upon the Ground; when their Sides are parallel, then the Reprefentations of thofe Sides will be parallel alfo: Thus the Reprefentation tx of TX, and os of OS, are parallel to their Originals, but feverally diminifhed in proportion to their Diftance from the Picture; and therefore the Reprefentation of their oblique Sides TO, XS, which muft join tx, os, to compleat the Reprefentation of the whole original Figure, cannot be parallel to their Originals, but will be oblique in the Picture, and would, if continued towards the Top of the Picture, converge into an imaginary Point C, exactly as high above the Bottom of the Picture, as the Eye is above the original Plane OP. Now thefe Points, into which we fuppofe the Reprefentations of the Sides of Objects do vanifh

Fig. 42.

Fig. 41.

vaniſh upon the Picture, are called by the general Name of Vaniſhing Points.

From hence then, we may form an Idea of the Nature of the Perſpective Plane or Picture, and of Perſpective Repreſentations; which Repreſentations are nothing more than the Section which the Picture makes with the Rays of Light in their Paſſage from original Objects to our Eyes; and that the whole of this Art, depends upon finding the exact Section, or true Shape, which that cutting of the Rays makes upon the Picture in all kinds of Situations, and in giving them their proper Force and Colour.

But to illuſtrate this by a very familiar Inſtance. Suppoſe a Spectator to be looking at a Proſpect without Doors, from within, through a Glaſs-Window; he will perceive not only the vaſt Extent which ſo ſmall an Aperture will admit to be ſeen by his Eye, but the Shape, Size, and Situation, of every Object upon the Glaſs: If the Objects are near the Window, the Spaces which they take upon the Glaſs will be proportionably larger than when they are at a greater Diſtance; if they are parallel to the Window, then their Shapes upon the Glaſs will be parallel alſo; but if they are oblique, then their Shapes will be oblique, and ſo on. And he will always perceive, that as he alters the Situation of his Eye, the Situation of the Objects upon the Window will be altered alſo: If he raiſes his Eye ever ſo high, the Objects will ſeem to keep pace with his Eye, and riſe higher upon the Window; and the contrary, if he places it ever ſo low. And ſo in every Situation of the Eye, the Objects upon the Window will ſeem to riſe higher or lower; and conſequently, the Depth of the whole Proſpect will be proportionably greater or leſs, as the Eye is elevated or depreſſed; and the Horizon will, in every Situation of the Eye, be upon a Level with it: That is, the Horizontal Line, or that imaginary Line which appears to part the Earth and Sky, will ſeem to be raiſed as far above the Ground upon which the Spectator ſtands, as his Eye is removed from the ſame Place.

Fig. 43. Let us now ſuppoſe two Planes ABab, CDcd, of the ſame Height, and parallel to each other, one to paſs through the Eye E, the other through any Point as e, and both to be perpendicular to the Ground ABCD; and let us imagine another Plane, abcd, to be laid upon theſe two Planes, ABab, CDcd, as in the Figure, and it will be evident, that this Plane abcd is parallel to the Ground ABCD, becauſe it lies upon two Planes ABab, CDcd, of the ſame Height. Now if we ſuppoſe this Plane, abcd, to be continued

tinued at an infinite Diſtance, and the Line cd to repreſent a Part of the real Horizon, and then imagine a Picture GLPP, to be placed between the Eye E, and the Horizon cd; then its Section HL, with the horizontal Plane abcd, will be the indefinite Repreſentation of the Horizon cd, upon the Picture; and this Repreſentation is called the Horizontal Line. Now ſince all Objects which lye flat upon the Ground, or are parallel to it, ſeem to vaniſh into the real Horizon, therefore the Repreſentation of all ſuch Objects upon the Picture, muſt vaniſh into this Horizontal Line; becauſe it is the perſpective Repreſentation of the real Horizon: And for the ſame Reaſon, the Ground, or whole Extent between the Eye and the real Horizon, will not appear to lye flat, but to riſe upwards. For let E be the Eye, ABCD the Ground, Fig. 44.
and HI the utmoſt Extent which the Eye can diſtinguiſh; now, I ſay, the Ground will not appear to lie flat, as A B C D, but to riſe upwards, like A B c d, 'till it cuts the Plane a b c d, which is drawn through the Eye E, parallel to the original Plane ABCD; and the Section c d, which the Planes A B c d and a b c d make with each other, will repreſent the real Horizon. And, as before, if we ſuppoſe a Picture, G L P P, to be fixed between the Eye and the ſaid Horizon; then the Section H L, which the Picture makes with the parallel Plane a b c d, will be the indefinite Repreſentation of the Horizontal Line upon the Picture; becauſe the Rays of Light, in their Paſſage from the Section cd, or real Horizon, would cut the Picture in the Line HL.

From hence then, we may ſee, the grand Principle on which Perſpective depends; namely, on finding thoſe Lines and Points into which Objects ſeem to vaniſh upon the Picture. And whoever will give himſelf the Trouble to underſtand the following ſhort Theory, will have maſtered all the Difficulty in Perſpective: For it only requires to have a clear Idea of the Nature and Property of vaniſhing Lines and vaniſhing Points, and a few other Requiſites as previous thereto; which he may partly conceive by what has been ſaid already, and by conſidering, that as the Horizontal Line H L, is produced by means of the Plane a b c d, which paſſes through the Eye parallel to the Ground, or original Plane; ſo, in the very ſame Manner, all other vaniſhing Lines are determined; namely, by imagining a Plane to paſs through the Eye, parallel to thoſe Planes whoſe Repreſentations are required upon the Picture. ---Again, in regard to vaniſhing Points; they are determined by drawing Lines from the Eye, parallel to the original Lines, 'till they

they cut the Picture; in order to which, we must always suppose these Lines to lie in some Plane, and then, having found the vanishing Line of that Plane, the vanishing Point of any Line, in that Plane, may be found also. And from hence we may observe, that the Horizontal Line is of the same Nature with any other vanishing Lines, and differs from them only in being more useful, because, many more Objects are perpendicular and parallel to the Picture, than oblique with it: And therefore, the great Stress which hath been laid upon this Line by most Writers, is not so very significant as they apprehended; for, in some Cases, it is of no use at all in a Picture. For let us consider a little. If vanishing Lines upon the Picture, are always to be produced by Planes passing through the Eye, parallel to original Figures, then no original Plane can have its vanishing Line in the Horizontal Line, unless it is parallel to the Ground; but, if any Object be obliquely situated with regard to the Ground, then, the Plane which is to pass through the Eye, parallel to the Original, in order to determine its vanishing Line, will be oblique with the Ground also; and therefore it cannot pass through the Horizontal Line, but will be either above, below, perpendicular to it, or cross it in an oblique manner: All which may be conceived by inspecting the following Figures. In Fig. 45, the original Object, TOSX, lies upon the Ground; therefore, the Plane, a b c d, which passes through the Eye E, parallel to the Ground, cuts the Picture in the Horizontal Line HL. In Fig. 46, the Original, TOSX, is supposed perpendicular to the Ground, and to be perpendicular to the Picture also; therefore, the Plane ABPD, which passes through the Eye E, parallel to the said Plane, will be perpendicular to the Ground and perpendicular to the Picture; and therefore will pass through the Center C of the Picture, and produce the vanishing Line PD, which will be perpendicular to the Horizontal Line HC. But, if the original Object is perpendicular to the Ground, and oblique with the Picture, as in Fig. 47, then its vanishing Line PD, will be perpendicular to the Horizontal Line HL, but, will not pass through the Center or Middle of the Picture, but will be on one Side of it. Again, if the square Object ABTS, Fig. 48, (which is inclined to the Ground, at the Angle ATO, but reclined to the Picture) have two Sides AB, TS, parallel to the Picture; then the Plane OPVL, which passes through the Eye E, parallel to the original ABTS, will produce a vanishing Line VL, above the Horizontal Line HC, and exactly parallel to it. But if the same Object,

V.

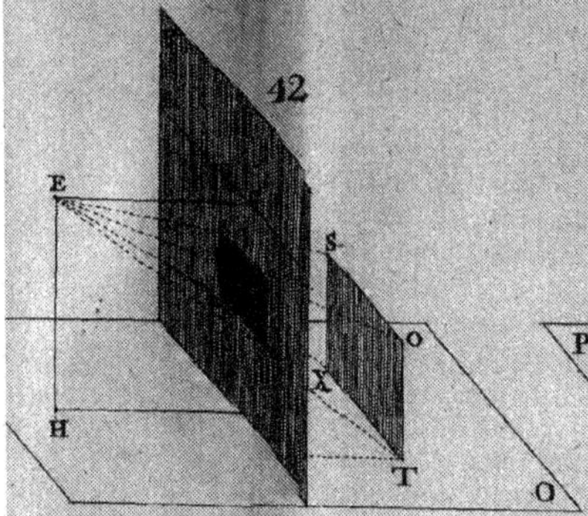

42

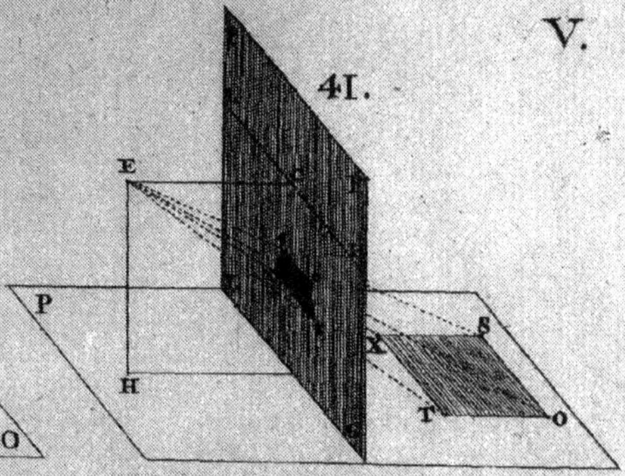

41.

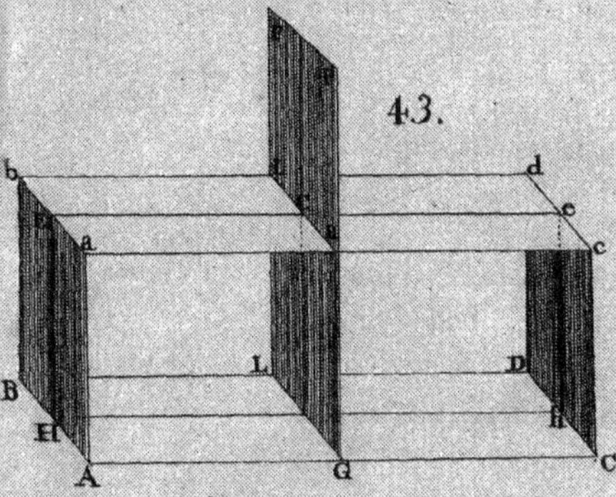

43.

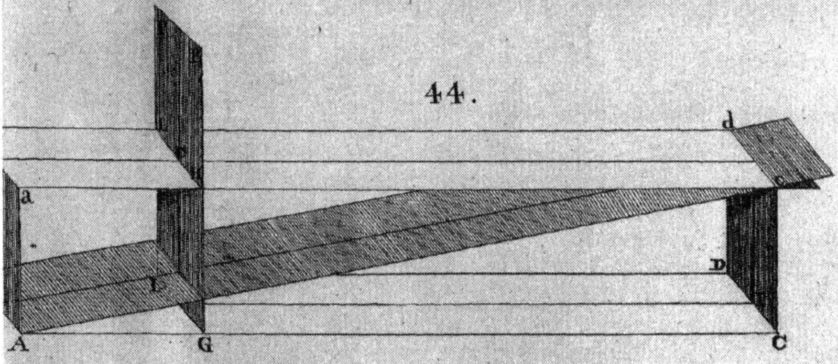

44.

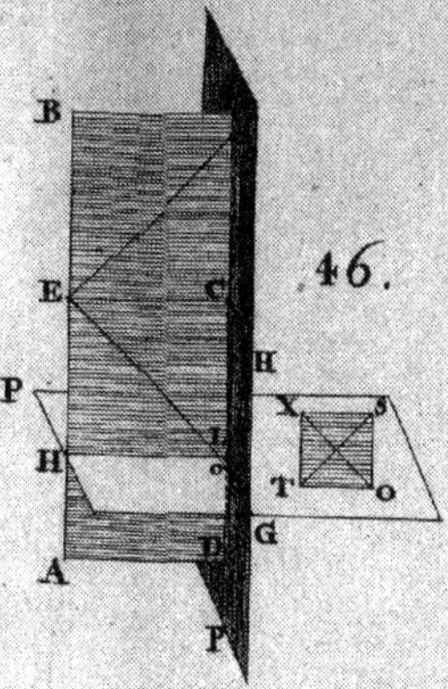

46.

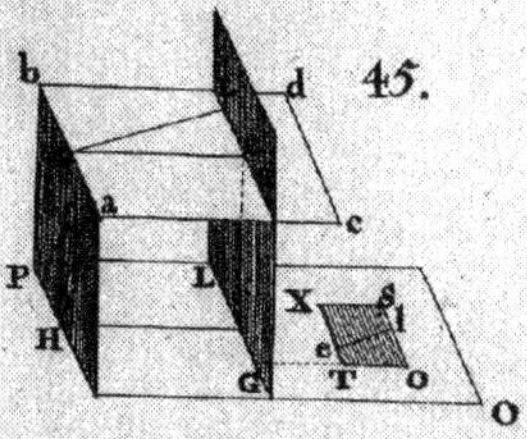

45.

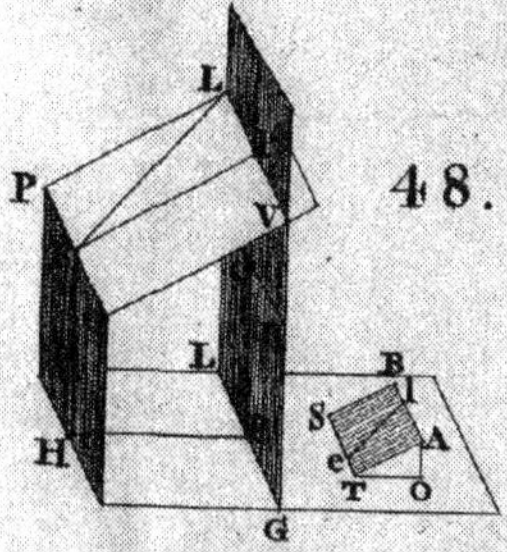

48.

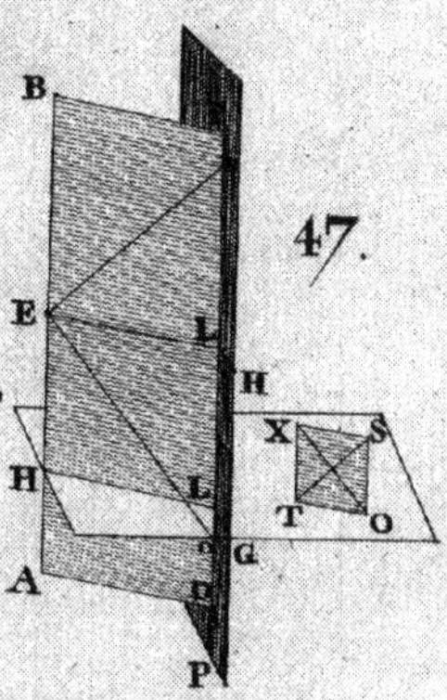

47.

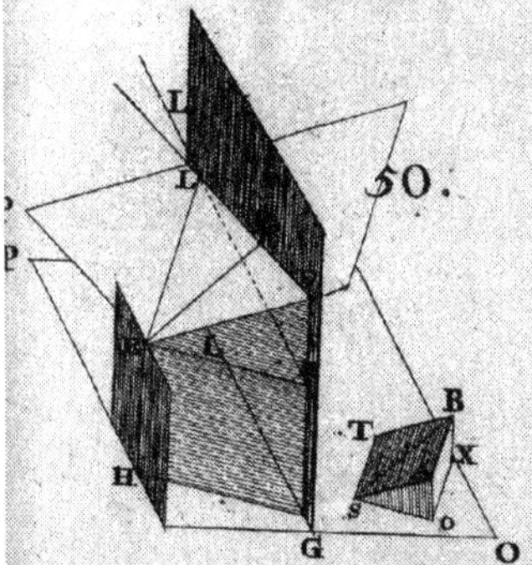

50.

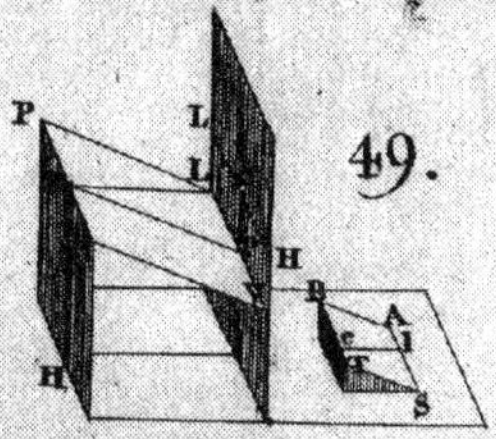

49.

Object, (Fig. 50.) be turned so as to have all its Sides oblique with the Picture, then the Plane EPLV, which passes through the Eye E, parallel to the original ABTS, will produce a vanishing Line VL, which will be aslant the Horizontal Line HL. Again; if the Object, ABTS, (Fig. 49.) be inclined both to the Ground and the Picture, but have its Sides AS, BT, parallel to the Picture, (as in Fig. 48.) then its vanishing Line, VL, will be parallel to the Horizontal Line HL, but below it. And so in regard to the vanishing Points of any original Lines: As these Lines are supposed to lie in some Planes, therefore, having found the vanishing Lines of those Planes, as above, the vanishing Point of any Line in those Planes may be easily found also; *viz.* by drawing Lines through the Eye, parallel to such Lines, 'till they cut the Picture: Thus, in Fig. 45, EL is drawn from the Eye E, parallel to the Original el, and therefore L is the vanishing Point of el upon the Picture. And so again in Fig. 47, Es, EL, and Eo, are parallel to the Originals ST, SX, OT and OX, and therefore will produce the corresponding vanishing Points; *viz.* s for the Line ST, L for the Lines SX and OT, and O for the Line XO. In like Manner the Points L, in Fig. 48, 49, 50, are determined; *viz.* by drawing the Lines EL, from the Eye, parallel to the Originals el and SB.---From hence, then, we may perceive, that the various Situations of Objects may be reduced under three general Heads; *viz.*

1. When they are perpendicular to the Picture, or parallel to the Ground.

2. When they are parallel to the Picture, or perpendicular to the Ground.

3. When they are obliquely situated, both as to the Picture and the Ground, or any other Plane upon which we suppose them: All which I shall now endeavour to explain in their several Orders, and apply them to Practice.

SECT. II.

DEFINITIONS.

1. THE *Point of Sight*, is that Point where the Spectator's Eye is placed to look at the Picture. Thus the Point E, of all the Figures in Plate 6, is the Point of Sight, or Place of the Eye.

Fig. 45. 2. If from the Point of Sight E, a Line, EC, be drawn perpendicular to the Picture GLHL, the Point C, where that Line cuts the Picture, is called the *Center of the Picture*.

3. The *Distance of the Picture*, is the Length of the Line EC, which is drawn from the Eye, perpendicular to the Picture.

Fig. 48, 49, 50. 4. If from the Point of Sight E, a Line EP be drawn perpendicular to any vanishing Line VL, the Point P, where that Line cuts the vanishing Line, is called the *Center of that vanishing Line*.

5. The *Distance of a vanishing Line*, is the Length of the Line EP, which is drawn from the Eye perpendicular to the said Line.

6. By *Original Object*, is meant the real Object whose Representation is sought, whether it be a Line, Point, or plane Figure: And by *Original Plane*, is meant that Plane upon which the real Object is situated; thus the Ground OP, is the Original Plane, and TOSX the Original Object. (Fig. 45.)

7. The Line GL, where an original Plane OP cuts the Picture GLHL, is called the *Section of the Original Plane*, or the *Ground Line*.

8. If any Original Line OT, be continued so as to cut the Picture; the Point G, where it cuts the Picture, is called the *Intersection of that Original Line*.

9. The *Vanishing Line of any Original Plane, &c.* is that Line, where a Plane drawn through the Eye, parallel to that Original Plane, cuts the Picture: Thus HL in this Figure, and VL in Fig. 48, 49, 50, are the vanishing Lines of their several Original Planes, TOSX and ABTS.

10. The *Vanishing Point of any Original Line*, is that Point where a Line drawn from the Eye, parallel to that Original Line, cuts the Picture: Thus EL, being parallel to the Original el, produces the vanishing Point L; and so on. (Fig. 48.)

THEOREM I.

Fig. 51. If two or more Planes, ABCD, EFGH, are parallel to each other, they will have the same vanishing Line HL.

For

For let GHLL be the Picture, E the Spectator's Eye, and ABCD an original Object.

Imagine the Plane HIKL to pass through the Eye E, parallel to the original Object ABCD, and it will cut the Picture in the Line HL, which will be the vanishing Line of the original Plane ABCD: And since the other original Plane EFGH, is parallel to ABCD, therefore the Plane HIKL is parallel to that also; and consequently HL is the vanishing Line of the Plane EFGH, and of every other Plane which is parallel to ABCD.

THEOREM 2.

The vanishing Points, H and L, of Lines AC, BD, in any original Plane ABCD, are in the vanishing Line HL, of that Plane.

From the Eye E, draw EH, EL, parallel to BD and AC; then because the original Plane ABCD, and the Plane HIKL, are parallel; therefore the Lines EH, EL, that are drawn from the Eye E, parallel to the original Lines BD, AC, will be in the Plane HIKL; and consequently must cut the Horizontal, or vanishing Line HL, in the Points H, L, and thereby produce the proper vanishing Points of the original Lines BD, AC.

THEOREM 3.

If the original Plane ABCD, is parallel to the Picture GHLL, it can have no vanishing Line upon it, and therefore its Representation will be parallel, as in Fig. 42. because its parallel Plane a b c d, which passes through the Eye E, can never cut the Picture, and consequently, will not produce a vanishing Line upon it. And so in regard to the Line BD: It can have no vanishing Point upon the Picture, but its Representation will be parallel to the Original, as o s, t x, in the above Figure. Fig. 52.

THEOREM 4.

The Representation a b, of a Line AB, is a Part of the Line GC, which passes through the intersecting Point G, and the vanishing Point C, of the original Line AB. Fig. 53, 54.

For imagine the Plane AHEF, to pass through the Eye E, and the original Line AB, and it will pass through both the intersecting Point G and the vanishing Point C, and cut the Picture in the Line GC: And if the visual Rays AE, BE, are drawn from the Object to the Eye, they must be in the Plane AHEF, and consequently, their Section a b with the Picture, will be in the Section GC of that Plane with the Picture; therefore, a b, which is a Part of the Line GC, is the Representation of the Line AB.

COROL. 1.

When the Original is perpendicular, as AB, Fig. 53, then its vanishing Point will be in the Center C of the Picture; because a Line drawn from the Eye perpendicular to the Picture, determines its Center; and therefore, since AB is perpendicular to the Picture, EC is parallel to it, and consequently will produce the Center C, for the vanishing Point of AB.

COROL. 2.

If the Original AB is in a Plane OPB, perpendicular to the Picture, but lies obliquely in that Plane in regard to the Picture,
Fig. 54. as AB; then its vanishing Point L, will be in the Horizontal Line HL, but on one Side of the Center C: And so whatever be the Situation of any original Line, its Representation upon the Picture will always be in that Line which is drawn through its Intersection and vanishing Point.

COROL. 3.

Fig. 55. For let AB be inclined to the original Plane OP, at the Angle ABD.

Continue AB 'till it cuts the Picture in G, and from the Eye E, draw EF parallel to it, which will cut the Picture in the vanishing Point F; then draw FG, and the visual Rays AE, BE, cutting FG, in a and b; then will the Line a b be the Representation of the Original AB, and is a Part of the Line FG, which passes through the intersecting Point G, and the vanishing Point F, of the Original AB. This, from what was observed above, is self-evident; because the Rays AE, BE, are in the Plane AFEG, which passes through the Eye and the original Object, and therefore must cut the Picture in the Section FG.

COROL. 4.

From hence it follows, that all Lines which are parallel to each other, but not parallel to the Picture, will have the same vanishing Point; because a Line which passes through the Eye, being parallel to one, is parallel to all the rest; and therefore can produce but one

VII.

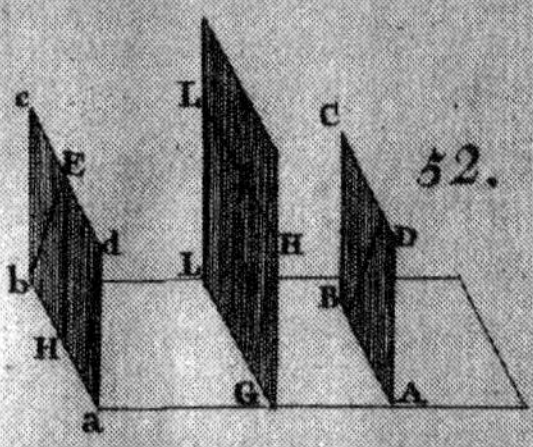

52.

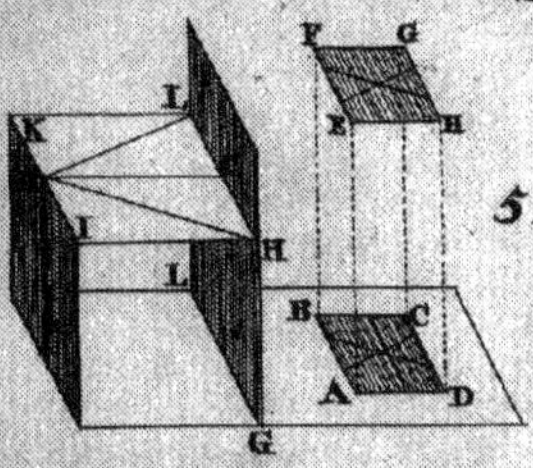

51.

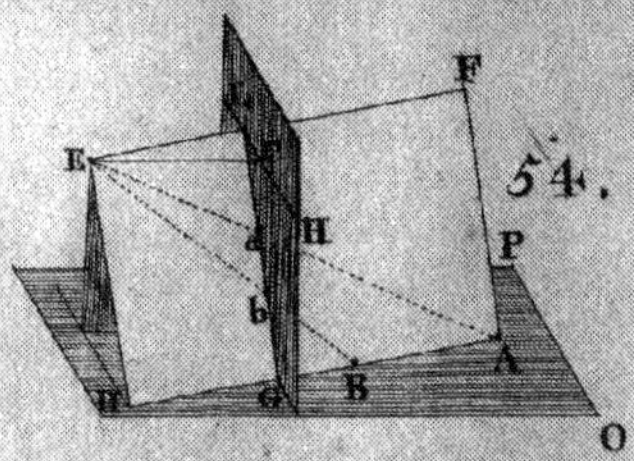

54.

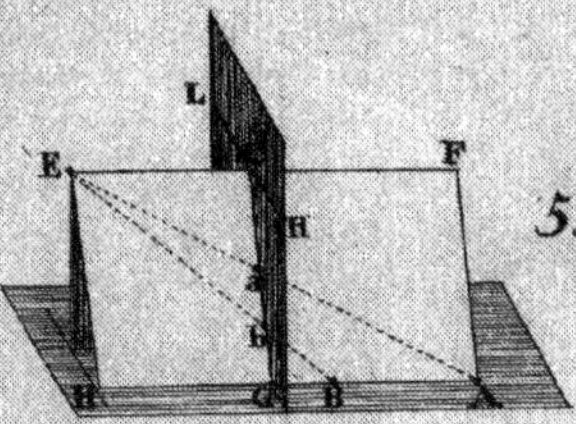

53.

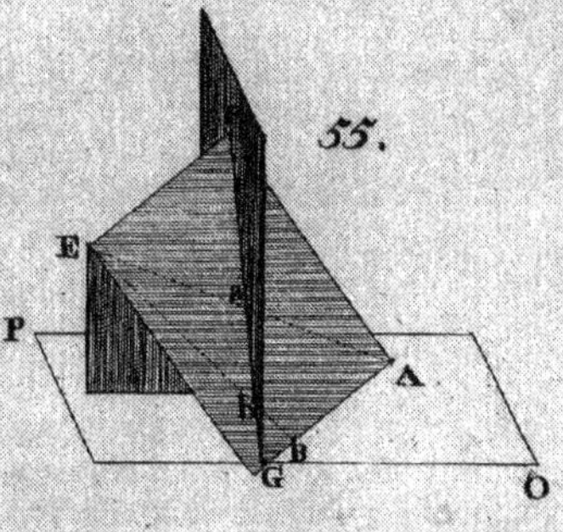

55.

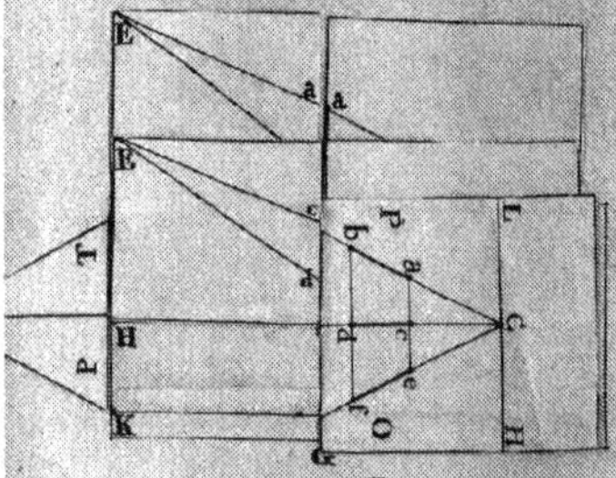

56.

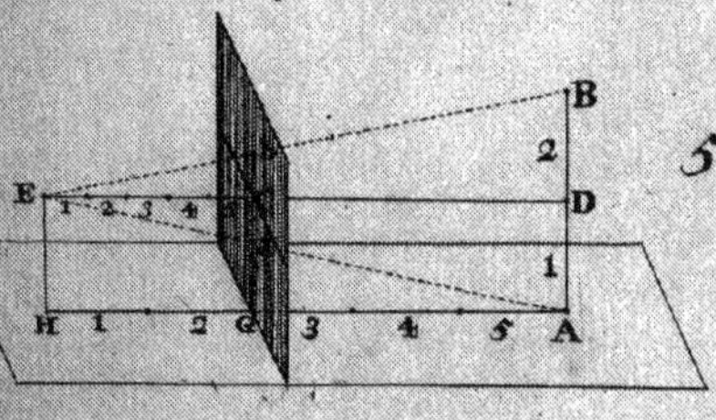

56. 2.

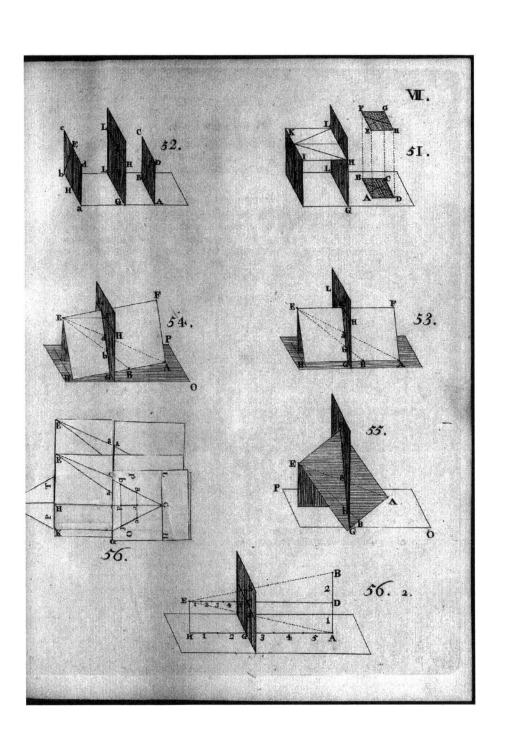

one vaniſhing Point, let the Number of parallel Lines be ever ſo many. This I have explained by Paper Planes, where OPHL is the Picture, TPE a Plane which paſſes through the Eye parallel to the Picture, and AB, CD, EF, three original Lines parallel to each other. Now if we raiſe the Picture OPHL, and the Plane TPE, 'till they are perpendicular to the original Plane AEKI, and then turn the other Planes, which paſs through the original Objects AB, CD, EF, 'till they coincide with the Eye at E; they will all meet upon the Picture in the Point C, which is the common vaniſhing Point of all the original Lines AB, CD and EF. And by obſerving the viſual Rays, which are drawn from the Extremities of every original Object to the Eye, at E, we may perceive that the Repreſentation of the Line AB, will be a b upon the Picture; of CD, cd; and of EF, ef: All which Repreſentations will tend to the Point C, as a common Center, and there vaniſh into the Picture. And we may moreover obſerve, that ſince the original Lines AB, CD, EF, are not only equal and parallel to each other, but at equal Diſtances from the Picture or Section GL; that therefore their Repreſentations will be at the ſame Diſtance from the Section, GL, of the original Plane, and between the ſame parallel Lines a e, b f. Fig. 56.

This laſt Theorem, and the Corollaries deduced from it, are the principal Foundation of all the Practice of Perſpective; and therefore the Reader will do well to make it very familiar to him: And to help his Reflections upon it, I have annexed the laſt Figure. But although I have confined myſelf in this Figure to an original Plane which is perpendicular to the Picture, yet the ſame Rules will ſerve for any other original Planes, be they ever ſo obliquely ſituated in regard to the Picture; provided they are parallel amongſt themſelves: As muſt appear extremely obvious, by a little Attention in examining the Figure.

THEOREM 5.

The Repreſentation a b, of any Line AB, that is parallel to the Picture, is to its original Line AB, as the Diſtance EC of the Repreſentation a b is to the Diſtance ED of the original Figure. For let the original Figure AB be two Parts, and the Diſtance ED (or which is the ſame Thing, AH) five Parts; and the Diſtance EC, (or HG) of the Repreſentation ab, two Parts; then will AB be to its Diſtance ED as five to two. For if we divide the Fig. 56. No. 2.

the Diſtance CE of the Repreſentation ab, into five Parts, then the Repreſentation ab will be equal to two of thoſe Parts; that is, as five is to two. Again, the Diſtance Ca, between the vaniſhing Point C, of a Line AO, and any Point a in its Repreſentation Oa; is to the Diſtance CO, between the vaniſhing Point C and the Interſection of that Line, as the Diſtance EC (or HO) of the Eye, is to the Diſtance HA of the original Point. For let HA be five Parts, and HO two Parts; divide OC into five Parts; and the Diſtance Ca, between the Repreſentation a of the Point A, will be two of thoſe Parts; therefore, Ca is to CO, as HO is to HA; that is, as two is to five: As is evident by inſpecting the Figure.

From hence, then, we may obſerve, that the perſpective Repreſentations of Objects are diminiſhed upon the Picture in an harmonical Proportion; and that, if the Length of any original Object, its Diſtance, together with the Diſtance and Height of the Eye, are known, that then the Appearance of thoſe Objects upon the Picture may be found by Calculation; which will be exemplified in the practical Part. Proceed we, therefore, in our propoſed Order *, to determine the Repreſentations of Objects which are in Planes variouſly ſituated in regard to the Picture.

SECT. III.

Of OBJECTS *which are in Planes perpendicular to the Picture.* †

Fig. 57. No. 1. LET ABCD be a ſquare Object lying flat on the original Plane OGLP, and let E be the Eye, and EC its Diſtance.

From what has been ſaid already it is manifeſt, that abcd is the Repreſentation of ABCD; for the Points a, b, c, d, are where the viſual Rays BE, &c. are cut by the Picture, as was obſerved in Fig. 41, 42. Or the Repreſentations ab, cd, are Parts of the Lines TC, SC, which are drawn from the interſecting Points T and S, and the vaniſhing Point C, of the original Lines AB, CD; as was ſhewn in Fig. 53, 54; and conſequently ad, bc, are the Repreſentations of their Originals AD, BC.

* Vide Page 25.

† The original Plane OGLP, which is perpendicular to the Picture, I ſhall always ſuppoſe the Ground, unleſs mention be made to the contrary; becauſe it will be more intelligible to the Generality of Readers, and becauſe I ſhall make great uſe of this Plane, and of its vaniſhing Line HL, as being the Horizontal Line.

Now

Now let us suppose the original Plane OGLP to be turned upon its Section GL; and the parallel Plane HIKL to be turned also upon the vanishing Line HL, 'till those Planes and the Picture become one strait Plane, like 𝔒𝔓𝔍𝔎; then it is manifest that the Eye E, will be transposed into the Point ℭ, and ℭC will be equal to its Distance. And if we moreover suppose the original Figure ABCD, to be drawn upon the under Side of the Plane OGLP, and exactly in the same Situation as 𝔄𝔅ℭ𝔇 in the Plane 𝔒GL𝔓; then, I say, if Lines are drawn from the several Points 𝔄𝔅ℭ𝔇 in this transposed Plane, to ℭ the transposed Place of the Eye, that their Sections a, b, c, d, with the Lines TC, SC, will be in the very same Points, in which those Lines are cut by the Rays, which go from the original Points A,B,C,D, in the Plane OGLP, to the Eye E: Thus the Ray BE cuts the Line TC in b; and if a Line is drawn from 𝔅 to ℭ, it will cut TC in the same Point b; and so of the rest. From whence it follows, that the Representation abcd, may be as exactly determined by thus transposing the Planes, as by those imaginary Rays of Light which go from the real Object to the Eye.

That the Sense of this Figure may be the more clearly comprehended, in Fig. 57, No. 2, are all the above Planes laid flat upon the Paper; and may easily be distinguished by the Letters which denominate each Plane. Thus OPLG is the original Plane, ABCD the original Object, T and S the Section of the Sides AB, CD, with the Picture GLHL: The parallel Plane is HIKL; and HL the vanishing Line of the original Object. C the Center of the Picture; E the Eye; and EC its Distance.---These Things being premised, let us apply them to Practice by drawing the above Representation.

From T and S draw TC, SC, and from the several Points A, B, C, D, draw Lines to the Eye at E, which will cut TC, SC, in the Points a, b, c, d; then draw ad, bc, parallel to HL, and the Representation is compleated. Fig. 57. No. 2.

From hence, then, it follows, that if the Situation, or Seat of an original Object, together with the Place of the Picture, and the Distance of the Eye, are known, that then the Representation of that Object may be easily determined: For let us now, without any Regard to the former Figure, call OPGL the Ground, ABCD an original Object, GLHL the Picture, HL the Horizontal Line, C the Center of the Picture, and CE the Distance of the Eye.

From

From the Eye E draw EC, parallel to the Sides AB, CD of the Original, which will cut the vanishing Line HL, in C, the Center of the Picture; because AB and CD are perpendicular to the Picture, that is, perpendicular to the Section GL; therefore C is the vanishing Point of AB and CD.---Continue the Sides AB, CD, 'till they cut the Section GL in T and S. From T and S draw Lines to C; then from the several Points A, B, C, D, draw Lines to E, which will cut TC, SC, in the Points a, b, c, d: Finally, draw the Lines ad, bc, which will give the Representation required.

This Representation may also be determined without drawing Lines from the original Points A, B, C, D, to the Eye E, by means of the Diagonal AC continued, and its parallel EN.----For Continue the vanishing Line HL, and the Section GL, at pleasure; continue also the Diagonal AC, 'till it cuts the Section in M: From E, draw EN, parallel to AC; and from N, where EN cuts the vanishing Line, draw NM, cutting TC, SC, in the Points a and c; then is a the Representation of A, and c the Representation of C; therefore from a and c, draw ad, bc, parallel to HL, and the Thing proposed is done.

Fig. 58. For let ABCD be an original Square, and AC, BD, Diagonals drawn in it; and let ABcd be its Representation upon the Picture.---C is the Center of the Picture, and CE its Distance.

Through E, draw EL and EH, parallel to the Diagonals AC, BD, cutting the vanishing Line in L and H; then are L and H the vanishing Points of those Diagonals; for there the Picture is cut by Lines which are drawn from the Eye parallel to the Originals AC, BD. And for the same Reason, (as we have observed before) C is the vanishing Point of AD, BC; and therefore, if Lines are drawn from the Sections A, B, to the vanishing Points H, C, L, their mutual Intersections c, d, with AC, and BC, will determine their several Representations: Thus Ad is the Representation of AD, Bc of BC, Ac of AC, and Bd of BD; and by drawing cd (which will be parallel to the Horizontal Line) the Representation of the whole Square will be compleated.

The practical Part is represented by the 59th Figure; where all the Planes are laid down, as before, with corresponding Letters to distinguish them.

From hence, then, we may observe, that any plane Figure may easily be drawn upon the Picture by resolving the whole into Triangles.

For

VIII.

57.2.

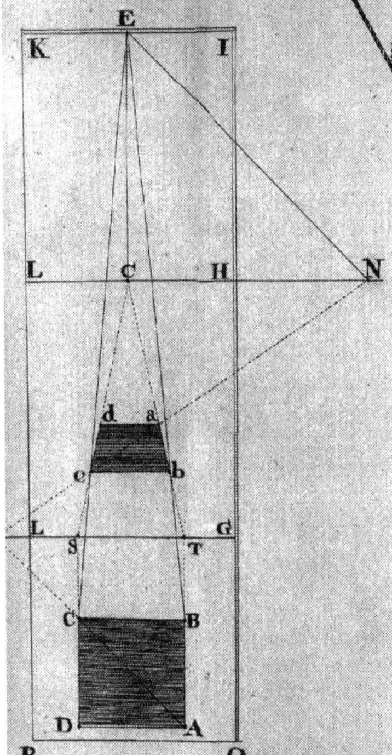

57.1.

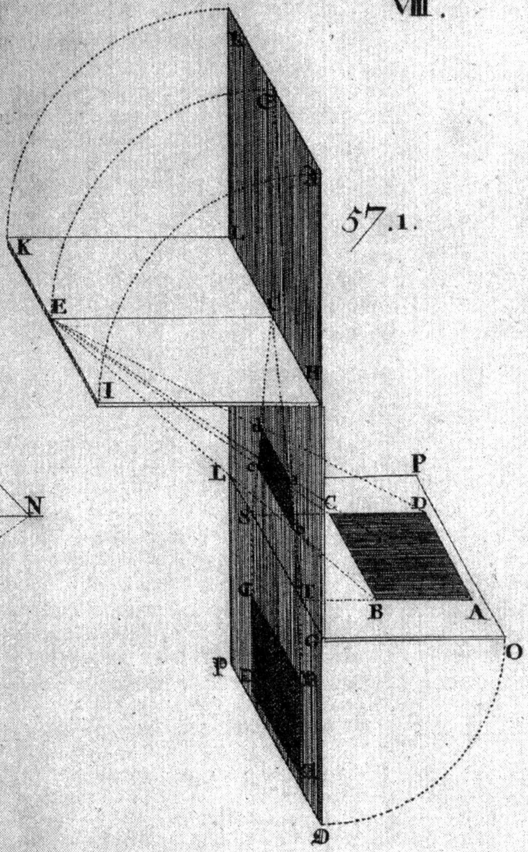

IX.

60.

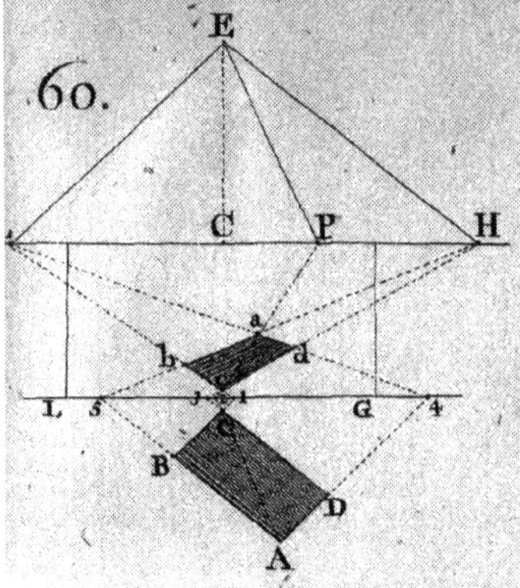

58.

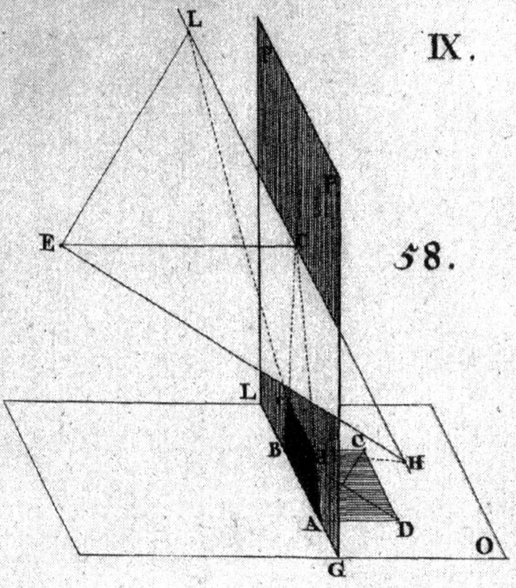

59.

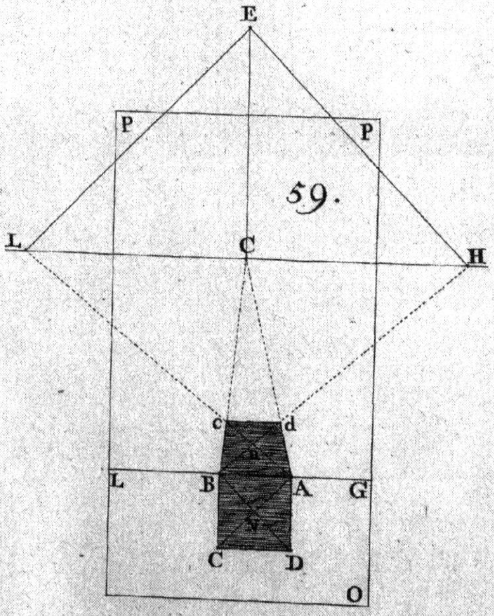

For let ABCD be a Square resolved into four Triangles, as AND, ANB, CND, CNB. Then, by means of the three vanishing Points H,C,L, which are found by drawing EC, EH, EL, parallel to AD, BC, AC, BD, the Representations of those Triangles may be found; as in the Figure. And so likewise in Fig. 60, the Representation of the Parallelogram ABCD, by means of the Points H, L; or the Triangles ABC, ADC, by means of the Points P, H, L, may be determined. Fig 59.

These two last Figures, though so very simple, contain the greatest Part of Practical Perspective: For, however original Planes are situated, or however any Lines are drawn upon them, their Representations may always be determined upon the Picture, by continuing the original Lines 'till they cut the Picture, and by drawing Lines through the Eye parallel to them. All the Difficulty lies in being careful to draw the Lines from the right intersecting and vanishing Points; which a little Practice will make extremely easy: And, therefore, here the Learner will do well to exercise himself with the Examples under this Head in Book II. Sect. 2.

SECT. IV.

Of OBJECTS *which are in Planes perpendicular to the Ground.*

HEre TOSX is a square Plane which stands upon its Side TO, perpendicular to the Ground Plane OP, and is also perpendicular to the Picture. Fig. 61.

Now let E be the Eye, C the Center of the Picture, and CE its Distance.—From the Eye E, draw EH parallel to TX or OS, and EC parallel to OT: Then because EC is parallel to TO and SX, therefore C is the vanishing Point of those Lines; and therefore, from C draw CL, cutting the Section GL in L; and then from L draw LH parallel to CE, which will compleat a perpendicular Plane CEHL, that passes through the Eye parallel to the original Object TOSX; and therefore CL, its Section with the Picture, is the vanishing Line of that original Plane. And since CE is by Construction perpendicular to CL, therefore C is the Center of the vanishing Line, and also the Center of the Picture, and CE is its Distance.

Again, continue CL at pleasure; and from the Eye E, draw EA, EB, parallel to the Diagonals OX, TS, which will cut the vanishing

Line AB in the Points A and B; therefore A and B are the vanishing Points of those Diagonals, by means of which the whole Representation may be determined. Thus G is the Section of the Side OT, and C its vanishing Point, therefore draw GC; then from T and O draw Lines to E, which will give the Appearance to of TO; and from t and o draw the Lines tx, os, parallel to the vanishing Line AB (that is, perpendicular to the Ground Plane) and continue them at pleasure: Finally, from A draw a Line through o, cutting tx in x, and from B draw a Line to t, which will cut os in s, then draw sx to its vanishing Point C, which finishes the Figure.

Fig. 62. But to apply this to Practice.---The Planes being supposed to be laid flat, as in Fig. 57. No. 2.

Then OT represents the Seat, or Plan, of the original Plane TOSX, in the last Figure, TG its Distance from the Picture, AEB the parallel Plane, E the transposed Place of the Eye, and CE its Distance.

From the Extremities O, T, of the Seat OT, draw T 1, O 2, at pleasure, but parallel to each other, cutting the Section in 1 and 2; make CB equal to the Distance CE of the Picture, and from B draw BH, parallel to T 1, O 2, cutting the horizontal Line in H: Then is H the vanishing Point of the Lines T 1, O 2; therefore draw H 1, H 2, and from G draw GC, which will be cut by the above Lines in the Points t, o; and thereby give to for the Representation of TO. Again, from t and o, draw the Lines tx, os, at pleasure, but parallel to the vanishing Line AB; then from A draw a Line through o, cutting tx in x; and from B draw a Line to t, which cutting os in s, will determine the last Angle of the Square; and therefore, by drawing sx to its vanishing Point C, the whole Representation will be compleated.---I have made use of both the vanishing Points A, B, to exercise the Learner, but one Point will do; thus, Ax determines the Side tx; therefore draw xC, which will cut os, and give the other Side os.

Fig. 61. Here let us observe, that when the Seat OT, of any Plane, is perpendicular to the Picture, the vanishing Line of that Plane will pass through the Center of the Picture, and be perpendicular to the horizontal Line: But, if the Seat OT, Fig. 63, of any perpendicular Plane, TOSX, be oblique with the Picture, then its vanishing Line, AB, will not pass through the Center of the Picture, but on one Side of it; nevertheless, it will always be perpendicular to the horizontal Line, and will pass through the vanishing Point L, of its Seat OT.

For

For, draw EL, parallel to OT, and it will cut the horizontal Line in L: From E and L, draw EH, LL, parallel to TX or OS; and from L, where LL cuts the Section GL, draw LH parallel to EL; then is the Plane LLHE parallel to the original Plane TOSX, and consequently perpendicular to the Ground; and therefore LL, its Section with the Picture, is the vanishing Line of that original Plane, and is perpendicular to the horizontal Line: And since the vanishing Point L is in the Section LL, therefore LL continued will pass through that Point, and consequently AB is the vanishing Line of the Plane TOSX. Again; since EL is perpendicular to the vanishing Line AB, therefore L is the Center of that vanishing Line, and EL its Distance; and therefore, from E draw EA, parallel to the Diagonal OX, and EB parallel to the Diagonal TS, cutting the vanishing Line in A and B; then are A and B the vanishing Points of those Diagonals; from whence the Representation may be compleated, as in the former Figure. Fig. 63.

But to apply this to Practice. Let the several Planes be supposed to be laid down as before.

Then TO is the Seat of the original Object, L its vanishing Point, C the Center of the Picture, EC its Distance, L the Center of the vanishing Line AB, and EL its Distance. Fig. 64.

From the Section G, draw GL to its vanishing Point, and from the Extremities T, O, of the Seat TO, draw two parallel Lines at pleasure, cutting the Section GL in 1 and 2; from E, draw E 3, parallel to T 1 and O 2, cutting the horizontal Line in 3; then draw 1 3, 2 3, which will give the Representation ot; again, from t and o, draw the Lines tx, os, parallel to the vanishing Line AB: And then, by means of the vanishing Points A and B, the whole Representation may be compleated, as in Fig. 62.

This Figure also deserves the Learner's particular Attention; for if he observes, in Fig. 62, the vanishing Line AB passes through the Center of the Picture, and therefore the Distance CE of that vanishing Line, is equal to the Distance of the Eye, or principal Distance: But in this last Figure, since the vanishing Line does not pass through the Center of the Picture, therefore, the Distance EL, of that vanishing Line, is greater than the principal Distance CE, and will be proportionably greater and greater, as the vanishing Line is removed farther and farther from the Center of the Picture. For the principal Distance EC, is one Side of a right-angle Triangle ECL; but EL, the Distance of the vanishing Line Fig. 64.

AB, is the Hypothenuse of that Angle, and therefore greater than either of the Sides EC or CL: From whence it follows, that if a Line CL be drawn from the Center of the Picture, perpendicular to any vanishing Line AB, the Point L, where that Line cuts the Picture, will determine the Center of that vanishing Line; and if a Line be drawn from the Eye to that Point, as EL, it will determine its Distance *.

Let us now, without any Regard to the Theory, find the Appearance of a square Object situated like TOSX, in Fig. 63.

Fig. 64. Let TO be the Seat of the Object proposed, HL the horizontal Line, C the Center of the Picture, CE the principal Distance, and GL the Section of the Ground Plane with the Picture. Continue the Seat OT, 'till it cuts the Section in G, and parallel to OT, draw EL from the Eye, cutting the horizontal Line in the vanishing Point L; then draw GL: Finally, draw T 1, O 2, and and also their Parallel E 3; by which means the Representation o t, may be found. Again, through the vanishing Point L, draw BA, perpendicular to HL, and continue the horizontal Line towards 𝕮, at pleasure; then, because CL is perpendicular to the vanishing Line AB, therefore L is the Center of that vanishing Line, and consequently, EL is its Distance: Therefore continue the Perpendicular CL, at pleasure, beyond the vanishing Line AB, and from L, with the Radius LE, describe an Arc A𝕮BE, cutting the vanishing Line in A and B, and CL continued in 𝕮; then are A and B the vanishing Points of the Diagonals o x, and t s, and 𝕮 is the proper Distance of the Eye: Therefore by drawing Perpendiculars from t and o, and Lines from A and B, through the same Points t and o, they will cut the Perpendiculars t x, o s, in x and s, and thereby give the Height of the Square; from whence, by drawing x L, it will be compleated.

From hence, then, it is manifest, that the Method for finding the Representation of an upright Plane, is exactly the same as that for determining the Appearance of a Plane which lies flat upon the Ground, only the Situation of the vanishing Line is different; but the Operation in both Cases is the very same; which may be conceived by turning the Figure, and imagining AB to be the horizontal Line, L the Center, and L𝕮 the Distance of the Picture: For then this Figure will be like Fig. 59. But that the Learner

* See Definition 2, Sect. 2. Chap. 1.—also Definitions 4, 5, Sect. 2, of this Chapter.

X.

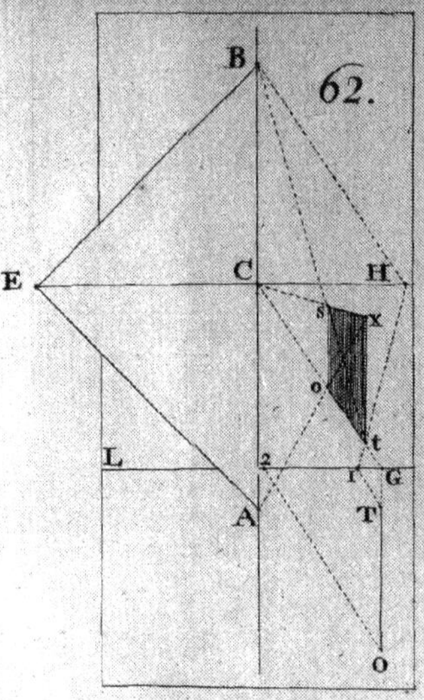
62.
B
E
C
H
s
x
o
t
L
2
1
G
A
T
O

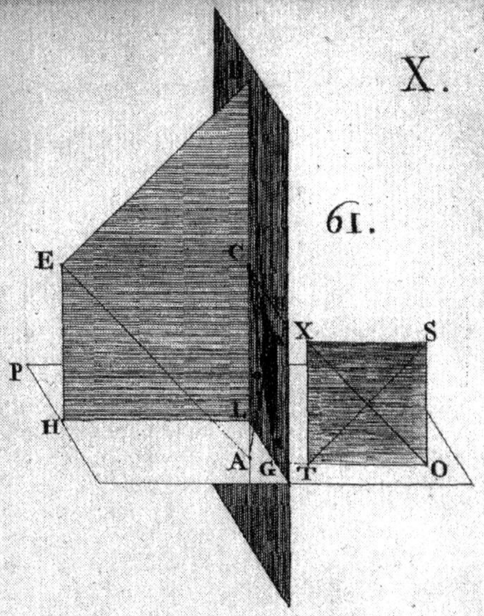
61.
E
C
X
S
P
L
H
A
G
T
O

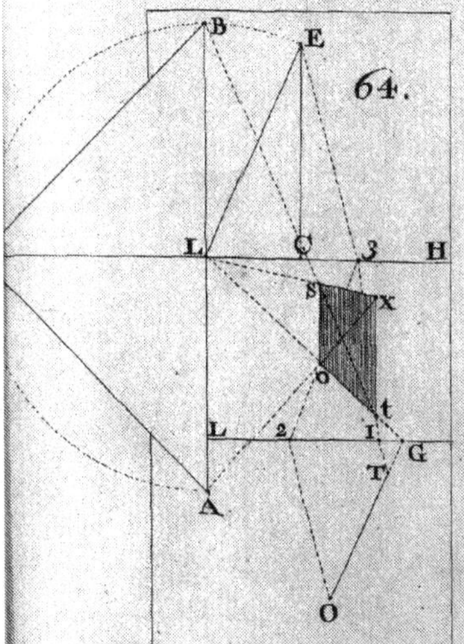
64.
B
E
L
C
3
H
S
X
o
t
L
2
I
G
T
A
O

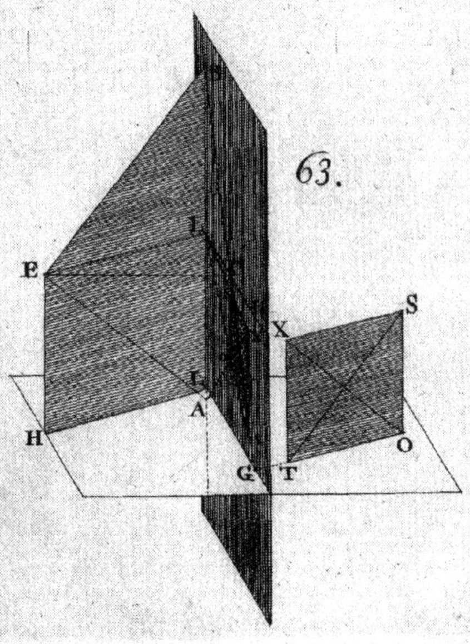
63.
L
E
X
S
I
A
H
O
G
T

may underſtand the Meaning of this more perfectly, he is deſired, before he proceeds any farther, to exerciſe himſelf with ſome Examples of this Kind; which he will find in Book II. Sect 3.

SECT. V.

Of OBJECTS *which are inclined to the Ground.*

THE Objects which come next under Conſideration, are ſuch as are neither perpendicular nor parallel to the Ground, but inclined to it; like the Roofs of Houſes, Pediments, and the like; the vaniſhing Lines of which cannot be the horizontal Line, nor any Line that is perpendicular to it.

For let TOSXYZ be the original Object, having one Side TOSX upon the Ground, and one Side TOYZ inclined to it, at the Angle YTX; and let the other Sides be perpendicular to the Ground.---E is the Eye, C the Center of the Picture, and CE its Diſtance. Fig. 65.

From E draw EC, parallel to XT or SO; then is C their vaniſhing Point: And becauſe TX is perpendicular to the Picture, therefore its vaniſhing Point C is the Center of the Picture. And ſince the Plane TXY, is perpendicular to the Ground, therefore its vaniſhing Line LD, is perpendicular to the horizontal Line; and therefore, through the vaniſhing Point C, draw LD, which continue at pleaſure, then from E draw ED, parallel to TY or OZ, which will cut the vaniſhing Line LD, and give D for the vaniſhing Point of the inclined Sides TY, OZ. And if a Line, VL, be drawn through D, parallel to the horizontal Line HC, it will be the vaniſhing Line of the inclined Plane, TYZO; becauſe, if a Plane was to paſs through the Eye, parallel to TYZO, it would cut the Picture in the Line VL. And ſince ED is perpendicular to the vaniſhing Line VL, therefore D is the Center of that vaniſhing Line, and ED its Diſtance.

To apply this to Practice. Let us ſuppoſe the Planes to be laid down as in the former Figures; only for Convenience, we have removed the Seat TOSX, farther from the Middle of the Picture. ----Here TOSX is the Seat of the original Object, HL the horizontal Line, E the Eye, C the Center of the Picture, and CE its Diſtance. Fig. 66.

Find the Repreſentation of TOSX, as before directed, by means of the Lines O 1, S 2, and their parallel DH: Then, parallel to the

the horizontal Line HE, draw a Line ab, Fig. z, at pleaſure, and through C draw the vaniſhing Line DL, perpendicular to the horizontal Line, at pleaſure alſo: With the Line ab, and at the Point b, make an Angle abc, equal to XTY, the Angle of Incli-
*Fig. 65. nation of the original Figure; * then from E, the Diſtance of the Eye or principal Diſtance, draw ED parallel to bc, cutting the vaniſhing Line in D; finally, from D draw Dt, Do, and from s draw sz, parallel to DL, which will cut oD in z; therefore, from z, draw zy parallel to to, or HE, and the Thing propoſed is done.

Or the vaniſhing Point D may be determined without the Figure z, by making an Angle at E, the Diſtance of the Eye, with the horizontal Line HE, equal to the Angle of Inclination, and then drawing ED.

In Fig. 65, the Plane TOZY is inclined to the Ground Plane, but reclined in reſpect to the Picture, and therefore its vaniſhing Line VL will be above the horizontal Line: But in Fig. 67, the inclined Plane TOZY is inclined to the Ground and to the Picture alſo; for which Reaſon, its vaniſhing Line VD will be below the horizontal Line.---The 68th Fig. repreſents the laſt Figure applied to Practice, the Operations of which are the very ſame with thoſe in Fig. 66; only the Seat TOSX, and the vaniſhing Point D, are inverted; that is, are below, inſtead of above the horizontal Line.

Fig. 65, 66, 67, & 68. From hence, then, it is evident, that D is the vaniſhing Point of all Lines which are parallel to the Sides oz, and ty; and therefore, when the Figure conſiſts only of parallel Sides, as oz and ty, there will be no Occaſion for drawing the vaniſhing
Fig. 65. Line VL or VD; ſince the vaniſhing Point D of thoſe Sides
—— 67. is only wanted. But if any other Lines are ſuppoſed to be drawn upon the inclined Plane, as in Fig. 69, then thoſe vaniſhing Lines become neceſſary; becauſe the vaniſhing Points of thoſe Lines will be ſomewhere in them. Which comes next under Conſideration.

Fig. 69. Let tozy be the Repreſentation of one inclined Plane, whoſe vaniſhing Point is D; and cdef another inclined Plane, whoſe vaniſhing Point is D; and let VDL be their vaniſhing Lines. ---E is ſuppoſed the Eye, C the Center of the Picture, and CE its Diſtance.--Continue the vaniſhing Line DD at pleaſure: Then, becauſe CD is drawn from the Center of the Picture, perpendicular to the vaniſhing Lines VL, VL, therefore D, D, are the Centers of thoſe vaniſhing Lines, and DE, DE, their Diſtance from the

the Eye; consequently if DI, DI, be made equal to DE, DE, then I, I, will represent the transposed Places of the Eye; and therefore if Lines are drawn from the Points I, I, parallel to any original Lines, they will cut the vanishing Lines VL, VL, and give the vanishing Points of such Lines. Thus, let it be required to find the vanishing Points of the Diagonals of a Square, t o 1 2, one of whose Sides t o is given.---Any where apart draw a Square, as X, at pleasure, but in such a Manner that its Sides, a b, c d, are parallel to the vanishing Line V L; and likewise draw its Diagonals. ---First for the Figure t o s z y.

From I, draw IL, IV, parallel to a c, b d; which will cut the vanishing Line in V and L; and from t draw t L, cutting o D in 2; from o, draw o V, cutting t D in 1; then draw 1 2 parallel with t o, and then is t o 1 2 the Representation of a Square upon the inclined Plane t o z y; and t 2, o 1, are the Representations of its Diagonals. And were it demanded to make the Length of the inclined Plane equal to several Times its Width, as in this Figure, we may do it by means of the Points V and L; because having determined one Square, all the rest are to be found in the same Manner.

Here let us take Notice, that if one vanishing Point of any Plane is determined, all the other vanishing Points of Lines which can be drawn any how in that Plane, will be somewhere in a Line which is drawn through that Point. Thus C is the vanishing Point of the Side o s, which lies upon the Ground, and the horizontal Line HE passes through that Point: Again, C is the vanishing Point of o s, which is one Side of the perpendicular Plane o s z; therefore DCD, the vanishing Line of that perpendicular Plane, passes through the Point C: And so again, D is the vanishing Point of the inclined Planes, and therefore VL, VL, their several vanishing Lines, will pass through the Points D, D; and consequently, all the Lines which can be drawn in either Plane, will have their vanishing Points somewhere in the vanishing Lines of those Planes. All which is explained by various Examples in the second Book.

Hitherto I have considered the inclined Planes, as having one or more of their Sides parallel to the Picture, for which Reason the vanishing Lines of those Planes are parallel to the horizontal Line. Let us now suppose the Plane to be situated in such a Manner as to have all its Sides oblique with the Picture, as in Fig. 70.

Fig. 70. Here TOZY, is a ſquare Plane every way oblique with the Picture; TOSX, its Seat on the Ground; YTX, its Angle of Inclination; E the Eye; C the Center of the Picture, and CE its Diſtance.---Draw the Horizontal Line HC, and continue it at pleaſure; then parallel to TX, or OS, draw EH, cutting the Horizontal Line in H; and then is H the vaniſhing Point of the Lines TX, OS. Again, parallel to TO, or SX, draw EL, cutting the Horizontal Line in L; then is L the vaniſhing Point of the Lines TO, SX; from whence the Repreſentation of its Seat may be found. Now ſince the Plane TYX is perpendicular to the Ground, its vaniſhing Line HV will be perpendicular to the Horizontal Line; therefore from the vaniſhing Point H, draw HV parallel to XY, and EV parallel to TY, cutting HV in V; then is V the vaniſhing Point of the parallel Sides TY, OZ; and ſince L is the vaniſhing Point of TO, it is alſo the vaniſhing Point of its parallel Side YZ, and therefore, a Line drawn through V and L, will be the vaniſhing Line, (as VL) of the inclined Plane TOZY. Here let us obſerve again, that if a Line, ED, be drawn from the Eye E, perpendicular to the vaniſhing Line VL, then D is its Center, and DE its Diſtance.

To apply this to Practice.---Imagine the ſeveral Planes to be laid down as before.

Fig. 71. Then, HL is the Horizontal Line, E the Eye, C the Center of the Picture, CE its Diſtance, HV the vaniſhing Line of the perpendicular Plane tyx; VL, the vaniſhing Line of the oblique Plane tozy, 𝕮 its Center, 𝕮𝕰 its Diſtance, and H, L, V, the vaniſhing Points of the ſeveral Planes; or, if you pleaſe, of the ſeveral Sides of ſuch a Figure.

Let ot be given for the neareſt Side. Continue ot, 'till it cuts the vaniſhing Line HL in its proper vaniſhing Point L: From L draw L𝕰, and from t and o, draw Lines to the vaniſhing Point V, and draw V𝕰: Then is V𝕰L a right Angle; which biſect, and draw E𝕯, cutting the vaniſhing Line VL, in 𝕯; then is 𝕯 the vaniſhing Point of the Diagonal of a Square: Therefore (ſince the inclined Plane was ſuppoſed to be a Square) draw 𝕯t, cutting oV in z; from L, through the Point z, draw Lzy, cutting tV in y; then draw yz, parallel to HV, which will compleat the whole Repreſentation, not only of the inclined ſquare Plane, but the whole Appearance of a Figure like 65, 67, but in a different Situation.

Since

Since this Figure is as difficult in regard to the Practice of Perspective, as any I can think of, I have annexed the Paper Planes in the 72d Figure, to help the Reader's Reflections upon it; and to assist him still further, we will now find the Representation of such an Object without any Regard to the Theory.

Let E be the Eye, C the Center of the Picture, CE its Distance, HL the horizontal Line, and t o one Side given of the inclined Face. Fig. 71.

Any where apart draw AB, Fig. X. parallel to the horizontal Line HL, and draw CB perpendicular to AB; then make an Angle at A, equal to the Angle of Inclination (as TYX in Fig. 70) and draw AC.---Continue o t to its vanishing Point L, and from L draw LE to the Eye; then at E make a right Angle with the Line LE, and then, because the Side which lies upon the Ground is square at the Corners, therefore H is the vanishing Point of the two Sides t x and o s, and L is the vanishing Point of the other two Sides t o and s x.---From the vanishing Point H, draw HV perpendicular to the horizontal Line, and continue the horizontal Line towards 𝕴. From H set off H𝕴, equal to the Distance HE of the vanishing Line HV; then from 𝕴 draw 𝕴V, parallel to AC in Fig. X; which will cut HV in V, and give HV for the vanishing Line of the perpendicular Plane t y x; and by drawing a Line through the Points V and L, we shall have VL for the vanishing Line of the inclined Plane t o z y: Therefore from C the Center of the Picture, draw C𝕮, perpendicular to the vanishing Line VL, and continue it at pleasure; then is 𝕮 the Center of that vanishing Line. Again, from C the Center of the Picture, draw CI perpendicular to C𝕮, and make CI equal to CE the principal Distance, and then draw I𝕮, which is the Distance of the vanishing Line VL; therefore, make 𝕮𝕰 equal to 𝕮I, and from the vanishing Points V and L, draw V𝕰, L𝕰, which will be a right Angle: Bisect the Angle 𝕰, and draw 𝕰𝕯, cutting the vanishing Line in 𝕯; then, as before, 𝕯 is the vanishing Point of the Diagonal of a Square t o z y, from whence the whole Representation may be compleated. Here also the Learner is referred for Examples to Book II. Chap. 2. Sect. 4.

Thus have I endeavoured to explain the Theory of Perspective, and to apply it to Practice by the most familiar and useful Examples, and in all the Variety of Instances which can come within the general Practice of Painting, &c. As for other Matters, which are out of the common Road, and which serve rather to perplex than benefit a Learner, I have purpoſely avoided them; and believe, I may venture to affirm, that whoever has attended to what has been ſaid, and exerciſed himſelf regularly with the Examples to which he was referred in the Practical Part, Book the Second, will find no kind of Difficulty in determining the Appearances of any Objects upon an upright Picture, let them be of ever ſo irregular a Figure, or howſoever they are ſituated

But thus far I have confined myſelf to the Appearance of Objects upon an upright Picture only, ſuch as are generally made choice of for Perſpective Repreſentations: But as there are ſome Caſes in which the Situation of the Picture is different, ſuch as Ceilings, inclined Walls, or the like, I ſhall now proceed to the Conſideration thereof, and ſhew, that the Repreſentation of Objects upon ſuch kind of Surfaces, is deducible from the ſame Principles, and conſequently, is to be determined after the ſame Manner; which is the Subject of the next Chapter.

XI.

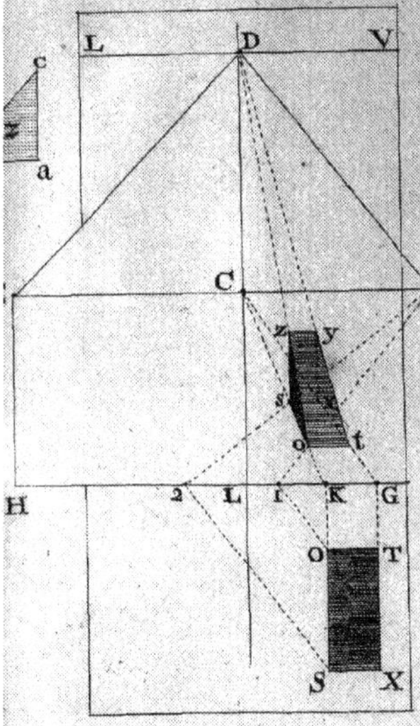
L D V
C H
z y
s u
o t
H 2 L I K G
O T
S X
c
a

66.

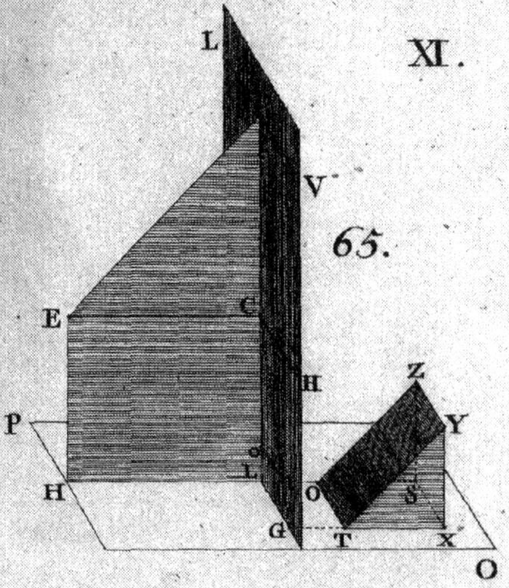
L
V
E C
H
Z
Y
P
o
L
O
S
H
G T X
O

65.

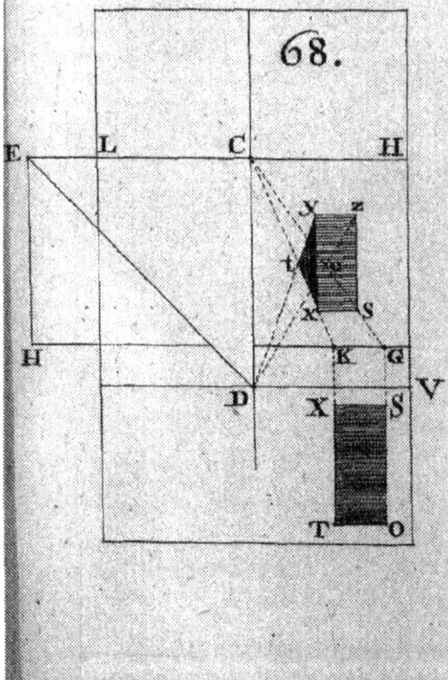
E L C H
y z
t u
x s
H K G
D V
X S
T O

68.

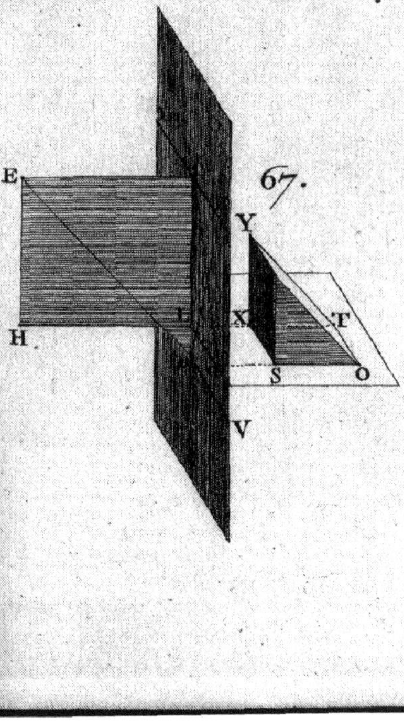
E
Y
X T
H
S O
V

67.

XII.

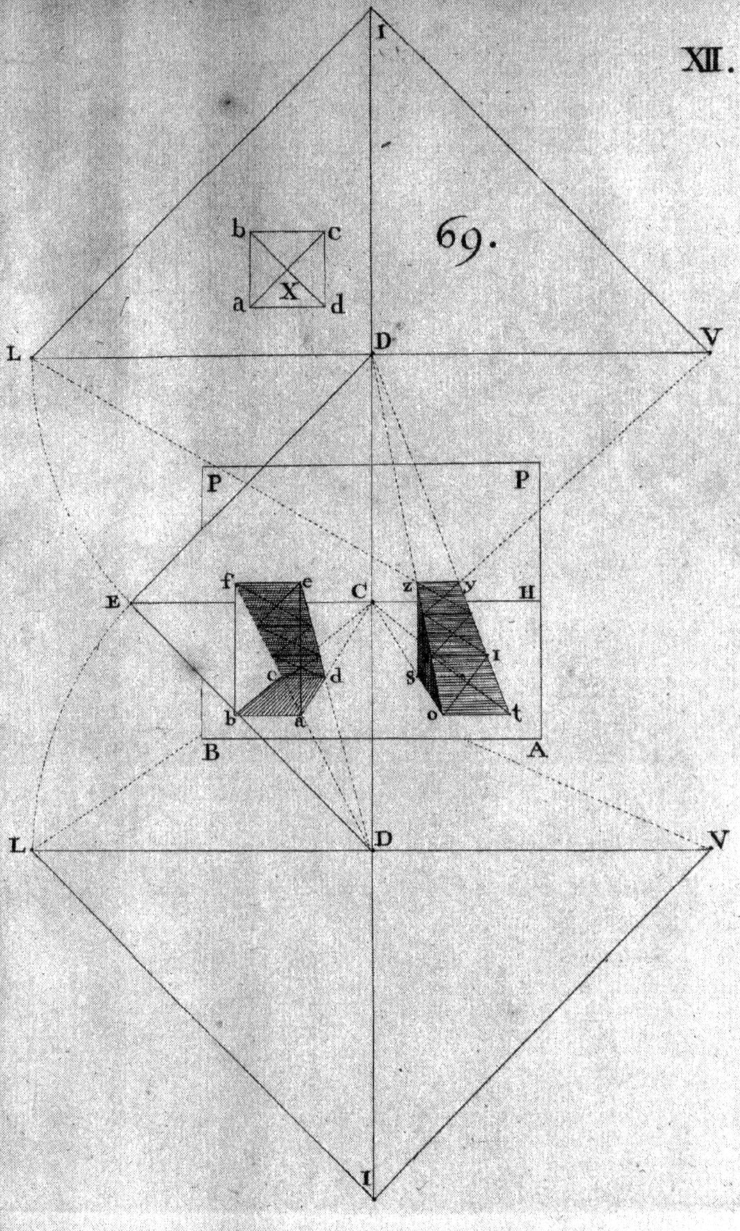

III.

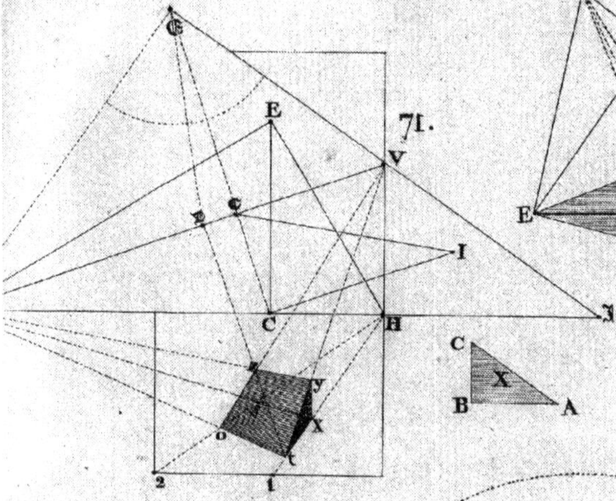

71.

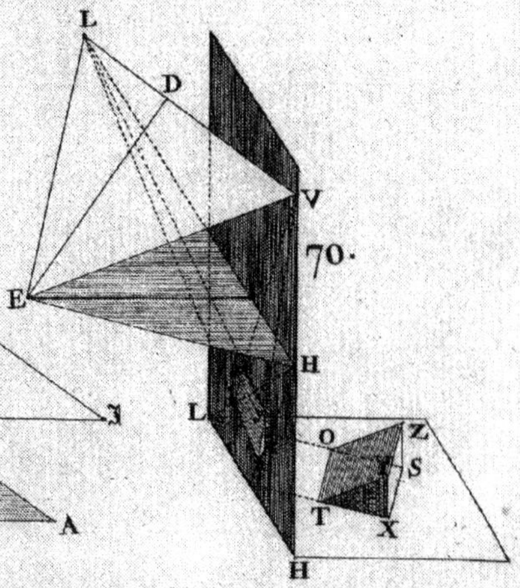

70.

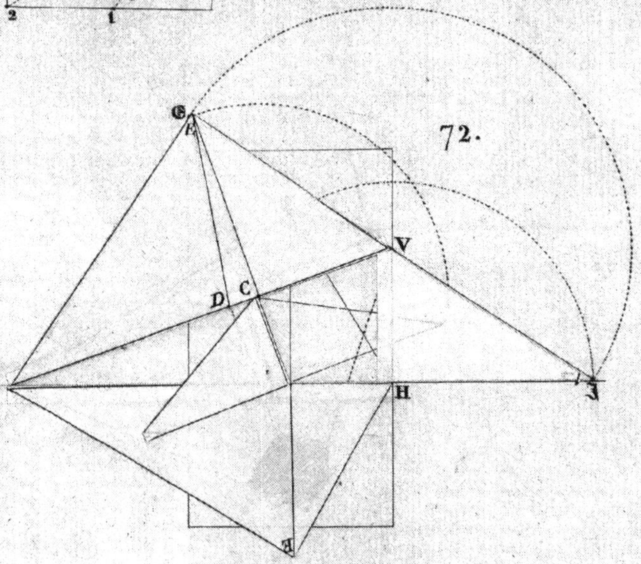

72.

CHAP. IV.

Of PARALLEL *and* INCLINED PICTURES.

SECT. I.

Of the PARALLEL PICTURE.

WHEN the Picture is perpendicular to the Ground, or any other Plane upon which the Spectator ſtands, I call it a perpendicular Picture; when it is parallel to the Ground, I call it a parallel Picture; and when it is inclined to the Ground, I call it an inclined Picture. The firſt of theſe Situations I have already conſidered at large, as being the moſt uſeful: Proceed we therefore to the Second, which principally relates to Ceilings or immoveable Pictures.

Now, whoever has attended to what hath been ſaid upon the upright Picture, will (I apprehend) find no ſort of Intricacy in this, becauſe, on either Picture, the Projection of Objects is determined in the very ſame Manner. But if there ſhould appear any Difficulty, it cannot be in the Operation, but in conſidering what Objects are proper and what not for ſuch kind of Pictures; and the Situation of thoſe Objects. For inſtance, to repreſent a Landſkip or any Objects which are ſuppoſed to be upon the Ground, is extremely improper for a Ceiling; for ſince the Picture is always ſuppoſed parallel to the Ground, and the Eye is placed between the original Object and the Picture, therefore the Rays of Light in their Paſſage from original Objects to the Eye, will not be cut by the Picture, and conſequently ſuch Objects can have no Projections upon the Picture; for which Reaſon they ought not to be repreſented. But any Objects which may reaſonably be ſuppoſed to exiſt in the Air, or any Story which can be ſupported either by Hiſtory or Fable, may be repreſented with the greateſt Propriety; as may likewiſe ſeveral Parts of Architecture, which may ſerve either for Ornament, or be uſeful as to the main Deſign. And in regard to the Situation of Objects, they are generally ſuppoſed to be erect, and therefore I ſhall principally conſider them in that Situation; which will be ſufficient for our Purpoſe, as it will give the Reader a very clear Idea of all that can be ſaid upon the Subject; and which, together with the Examples under this Head in the Second

Book, will enable him to find the Reprefentation of all Objects upon a Ceiling with the fame Facility as he can determine thofe upon an upright Picture.

Fig. 73. Let KMNO be the Ground, E the Eye, EH its Height, DGLP the Picture, (which we will fuppofe a Ceiling) C the Center of the Picture, CE its Diftance, and GACL a Plane perpendicular to the Picture whofe Reprefentation is required.

From the Section GL, draw GC, LC; then from A and C draw AE, CE, cutting GC, LC, in a and c; then draw a c, which will compleat G a c L, the Reprefentation of the original GACL; which will, to an Eye placed in E, appear to be erect.

Let us now turn the Figure in fuch a Manner that the Picture may become an upright one; then ACMK is the Ground Plane, E the Eye, EC its Diftance, EI its Height, C the Center of the Picture, VL the horizontal Line, and G a c L the Reprefentation of GACL, which lies upon the Ground. From hence then it is evident, that in order to determine the Appearance of any perpendicular Plane upon the parallel Picture, we muft proceed in the very fame Manner as in finding the Reprefentation of an Object which lies flat upon the Ground in the perpendicular Picture; for in both Cafes, the original Plane ACLG is perpendicular to the Picture, only the Situation of the Picture is different in regard to the Eye, and therefore the Reprefentation in both Cafes will be the fame, as is manifeft by infpecting the Figure.

But fuppofe the original Plane be parallel to the Picture; then the Reprefentation will be like the Original, and muft be found by the fame Rules as Objects thus fituated are determined upon the perpendicular Picture.

Fig. 75. Thus, let LGPO be the Picture, E the Eye, C the Center, and CE its Diftance, and ABCD the original Plane parallel to the Picture.

From A, B, C, D, draw Lines perpendicular to the Picture, interfecting it in the Points G, L, P, O; then from thofe Points draw Lines to the Center of the Picture; and from the Points A, B, C, D, draw Lines to E, which will interfect GC, LC, PC, and OC, in a, b, c, d, and thereby determine the Reprefentation required.

Now let us turn this Figure alfo, and call ABMK the Ground Plane; then this Picture is an upright one, and the Reprefentation a, b, c, d, of the parallel Plane ABCD, in either Situation of the Picture is the fame; and confequently the Reprefentation of all parallel

parallel Objects are to be determined after the ſame Manner as in the upright Picture.

Now, ſince the Rules for drawing the Appearance of Objects upon the parallel Picture, are exactly the ſame as thoſe for drawing the Appearance of Objects upon the perpendicular Picture, it follows, that the ſame Rules will do in both Caſes, and therefore the Artiſt has nothing more to remember than this, *viz.* thoſe Objects which in the parallel Picture are to be repreſented as erect, muſt be determined as thoſe which lie flat upon the Ground in the perpendicular Picture; thoſe which are parallel in one Picture, as thoſe which are parallel in the other; and thoſe which are oblique, after the ſame Manner: Or in other Words, however original Planes are ſituated, the Repreſentations of them muſt always be determined by imagining a Plane to paſs through the Eye parallel to thoſe Planes, which will give their ſeveral vaniſhing Lines, from which the whole Repreſentation may be compleated. Thus, the Plane FGVL, which paſſes through the Eye E, parallel to the original Plane ACLG, produces the vaniſhing Line VL of that Plane; and therefore having the Diſtance EC of that vaniſhing Line, the Repreſentation of any Lines which can be drawn in the original Plane are eaſily found alſo. Fig. 73.

And here we may obſerve, that if the original Plane ACLG were infinitely extended, the Triangle GLC would be its indefinite Repreſentation, and conſequently the Appearance of all Lines which can be drawn in that original Plane, will be ſomewhere within that Triangle. And ſo likewiſe, if perpendicular Planes are erected on the other Sides LP, PD, DG, of the Picture, their indefinite Repreſentations will be the ſeveral Triangles LCP, PCD, and DCG, and the Center C will be their common vaniſhing Point.--- For draw the original Plane ACLG upon the Side LG of the Picture, and let every thing elſe remain as in the former Figure. Fig. 74. ---Through E draw the Plane FHGLV, parallel to the Plane ACLG, which will cut the Picture in VL; then is VL the vaniſhing Line of that Plane. Again, from E draw EC, perpendicular to VL; then is C the Center of the Picture. And ſince EC is parallel to AG, BS and CL, therefore C is the vaniſhing Point of thoſe Lines; and therefore, from C, the Center of the Picture, draw Lines to G, S, L; and from A, B, C, draw Lines to E, which will cut the former Lines in the Points a, b, c; then is aG the Repreſentation of AG, bS of BS, and cL of CL; and GacL is the whole Repreſentation of the original Plane ACLG.

And

And after the fame Manner any other Lines, as xz, may be found upon the Picture.

And from hence alfo, we may obferve, that if perpendicular Planes are fet on each Side of the Picture, the Reprefentation of thofe Planes will appear like the Sides of a Room continued upwards; from whence it follows, that by fuch Deceptions as this, a Room may be made to appear of any Height, by drawing a Reprefentation of this Kind upon a Ceiling with Accuracy and Judgment, and viewing it from the proper Point. One Example of which I fhall give in this Place, by way of Practice, and then refer the Reader again to the fecond Book for more Examples of this Sort.

Fig. 76. Let GLPO be a Ceiling, E the Eye, EC its Diftance, and C the Center of the Picture.

Through the Center C draw Lines parallel to LP, LG, and continue them at pleafure; then with the Diftance CE defcribe a Circle, cutting thofe Lines in D, F, H: Then DCH is the vanifhing Line for the original Planes, which ftand upon the Sides GL and OP; and ECF is the vanifhing Line of the Planes which ftand upon the Sides GO and LP; and the feveral Lines EC, DC, FC and HC, are the Diftance of the Eye from thofe Lines. Having fettled the vanifhing Lines of the four Sides, their Center and Diftance, it matters not upon which Side we begin to work; for upon any Side, as GL, draw out one of the original Planes, as ACLG, and upon it draw the Lines XZ, BS, which will make it like the Plane ACLG, Fig. 74. From the feveral Sections G, S, L, draw Lines to C; and from A, B, C, draw Lines to E, cutting GC, SC, LC, in the Points a, b, c; then from a to c draw ac, and then will Ga be the Reprefentation of GA, Sb of SB, and Lc of LC: Therefore, GacL is the Reprefentation of the whole original Plane GACL, and the Triangle GCL is the Reprefentation of that Plane infinitely extended.---In like Manner xz is the Reprefentation of its Original XZ.

Or the Operation may be fhortned thus. From the extreme Point B of any Perpendicular in the original Plane, draw a Line, BI, at pleafure, cutting the Section in I; then from E draw EK parallel thereto, cutting the vanifhing Line DH in K; from the Section S, of the Perpendicular SB, draw SC; and from the Section I draw IK, cutting SB in b: Then is bS the Depth of the Reprefentation; therefore, by drawing GC, LC, and by drawing a Line through b, parallel to GL, the Thing propofed is done.

Now,

Now, in order to transfer this Reprefentation unto all the other Sides, proceed thus.

From O and P draw Lines to the Center C; then will the remaining Part of the Ceiling be divided into three Triangles, GCO, OCP, PCL; which Triangles may reprefent three Planes perpendicular to the Ceiling, infinitely extended, and at right Angles with each other; and GC, OC, PC, and LC, reprefent the joining of thofe Planes: For GC and LC are the Reprefentations of GA and LC infinitely extended; and therefore, having found the Depth (as G a) of the Reprefentation of any given Plane, as above, from the Point a, which determines that Depth, draw a Line, as a e, parallel to O G; and from e, where a e cuts OC, draw another Line e d parallel to O P; and from d, where e d cuts P C, draw d c, which will cut L C in c; then will G a e O, O e d P, and P d c L, be the Reprefentations of three perpendicular Planes of the fame Height as ACLG, and fituated in the fame Manner; that is, upon the feveral Sides GO, OP, and PL; and confequently, to an Eye placed at E, and at the Diftance E C, the Sides of a Room will appear to be continued above the Ceiling by the Length of the Perpendicular GA, *i. e.* the Height of the original Plane A C L G.

SECT. II.

Of the INCLINED PICTURE.

I Have before obferved, that by an inclined Picture, I would be underftood to mean when the Perfpective Plane is neither perpendicular nor parallel to the Ground, but inclined to it. Indeed, this Situation of the Picture is very feldom made ufe of, yet as there are fome Cafes which may require the Knowledge of this kind of Perfpective, I have therefore given it a Place in this Work.

Let O P H be the Ground or original Plane, H L G L the Picture, inclin'd to the Ground Plane at the Angle P L L; and let E be the Eye, EH its Height, and H its Seat upon the Ground. Fig 77.

Continue the Picture HLGL downwards at pleafure, as GLFO. From the Seat H of the Eye draw HS perpendicular to the Section GL, cutting GL in S; then through S draw S D, perpendicular to GL alfo, and continue it at pleafure towards FO; and then from E draw E D, parallel to H S, cutting the Picture in D, and continue EH 'till it cuts DS in V; then from V draw V I, parallel to E D, and from D draw D I, parallel to EV: And then will EDIV be a

Plane which paſſes through the Eye perpendicular to the Ground Plane OPH, interſecting the Picture in the Line DV; and therefore the Section DV will be the vaniſhing Line of all Planes that are perpendicular to the Ground Plane and parallel to the Plane EDIV; and for the ſame Reaſon, V will be the vaniſhing Point of all Lines that are perpendicular to the Ground Plane OPH, becauſe EV which is drawn through the Eye parallel to thoſe Lines, will cut the Picture in the Point V: For as in the upright, or parallel Picture, ſo alſo in this, the vaniſhing Line of any original Plane muſt be determined, by imagining a Plane to paſs thro' the Eye parallel to that original Plane 'till it cuts the Picture. And ſo alſo in regard to the Center and Diſtance of the Picture, or the Center and Diſtance of a vaniſhing Line; the firſt is found by drawing a Line from the Eye, as EC, perpendicular to the Picture, and the latter, by drawing a Line from the Eye, as ED, perpendicular to that vaniſhing Line: The Method for doing either is as follows.

1. *For the Center and Diſtance of the Picture.*

Having continued the Picture downwards as above directed, and drawn the vertical Plane EDIV; from E, draw EC, perpendicular to the Section DV; then will C be the Center of the Picture, and CE its Diſtance: For ſince the vertical Plane cuts the Picture at right Angles, and ſince EC is in that Plane, and perpendicular to the Section DV, therefore EC is perpendicular to the Picture alſo, and conſequently C is the Center of the Picture, and CE its Diſtance.

2. *For the Center and Diſtance of a vaniſhing Line.*

Let the Plane ABHL paſs through the Eye E, parallel to the Ground Plane OPH, and it will cut the Picture in HL, which Line HL is the vaniſhing Line of the original Plane OPH; and if from E, a Line, as ED, be drawn perpendicular to HL, then D, where it cuts HL, is the Center of that vaniſhing Line, and DE is its Diſtance.

Fig. 78. Now, let it be required to find the Repreſentation of the original Plane ABGL upon the inclined Picture GLHL; and let E be the Eye, H its Seat upon the original Plane, EC its Diſtance, and C the Center of the Picture.

From H, the Seat of the Eye, draw HS, perpendicular to the Section GL; from S, draw SD perpendicular to GL, and continue it at pleaſure; then from the Eye E, draw ED parallel to HS, cutting SD in D; finally, through D, draw HL, parallel to GL,

GL, then is HL the vanishing Line of the original Plane ABGL, and D is the vanishing Point of the Sides AG, BL; therefore, from G and L draw GD, LD, and from A and B draw AE, BE, cutting GD, LD, in the Points a and b; then is GabL the Representation of the original Plane GABL.

To apply this to Practice.---Let GLNM be the Picture laid flat, as in some of the preceding Figures.---Bisect the Bottom GL, and draw cD perpendicular thereto, and continue it at pleasure: Then from the 78th Figure take SC, CD, and transfer them unto cD in this Figure, beginning at the Point c; draw HL; then is C the Center of the Picture, cD the Height of the vanishing Line, and D its Center. Again, make DE equal to the Distance of the Eye, and AG equal to the Length of the original Plane, (that is, equal to AG Fig. 78.) then from G and L draw GD, LD, and from A draw AE, cutting GD in a; finally, from a draw ab, parallel to GL; which will compleat a Representation GabL, exactly like GabL Fig. 78. Fig. 80.

Or it may be done thus.---From the Center C draw CE, parallel to GL, and make CE equal to the Distance of the Picture, and ED equal to the Distance of the vanishing Line HL; then from D, with the Radius DE, describe the Arc ELEH; and from G, with the Radius GA, describe the Arc Ac; and then from c and H draw Hc, which will cut GD in a, and give the Depth of the Representation; from whence the whole may be compleated.

In like Manner, let it be demanded to find the Projection of a Line AB, which stands perpendicular to the Ground Plane OPH. Fig. 79.

From B, the Seat of the Line AB, draw a Line BH to the Seat of the Eye H; and from V draw Vd, through the Section c, and continue it at pleasure; then from A and B draw Lines to the Eye E, cutting Vd in a and b; and then is ab the Representation of the Original AB. For since EV is parallel to the Original AB, therefore the Point V, where it cuts the Picture, is the vanishing Point of AB, and of all other Lines which are parallel to AB: And if we imagine a Plane ABHE to pass through the original AB, and the Line HE, it will cut the Picture in ca; and therefore, since the Rays AE and BE are in that Plane, the Section ab will be the Representation of AB.

To apply this to Practice.---Let MNGL be the Picture, laid flat as before. Then C is its Center, CE its Distance, V the vanishing Point of Lines perpendicular to the Ground Plane, HL the vanishing Line of Planes parallel to the Ground Plane, D the Fig. 81.

 Center

Center of that vanishing Line, and DE its Distance. Now, let it be required to find the Representation of a square Plane which stands perpendicular to the Ground Plane, having one Side, a b, of the Representation given.

From D, the Center of the vanishing Line HL, and with the Distance DE, describe an Arc ELFH, cutting the vanishing Line in H and L; then is H the vanishing Point of the Sides a d, b c: Therefore, draw a H, b H, and from H draw HV; so will HV be the vanishing Line of a Plane perpendicular to the Ground; and by finding A (the vanishing Point of the Diagonal of a Square) the whole Representation may be determined.

The 82d Figure represents a Cube upon the inclined Picture: For having determined the Appearance of one Face a b c d, as in the last Figure, the whole Representation may be compleated, by means of the vanishing Lines HL, HV, and LV, and the vanishing Points of the Diagonals, B, D, G.

I have hitherto considered the Picture as reclined from the Eye; let us now suppose it to be inclined to the Eye, as in Fig. 83, where E is the Eye, LV the Picture, C its Center, CE its Distance, V the vanishing Point of Lines perpendicular to the Ground, and DL the vanishing Line of Planes parallel to the Ground.---In the 84th Figure the Picture is laid flat, and the Representation of one Face of a Cube is determined: And in the 85th Figure, the Projection of the whole Cube is compleated.---These Figures need no Explanation, being only as it were the Reverse of the others; and therefore a little Attention must render them extremely obvious.

From hence then it follows, that the Method of determining the Representation of a Cube upon an inclined Picture, is exactly the same as in finding the Appearance of a Cube any ways inclined to the Ground; and therefore the Rules which serve for the one will serve for the other also: For which Reason the Learner is desired to compare this with what has been said in Sect. 5. Chap. 3.

SECT.

XIV.

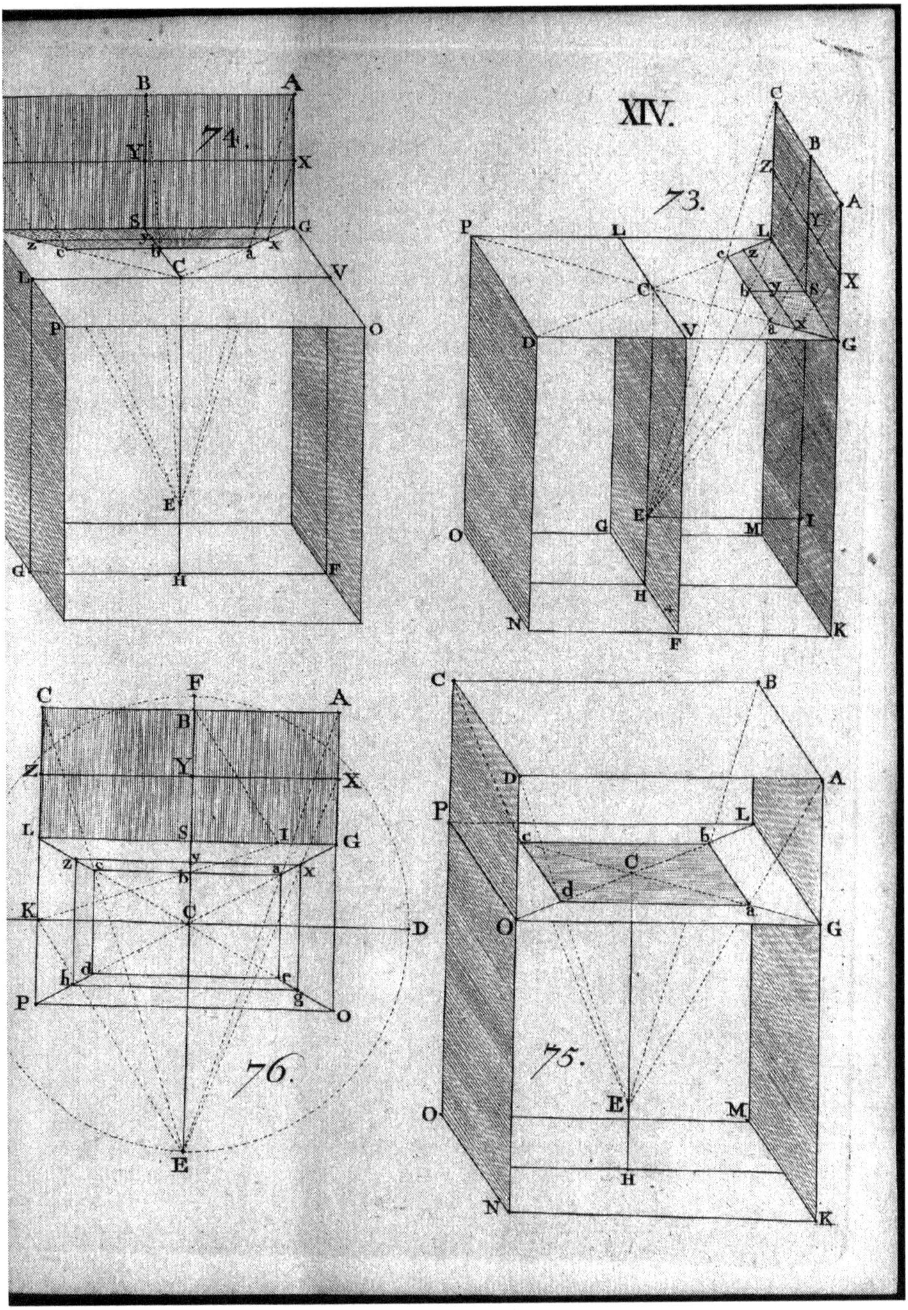

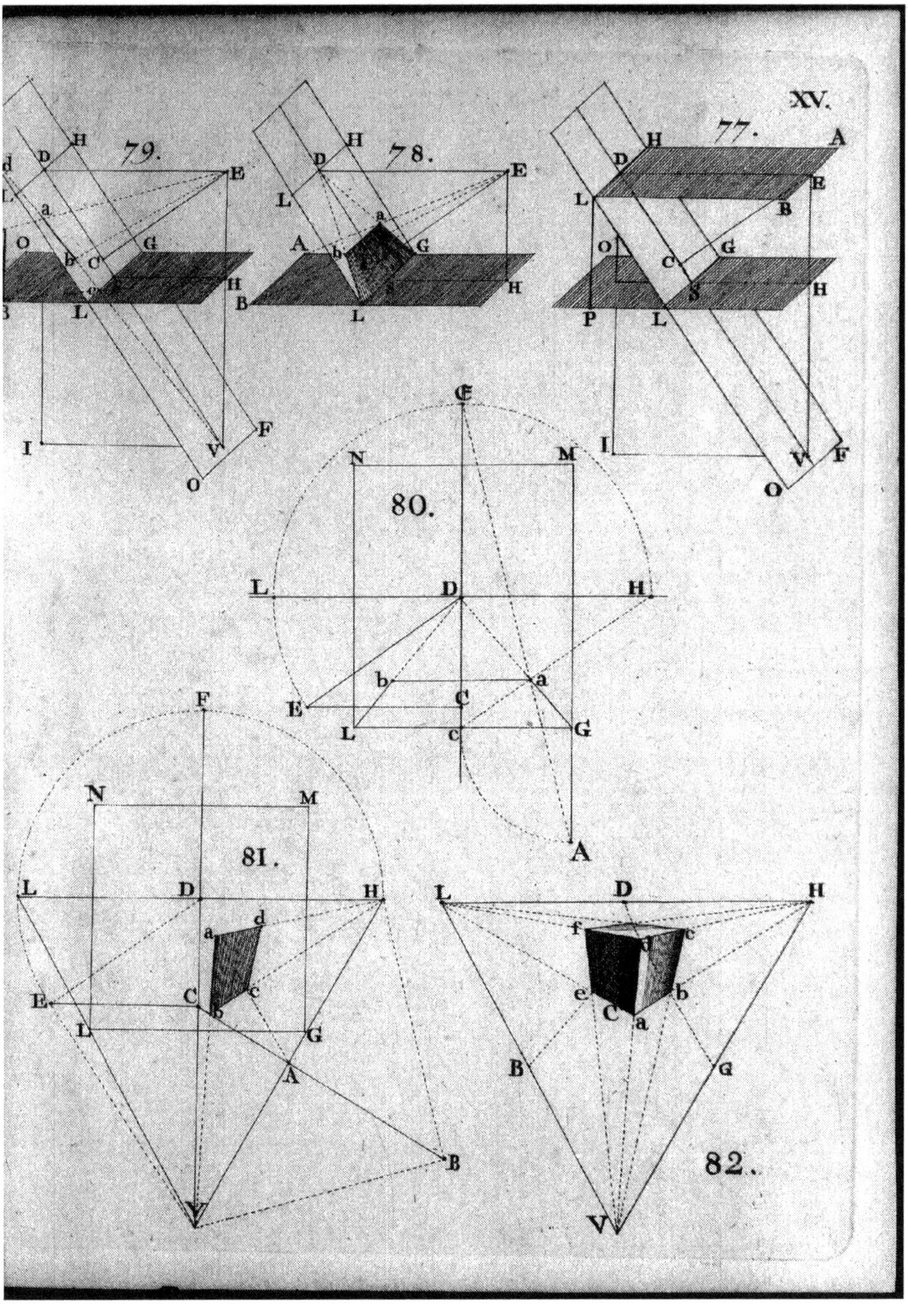
XV.
77.
78.
79.
80.
81.
82.

XVI.

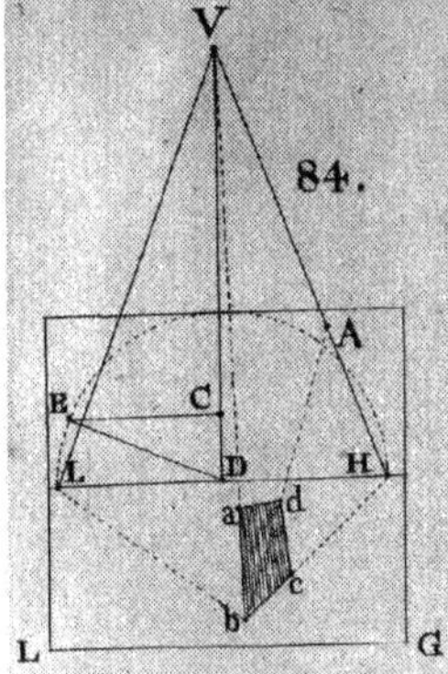

84.

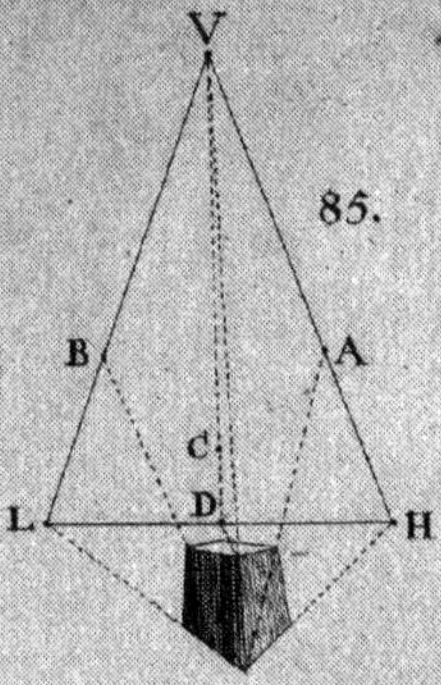

85.

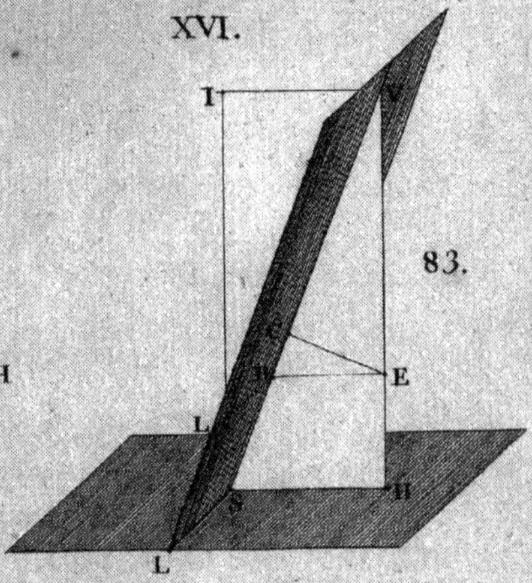

83.

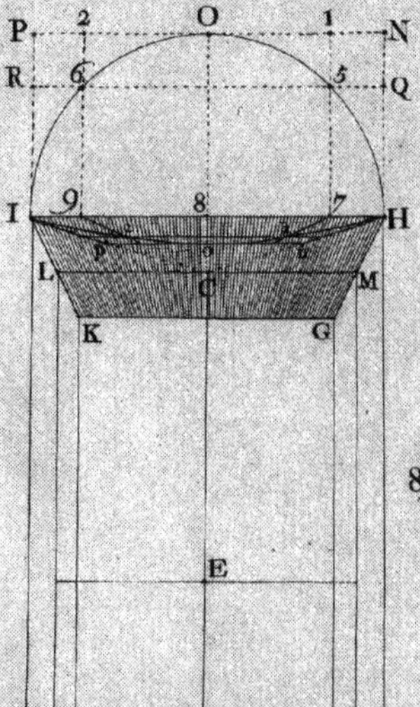

87.

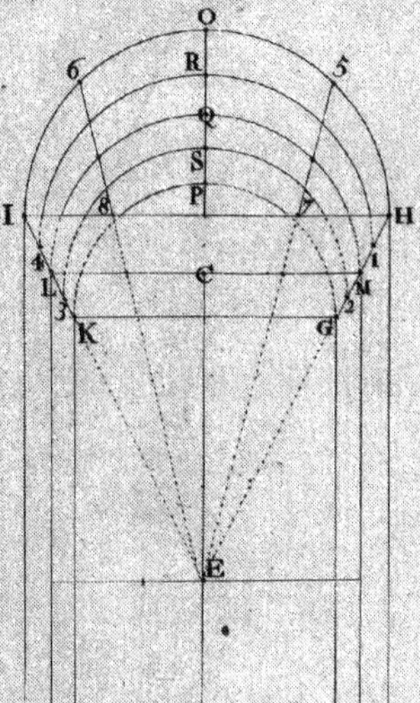

86.

SECT. III.

Of VAULTED ROOFS, DOMES, *&c.*

TO draw Perspective Representations upon vaulted Roofs, Domes, or any other uneven Surfaces, has always been esteemed a Work of great Difficulty; and among all the Methods which have been given us for this Purpose by different Authors, none seems so practicable as that by Mr. *Hamilton*, in his ingenious Treatise intitled STEREOGRAPHY; where he directs us to *Reticulate the proposed Surface, in such a Manner as may be best suited to its Shape, and can with the most Ease be done; then to draw out, on a Plane properly chosen, a Picture of the intended Design, by way of Model; after which, to draw on this Model, the Image of that Reticulation, by the common Rules of Perspective; which will divide the Design on the Model, into such Parts, as are proper to be transferred into each corresponding Cell of the original Reticulation; and finally, by means of this Reticulation, to transfer the Work unto the Dome or Roof, in the same Manner as one Picture is copied from another, by the common Methods of Reticulation.

Thus, suppose it was required to paint some perspective Representation upon a vaulted Roof, HOIKPG.

Let this Figure be a Model drawn out upon Paper, of a vaulted Roof; and let GHIK represent a Plane, which is supposed to pass through the Foot of the Arch, parallel to the Horizon. Fig. 86.

Now, if we suppose the Spectator's Eye to be placed directly under the Middle of it at E, and then imagine a Plane ABLQM to pass through the Eye, perpendicular to the Ground Plane AB, it will cut the Picture in ML; and therefore, by drawing EC perpendicular to the Section ML, we shall have C for the Center of a parallel Picture, and CE for its Distance.----Let us next divide the Roof into any Number of Squares, or Parallelograms, as in the Figure; and then imagine a Line to be drawn from the Angle of every Square to the Eye E; and it must appear extremely evident, that the Sections of these Lines with the Plane, or parallel Picture GHIK, will be the Projection of those Points upon the Picture; and it must also appear as obvious, that, when the Projection of the Angle of every Square is determined upon the Pic-

* To Reticulate any Surface, is to divide it into Squares like Net-Work

ture, the whole Representation of those Squares may easily be compleated. But farther, since the perpendicular Plane ABLQM passes through the Eye, and cuts the Picture in a strait Line; therefore the Projection MCL, of the Arch MQL, will be a strait Line upon the Picture; but the Projection of all the other Arches, 1R4, HOI, &c. will be curve Lines. Again, since the transverse strait Lines 7 5, PO, 6 8, are parallel amongst themselves, and are also parallel to the Picture; therefore the Representation of those Lines upon the Picture, will be strait Lines, and parallel to each other.

These Things being premised, let us now suppose this Figure removed to the 87th Figure.---About the Arch HOI, describe the Parallelogram HIPN; and through the Points 5, O, 6, draw the Lines 1 7, O 8, 2 9, perpendicular to the Picture, and cutting the Picture in the Points 7, 8, 9; then through 5, 6, draw QR parallel to HI, and from the several Sections H, 7, 8, 9, I, draw Lines to C, and from N, O, P, Q, R, draw Lines to the Eye E, which will determine the Projection of the Parallelogram; by which means the Representation H a o c I, of the Arch HOI, may be compleated. After the same Manner, the Projection of all the other Arches may be found; but as one is sufficient for our Purpose, we will now suppose this parallel Picture to be laid down flat in the 89th Figure, where C is the Center, CE the Distance of the Picture, and H, 7, 8, 9, I, the Sections of the Perpendiculars NH, 1 7, &c. in Fig. 87.

Continue IH (Fig. 89,) at pleasure, towards N, and make HQN in this Figure equal to HQN in the 87th Figure; then from H, 7, 8, 9, I, draw Lines to C, and from N and Q draw Lines to E, which will cut HC in n and t, and thereby give the Depth of the Parallelogram HnpI; by which Means the Points H, a, o, c, I, will be determined: Which being so many Points in the Representation of the Curve, they will be a sufficient Guide for drawing it, as in the Figure. After the same Manner, the Representation of the other Front Arch is to be found: From whence it follows, that the Projection of the whole curved Roof upon this parallel Picture, will be contained within the two curved Lines HoI, GgK, and the two strait Lines GH and IK; and therefore GHoIKg is the whole Space allotted for the Design. Now having determined this Space, let us next find the Projection of the several Squares which were supposed to be drawn upon the original Roof.

From

From a, o, c, draw Lines parallel to the Side GH, or IK; then will af, og, cd, be the Projections of the transverse Divisions (or strait Lines) which are parallel to the Picture; and by dividing the several Lines HG, af, og, cd, and IK, into four equal Parts, we shall have the Points given, through which the other Curve Lines are to be drawn, as in Fig. 88; by which Means the whole Representation may be compleated.

If it be required to paint any Perspective Representation upon a Dome, that also may be done after the same Manner, *viz.* by imagining the Dome to be divided into several perpendicular Sections, drawn at equal Distances from the Base, through the Center of the Dome; and by supposing those Sections to be cut by other Sections, which are made by Planes that are supposed to pass through the Dome parallel to the Horizon: Then by making a Model upon Paper in a given Proportion, and taking the Distance of the Eye accordingly, we may find the Projection of those Sections upon the parallel Plane, as in the former Figures: For then we shall have a parallel Picture, which we suppose passes under the Bottom of the Dome, properly reticulated, and by that Means, whatever is drawn upon it, may be transferr'd unto the real Dome or Cupola.

Thus, let ABDE, Fig. 90, represent the circular Plane (or parallel Picture) which we suppose to lie under the Bottom of the Dome; and let AacegfdbB, Fig. 91, represent one of the perpendicular Sections above-mention'd; and let us imagine the Dome to be divided perpendicularly by four of these Planes, and horizontally by four Planes, the Sections of which horizontal Planes are expressed by AB, ab, cd, ef: Then let us divide the Circumference of the Plane, or Picture, ABDE (Fig. 90) into eight equal Parts, and from each Part draw Lines through the Center C; and then will these strait Lines be the Projections of the perpendicular Sections upon the Picture. And in order to find the Projections of the parallel Sections; from C, the Center of the Picture, draw CE Fig. 91.
perpendicular to AB, and equal to the Distance of the Eye; then from ab, cd, ef, and g, draw Lines to the Eye E, which cutting the Picture, will give 16 for the Projection of ab, 25 for that of cd, 34 for that of ef, and C the Center of the Picture for g the Center of the Dome; therefore, from the Line AB transfer the several Divisions A1, 12, &c. unto the Line AB in the 90th Figure; and from the Point C, describe the several concentric Circles through the Points 1, 2, 3; and so will the whole Picture be properly divided for the Work: For each Reticulation upon the Picture,

Picture, is the exact Projection of its corresponding and original Reticulation upon the Dome; and therefore, all that now remains is, only to divide the Picture into an agreeable Number of Parts, and to consider each Part as a parallel Picture, whose perpendicular Sides will vanish into the Center of the Picture; and to be always careful to take the Center of the Model perpendicular to the supposed Place of the Eye; and the Distance to be work'd with, must be the same as that between the Eye and the Plane AB, Fig. 91, as well for describing the Model itself, as for the Reticulation.

We have hitherto considered the Eye as placed under the Center of the Dome, in which Case the Reticulation upon the parallel Picture is done with great Ease: But if it were placed obliquely, the Reticulation would become a little more troublesome; in regard that in such a Position of the Eye, the perpendicular Sections of the Dome would not form strait Lines upon the parallel Plane, but Curves.

Fig. 92. Thus, let AgB, be a perpendicular Section of the Dome, and ab, cd, ef, its Sections with the horizontal Circles, as before; and let E be the Place of the Eye.

Then Lines drawn from E, to the Vertex g of the Dome, and to the Centers and either Extremity b, d, f, of the horizontal Diameters, will cut the Base of the Dome AB in corresponding Points; which being transferred by Perpendiculars to the Diameter AB of the parallel Plane, will give the apparent Vortex C, and the Centers and Radii of the Images of the horizontal Circles, on the parallel Plane; and these being drawn, and each divided into the same Number of equal Parts, as the Base of the Dome is supposed to be, Curve Lines drawn through the corresponding Divisions of these Circles, will give the Projections of the several perpendicular Sections of the Dome, as in the Figure.

For as the horizontal Circles are all supposed parallel to the circular Plane ADBE, it is evident their Projections will still remain Circles, and their Subdivisions will be equal, like those of their Originals.

And here all the perpendicular Sections of the Dome form Curves upon the parallel Plane, except the Section AgB, which is projected into the strait Line AB, the Eye being supposed to lye in the Plane of that Section. But in Painting on curvilinear Grounds, the most direct Situation of the Eye ought always to be chosen, that the Design, when painted, may appear the more agreeably; and indeed, in all such Works, the Design ought, as much as possible,

88.

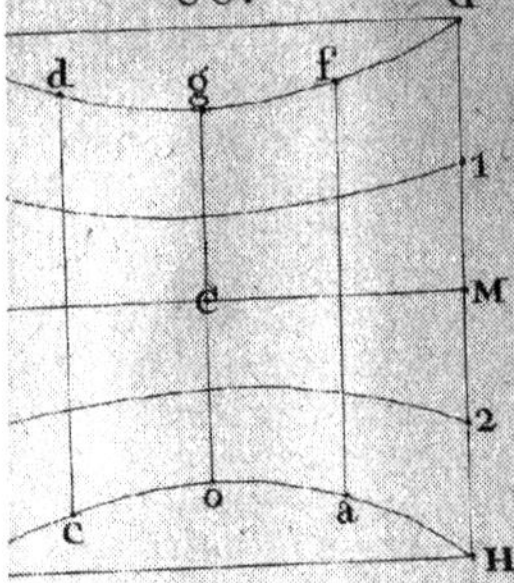
G
d
g
f
1
e
M
2
c
o
a
H

89.

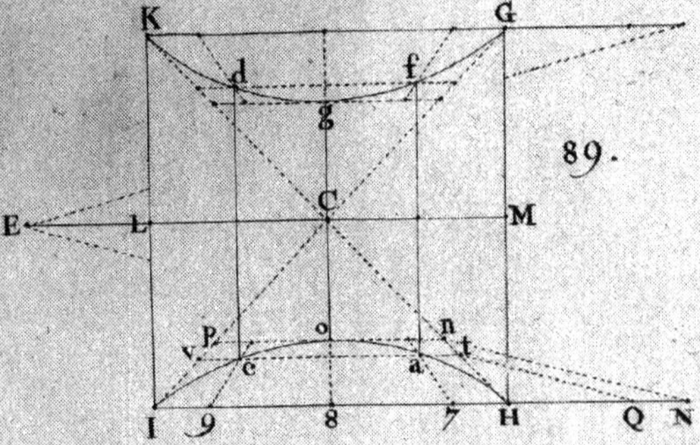
K
G
d
f
g
C
E
L
M
p
o
n
v
c
a
t
I
9
8
7
H
Q
N

91.

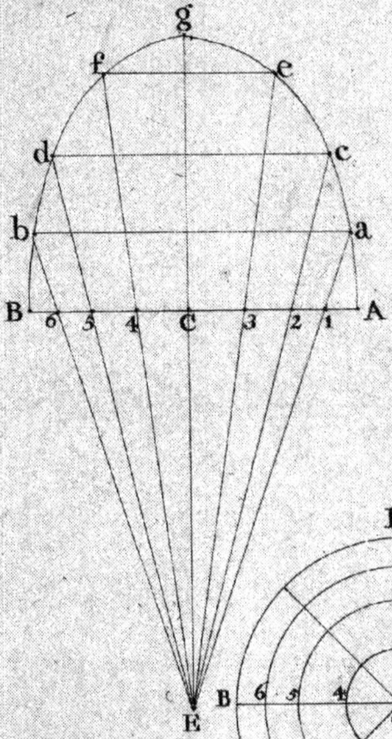
g
f
e
d
c
b
a
B
6
5
4
C
3
2
1
A
E

92.

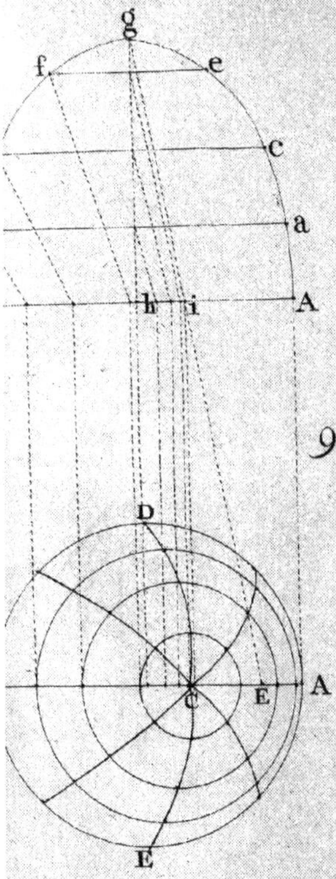
g
f
e
c
a
h
i
A
D
C
E
A
E

90.

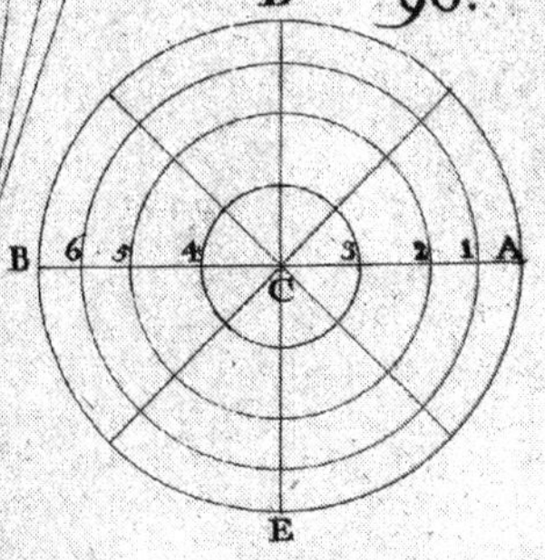
D
B
6
5
4
3
2
1
A
C
E

fible, to be fuited to the Shape of the Surfaces, and to confift principally of ornamental Architecture fitted to it, (putting the Hiftorical Part into fmall Compartments, to be difpofed in proper Places) or elfe of fome Aerial View, where the Sky and Clouds, with other Objects proper for that Situation, may be defcribed; in which Cafe, the principal Objects not being confined to regular Figures, there will be lefs Danger of their appearing diftorted by the Shape of the Surface painted upon.

But when a Cupola, Dome, or Vault, is to be defcribed on a flat Ground, there may be a greater Liberty taken in placing the Eye; which may have either a direct or oblique Pofition, as the Artift judges beft for the View he intends to reprefent, and will not be liable to thofe Inconveniencies which attend Painting upon an uneven Ground.

CHAP.

CHAP. V.

The PERSPECTIVE *of* SHADOWS.

THE Meaning of the Word Shadow is too obvious to need any Explanation; and therefore I ſhall not trouble the Reader about its Etymology, nor ſhall I conſider that infinite Variety of Shadows which may be projected by different Planes; but proceed to ſhew, that the Perſpective of Shadows upon the Picture, is to be determined after the ſame Manner as the Perſpective of Objects, being founded upon the ſame Principles, and deducible from the ſame Rules: It is therefore very ſurprizing, that almoſt every Author who has handled this Part of Perſpective, ſhould have committed ſuch egregious Miſtakes, in giving ſuch Rules as are falſe in Theory, and in Practice the moſt abſurd.

But to proceed. All Shadows are produced by the Interpoſition of ſome opake Objects, which ſtop the Progreſs of the Rays of Light in their direct Courſe from any luminous Body or Point. And ſince the Rays of Light do always proceed in ſtrait Lines, therefore, when they paſs over the Extremities of an Object, they leave a Space unilluminated, which Space is called, *the Projection of the Shadow of that Object*: And 'tis the Buſineſs of this Part of Perſpective, to determine the Appearance of that Projection upon the Picture. In order to do which, we muſt firſt conſider whether the Light be ſuppoſed to come from the Sun, a Candle, or any other luminous Point: If from the Sun, then, from its immenſe Diſtance with reſpect to us, the Rays may be conſidered as parallel; but if from a Candle, as flowing from a Point in a diverging Manner.

And in regard to the Theory of the Perſpective of Shadows; there needs but little more to be ſaid than what has been already advanced upon the Perſpective of Objects: For ſince every Ray of Light is to be conſidered as a ſtrait Line, that Line may be conceived to lie in ſome Plane; and therefore, if the Repreſentation of that Plane can be eaſily found upon the Picture, the Repreſentation of a Line which is in that Plane, may be eaſily found alſo.

And here let us obſerve, that the Planes in which I ſhall ſuppoſe the Rays of Light to be, will always be conſider'd as perpendicular to to the Horizon, as that will be fitter for our Purpose, and render the Thing more intelligible.

If the Rays of Light come from the Sun in Planes parallel to the Picture, they then can have no vanishing Point; in this Case, therefore, the Shadows will be parallel in the Picture: But if they come in Planes not parallel to the Picture, then because a Line drawn from the Eye parallel to those Rays will cut the Picture in some one Point, therefore they will have a vanishing Point upon the Picture, which will be the common vanishing Point for all the Rays in that Direction, whether they be all in one Plane or in any Number of Planes, provided those Planes are parallel to one another.

SECT. I.

Of SHADOWS *projected by the* SUN.

LET HP represent a Plane parallel to the Horizon, or, if you please, call it the Ground Plane, and let ABCD represent a Plane of parallel Rays, as EL, Dd, *&c.* each Ray making an Angle, RLA, with the Ground Plane. Fig. 93.

Now, in order to find the Perspective of any Shadow upon the Picture, two Things are necessary to be given;* *viz.* the Inclination, or Angle, which any System of Rays makes with the Ground Plane, and the Situation of the Plane (in respect to the Picture) in which those Rays are supposed to be. As to the Angle of Inclination, that may be given by a single Ray only; for since the Rays RL, Dd, *&c.* are all supposed parallel amongst themselves, therefore the Angle RLA, which any single Ray RL makes with the Plane HP, is common to all the rest: And as to the Situation of the Plane of Rays, that is to be chosen at the Discretion of the Artist, so as to be most productive of Effect as to his main Design.

LEMMA I.

If the Rays of Light come from behind the Picture towards the Spectator's Eye, then the vanishing Point of those Rays will be above the horizontal Line.

Let PQ be the Ground Plane, GO the Picture, E the Eye, EC the Distance of the Picture, C the Center of the Picture, HC the Fig. 95.

* What is here said to be given, is exclusive of the Distance of the Eye, the Center of the Picture, *&c.* which, it is presumed, will be taken for granted, without mentioning them.

horizontal Line, ABOD a Plane of parallel Rays intersecting the Picture at right Angles in the Line BO; and let RL be a Ray of Light, and RLA the Angle of Inclination which the Rays make with the Ground Plane.

Through the Eye E, draw EF parallel to any of the Rays, as RL, cutting the Picture in F; then is F the vanishing Point of all the Rays of Light; for EF being parallel to one Ray, is parallel to all the rest.---Now, since the Plane of Rays ABOD is perpendicular to the Picture, and passes through C the Center of the Picture, therefore the Plane BFEH, which passes through the Eye, will be perpendicular to the Picture, and will pass thro' its Center also; and therefore BO, the common Section of these two Planes, will be the indefinite Representation of the Plane ABOD; and consequently, F, where EF cuts the Picture, will be the vanishing Point of the Rays RL, *&c.*

COROL. 1.

Since the Plane of Rays passes through the Center of the Picture, the vanishing Point of the Rays will be in a Line drawn from the Center of the Picture perpendicular to the horizontal Line.

COROL. 2.

From hence also we may perceive, that C may be the Representation of the Seat of the luminous Point; for the Seat of the real Luminary is supposed to be in a Plane parallel to the Plane of the Horizon; and therefore, if we consider A, the Seat of R, as at an immense Distance, and suppose R a real luminous Point, then will C be the Representation of the Seat R; that is, the Representation of the Seat of a luminous Point upon the Picture, which is supposed to be at an immense Distance from it: Or, in other Words, since C is the vanishing Point of LA infinitely extended, therefore, it is also the vanishing Point of any Point in that Line at an immense Distance.

COROL. 3.

And here likewise we may observe, that in order to find the vanishing Point of a Ray of Light, or of any Number of parallel Rays, we need only have the Angle of Inclination given; then by setting off the Distance of the Picture upon the horizontal Line, and making an Angle at that Point of Distance with the horizontal Line, equal to the given Angle of Inclination, we may determine the

the vaniſhing Point of thoſe Rays; as is ſhewn in the 98th Figure; which will be more fully explained hereafter.

LEMMA 2.

In the laſt Figure we conſider'd the Rays as coming in a Plane perpendicular to the Picture; we will now ſuppoſe them to come in a Plane oblique with the Picture.

Let ABOD be a Plane of Rays which cuts the Picture obliquely in the Line OB, every thing elſe remaining as in the former Figure. Fig. 96.

Through the Eye E draw the Plane HLLE parallel to the Plane of Rays, cutting the Picture in LL; then continue LL upwards beyond F, at pleaſure, and from E draw EF parallel to the Ray of Light RL; then is F the vaniſhing Point of that Ray, *&c.*

COROL. I.

From hence it follows, that when the Light comes from behind the Picture, the Shadows of Objects will be thrown towards the Bottom of the Picture.

LEMMA 3.

When the Rays come from behind the Spectator's Eye towards the Picture, (that is, when the Spectator is between the real Luminary and the Picture) then the vaniſhing Point of thoſe Rays will be below the horizontal Line.

Let FHIL be the Picture, E the Eye, C the Center of the Picture, and EC its Diſtance; and let ABOD be a Plane of parallel Rays whoſe Seat upon the Ground Plane is in the right Line LH continued: Or in other Words, ſuppoſe the Plane of Rays was continued towards the Picture in the Line BL, it would paſs thro' the Eye E, and would cut the Picture in the Line LI. Fig. 97.

Through the Eye E, and its Seat H, draw EC, HL, parallel to AB or CD; and from L, where HL cuts the Section GL, draw LC parallel to AD; then is EHLC a perpendicular Plane which paſſes through the Eye parallel to the Plane of Rays ABOD, cutting the Picture in LC; therefore LC continued will be the indefinite Repreſentation of the Plane ABOD, and it will alſo be the vaniſhing Line of all the Rays which can come in that Plane; and if EF be drawn parallel to RL, then is F the vaniſhing Point of that Ray, and C the Repreſentation of its Seat upon the horizontal Line HL.

 For

For suppose the Plane ABOD to be transposed into the Line XZ, then it will be like the Plane ABOD in the 95th Figure, with this Difference only, that the Rays coming in a contrary Direction, will have their vanishing Point upon the Picture below the horizontal Line.

COROLLARY.

When the Light comes from behind the Spectator's Eye towards the Picture, the Shadows of Objects upon the Picture will be thrown towards the horizontal Line; and since the Light is generally supposed to come upon the Front of the Picture, and not from behind it, therefore these Kind of Shadows are most generally used.

I should have been more particular in the Explanation of this Figure, if there appeared the least Difficulty to me in understanding it: Indeed, as the Eye is supposed to be between the Picture and the original Object, it may seem to contradict our general Definition of Perspective, in which we have always consider'd the Picture as placed between the Eye and the original Object; and therefore this Lemma may appear not to be so aptly drawn from the preceding Theorems* as it really ought to be: Yet, since the Method for determining a vanishing Line, or Point, is the same in either Case, *viz.* by imagining a Plane to pass through the Eye, parallel to the original Plane, 'till it cuts the Picture, &c. I have, therefore, only explained that single Article, and endeavoured to make myself understood, in the most familiar Manner; not much regarding strict mathematical Demonstration, nor yet that Order or Method which would be necessary were this Treatise purely Mathematical.

LEMMA 4.

When the Rays of Light come in Planes parallel to the Picture, they can have no vanishing Point; because a Plane which passes through the Eye parallel to those Planes, and which in other Cases would cut the Picture, and thereby produce a vanishing Line, in this Case can never cut the Picture, and therefore cannot produce any vanishing Line: From whence it follows, that when the Rays come in this Direction, the Appearance of their Shadows upon the Picture will be parallel, for the very same Reason that the Repre-

* Chap. 3, Sect. 2, of this Book.

sentation

ſentation of any original Plane which is parallel to the Picture, is exactly like its Original.

We will now give ſome general Rules for applying to Practice what has been ſaid upon this Head. In order to do which, let AB repreſent a Picture laid flat, as in the preceding Examples; Fig. 98. and let HL be the horizontal Line, C the Center of the Picture, and CE its Diſtance.

METHOD 1.

To find the vaniſhing Point of a Ray of Light, when it is ſuppoſed to come from behind the Picture towards the Spectator's Eye, in a Plane like ABCD, Fig. 95, which cuts the Picture in its Center;

Any where apart, draw NP parallel to the horizontal Line HL, Fig. 98. and draw NO, at pleaſure, for the Ray of Light; then is ONP the Angle of Inclination.---Through C the Center of the Picture, draw EK perpendicular to HL, and continue it at pleaſure; then make CH equal to the Diſtance EC, and from H draw HD parallel to the Ray NO, cutting CE in D; and then is D the vaniſhing Point of the Rays of Light. For ſince EK is the vaniſhing Line of the Plane of Rays, C the Center of that vaniſhing Line, and CH equal to its Diſtance, therefore H may be conſidered as the Eye; and conſequently, ſince HD is drawn from that Point parallel to the original Line NO, the Point D, where it cuts the vaniſhing Line ED, is the vaniſhing Point of that original Line.

METHOD 2.

When the Rays come from before the Picture, as in Fig. 97;

Every Thing remaining as before,--Let TW be a Ray of Light, Fig. 98. and VTW its Angle of Inclination.---From H draw HK, parallel to the Ray TW, cutting the vaniſhing Line EK in K; then is K the vaniſhing Point required.

METHOD 3.

When a Ray of Light comes from behind the Picture in a Plane oblique with the Picture, as in Fig. 96;

Let IG be the vaniſhing Line of a Plane of Rays, RS a Ray Fig. 98. of Light, and RSQ its Angle of Inclination.---Continue the horizontal Line beyond L at pleaſure, and from F, the Center of the vaniſhing Line, draw FE; then is FE the Diſtance of that vaniſhing

nishing Line; therefore by making FL equal to the Distance FE, and by drawing LI parallel to the Ray RS, we shall have I for the vanishing Point of that Ray.

METHOD 4.

When a Ray comes from behind the Spectator's Eye towards the Picture, in a Plane oblique with the Picture.

Fig. 98. Let IG be the vanishing Line of that Plane, ZY a Ray of Light, and XYZ its Angle of Inclination.---From L, the transposed Place of the Eye, draw LG parallel to the Ray ZY, which will give G for its vanishing Point.

COROLLARY.

From hence let us remember, that the Center C, or F, of a vanishing Line EK, IG, of a Plane of Rays, will be the vanishing Point of all Shadows which are cast by perpendicular Objects upon the Ground; because that Point * must be in the horizontal Line, and also in the vanishing Line, of the Plane of Rays; such are the Points C and F.

To find the Shadow of an Object which is supposed to stand perpendicular to the Ground, when the Rays come in Planes parallel to the Picture.

Fig. 99. Let FG be the Picture, AB the Representation of a perpendicular Object whose Shadow is sought; and let HL be a Ray of Light, whose Inclination with the Ground is equal to the Angle HLC.---Through B, the Seat of the Object, draw Ea at pleasure, but parallel to the horizontal Line; and through A draw Ra parallel to the Ray HL, cutting Ea in a; then is Ba the Shadow of BA.

Fig. 100. Again, Let abcd be a perpendicular Plane, whose vanishing Point is C the Center of the Picture, and let HL be a Ray of Light.---Through the Seats a, b, of the Perpendiculars ad, bc, draw af, be, parallel to the horizontal Line, and through d, and c, draw Lf, Re, parallel to the Ray HL, cutting af, be, in f and e; finally, from f and e, draw fe, then is abef the Shadow of the Plane abcd, and fe continued will vanish into C, the vanishing Point of ab, and cd.

* See the Appendix to Shadows, Book II.

Now,

Now, when the Shadow of any perpendicular Object is produced by Rays which are supposed to come in Planes parallel to the Picture, that Shadow may be found by Calculation: Thus, when the Angle of Inclination is 45 Degrees, then the Shadow will be equal to the Height of the Object, as in the two last Figures; therefore, by putting Unity for the Height of the Object, we may have the following Proportions, *viz.*

Angle of Inclination.			*Length of the Shadow.*
Deg.	Min.		
90	00		No Shadow.
78	45		1-5th Part of the Object.
67	30		2-5ths ditto.
56	15		7-10ths ditto.
45	00	is	The Height of ditto.
33	45		1 2-4ths. once the Length of ditto and Half.
22	30		2 4-9ths. twice the Len. of ditto and 4-9ths.
11	15		5 Times the Length of ditto.
00	00		Infinite.

From hence, then, we see the Reason why the Shadows produced by the Sun are very long in a Morning and Evening, and why they grow shorter and shorter the nearer the Sun approaches to the Meridian.

The foregoing Rules applied to Practice.

To find the Shadow of an Object, when the Light comes from behind the Spectator towards the Picture.

Let AB be the Picture, C its Center, CE its Distance, IK a Ray of Light, D the vanishing Point of the Rays of Light, a b c d a perpendicular Plane whose Shadow is sought, and L the vanishing Point of the Shadow which is cast upon the Ground by the perpendicular Sides ad, bc. Fig. 101.

From a and b, the Seats of the Perpendiculars ad, bc, draw Lines to L, the vanishing Point of the Shadow; and from d and c, the Extremities of ad, bc, draw Lines to D, the vanishing Point of the Rays; then from where they cut aL and bL, draw ef, and then is abfe the Shadow of abcd; which if continued will vanish into C, the vanishing Point of ab, cd.

To

To find the Shadow of a perpendicular Object when the Light comes from behind the Picture.

Fig. 102. In this Figure, H is given for the vanishing Point of the Shadow, KI for a Ray of Light.----Draw FD parallel to IK, which will give D for the vanishing Point of the Rays of Light; then from the Point H of the Shadow, draw Lines through all the lower Corners, a, e, f, of the Object, and continue them at pleasure; then from D, the vanishing Point of the Rays of Light, draw Lines through the upper Corners b, c, d; which will give the Points g, h, i, from whence the Shadow a g h i f, may be compleated.

In the two last Figures, I have drawn out every Line and Point which is necessary in the Work, and have also added the Angles IGK, IKL, for the Inclinations of the Rays, to make the Thing more intelligible.

Here let us observe, that as the Shadow of every perpendicular Line, will vanish into the vanishing Point of the Shadow; so also the Shadow of every oblique Line, will vanish into the vanishing Point of that Line: Thus a g is the Shadow of the Perpendicular a b, and g h of the oblique Line c b; and g h, c b, will both vanish into G: For since the Shadow is cast upon a Plane perpendicular to the Object which projects it, therefore the Shadow h g, and the Edge c b, are to be considered as parallel, and consequently will tend to the same vanishing Point.

I have hitherto considered Shadows as projected upon the Ground, and the Planes which project them as perpendicular to it; but by the same Rules any other Shadows are to be determined, whether the Planes upon which they are cast are perpendicular, parallel, or oblique, or however the original Objects are situated: And therefore, thus much might have sufficed to explain the Theory and Practice of Shadows, so far as is generally necessary in a Picture; but that this Part of Perspective may be made as familiar as possible, I have added several useful Examples in the Practical Treatise, Book the Second.

XVIII.

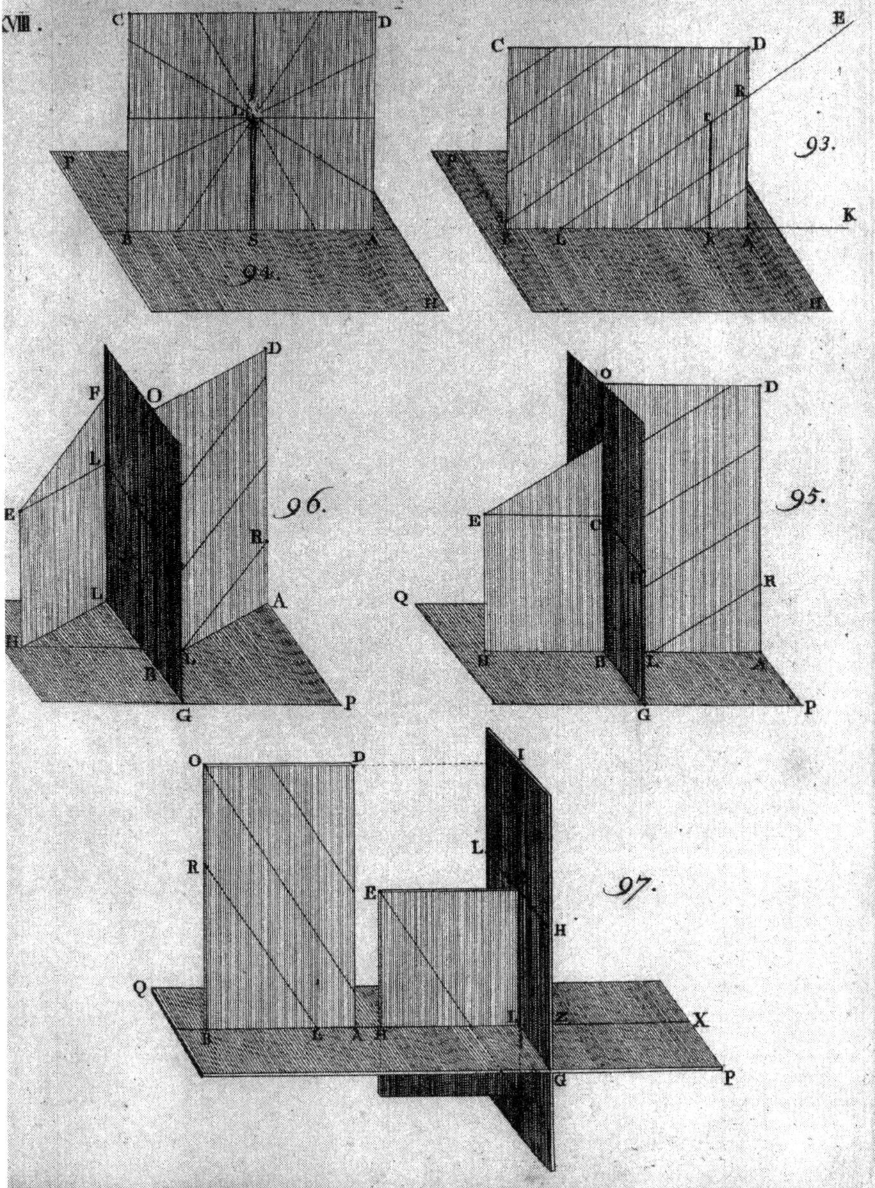

C
D
L
F
B
S
A
94.
H
C
D
E
R
93.
F
K
L
A
H
D
F
O
L
96.
E
R
L
A
H
B
G
P
O
D
95.
E
C
R
Q
H
B
L
A
G
P
O
D
I
L
R
97.
E
H
Q
B
L
A
H
I
Z
X
G
P

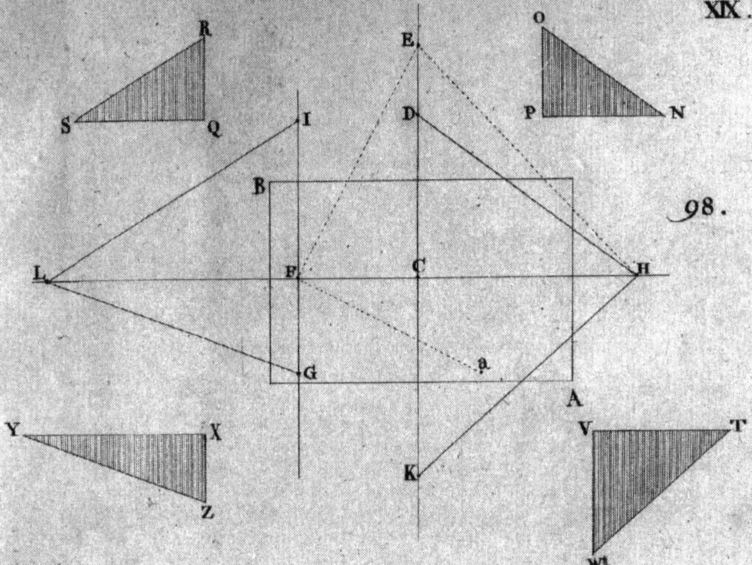

98.

100.

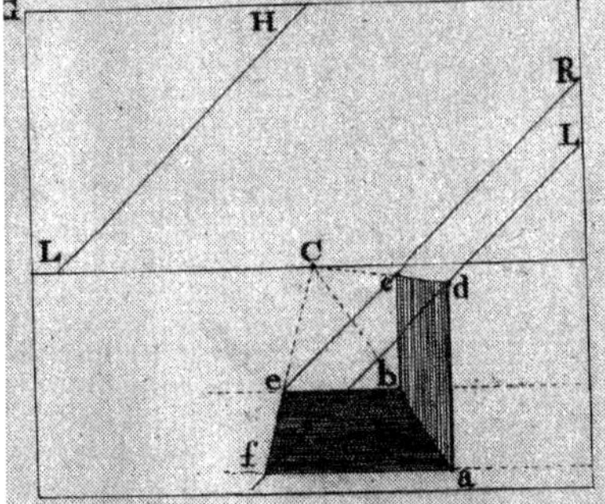

99.

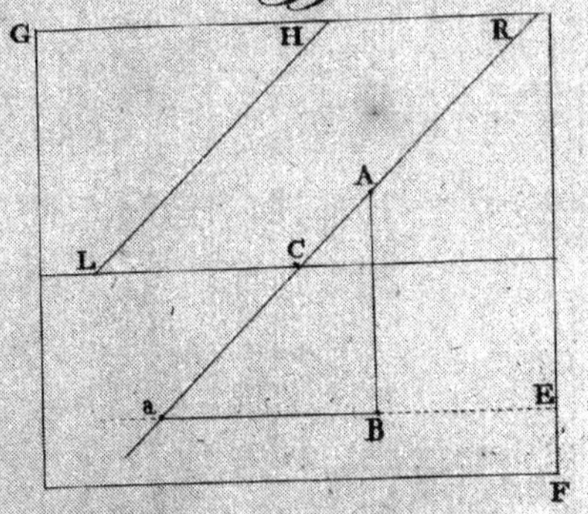

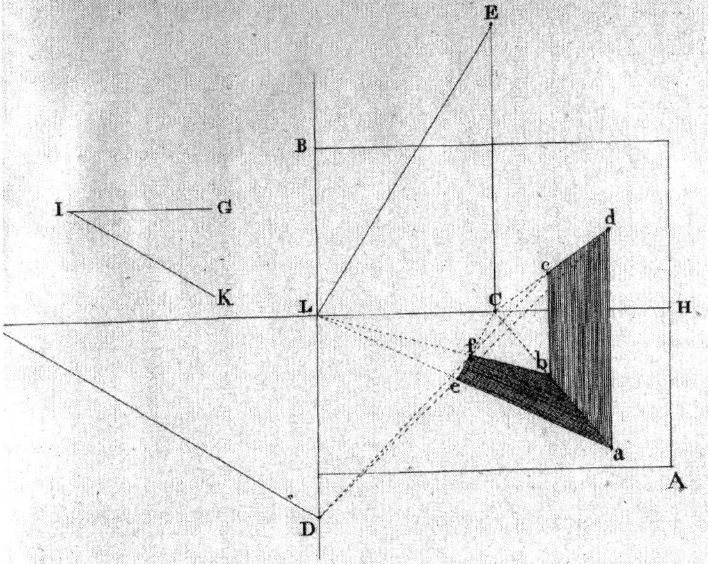

101.

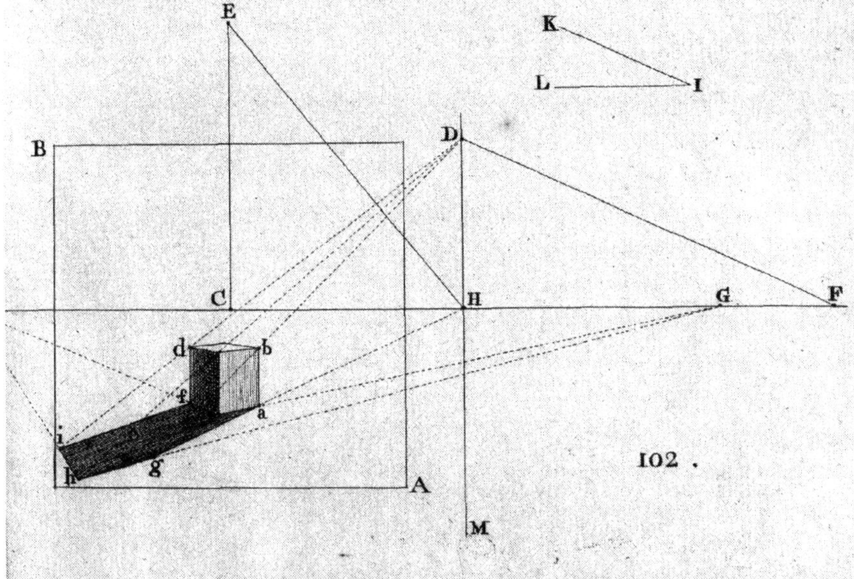

102.

104.

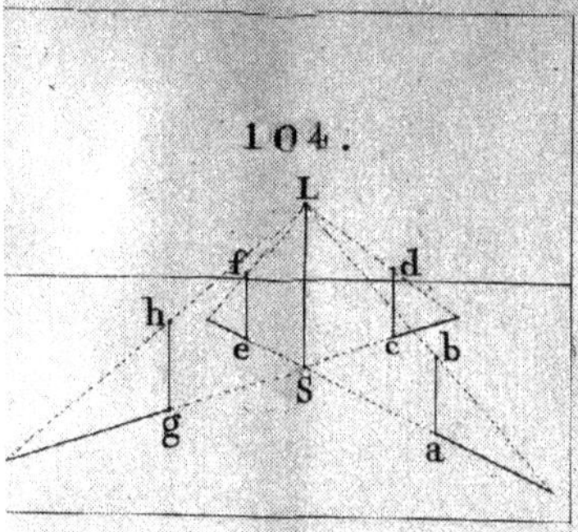

103.

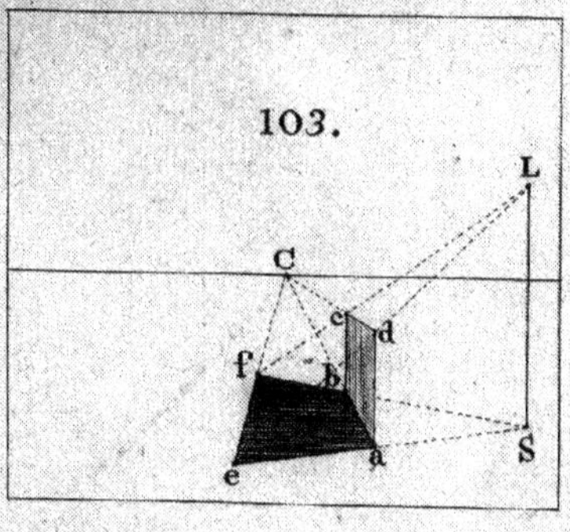

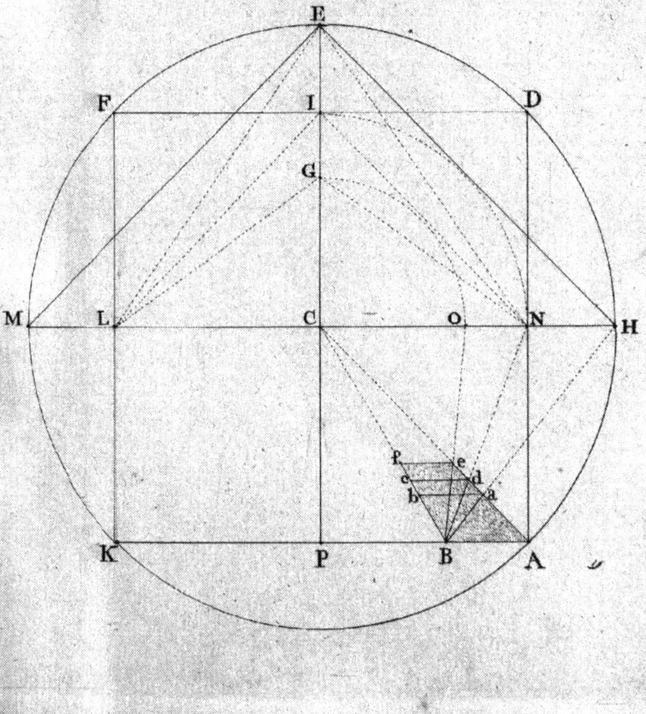

105.

SECT. II.

Of SHADOWS *projected by the* CANDLE, LAMP, *&c.*

THE Rays of Light from a Candle may be conceived to flow from a ſingle Point, like the ſeveral Radii of a Circle from its Center. The 94th Figure repreſents a Plane of theſe Rays, which is ſuppoſed to ſtand perpendicular to the Ground Plane HP; where L is the luminous Point, and S its Seat upon the Ground.

Now ſince theſe Kinds of Light are but ſeldom choſen for a Picture; and ſince the Method for determining Shadows projected in this Manner, is extremely eaſy; there needs but very little to be ſaid upon it: I ſhall therefore treat this Section with the utmoſt Brevity.

The firſt Thing neceſſary in order to determine the Shadow by a Candle, is, to give a luminous Point, and its Seat in the Picture; then by drawing Lines from thoſe Points through the Extremities of any Object, their mutual Interſections with each other will give the Appearance of that Shadow.

Thus, let L be a luminous Point, S its Seat, and a b c d the Repreſentation of a ſquare Plane: From S and L draw Lines through the Extremities a, b, c, d, and their Interſections at e and f will give the Shadow a e f b. Fig. 103

Again, let L be a luminous Point, S its Seat, and ab, cd, ef, gh, be the Repreſentations of ſeveral perpendicular Objects whoſe Shadows are ſought: Fig. 104.

From S and L draw Lines through the Extremity of each Line, and the Points where they cut each other, will ſhew the Length of the Shadows, as in the Figure.

CHAP. VI.

Of the Distance and Height of the Eye, of the Size of the Picture, and of the true Point of Sight, &c. with some Considerations upon the Appearance of circular Objects upon the Picture.

1. *Of the* DISTANCE *of the* EYE.

THE choosing a proper Distance for the Eye is so essential in all Perspective Representations, that without a nice Observance thereof every Object will appear unnatural and preposterous, be the Rules by which it was drawn ever so true in Theory, or so exactly observed in Practice. And the Reason of this will appear extremely obvious, if we consider that there is a certain Distance at which the Eye can see an Object with more Distinctness than in any other Point of View. Now, That Distance may be called the *true Point of Sight* in respect to That Object; and what is said of one Object will hold equally true of any Number of Objects: And therefore, as it is the Business of Perspective to draw the Representations of Objects, as they appear to the Eye, under the most agreeable Shape, it follows, that the Distance to be work'd with upon the Picture, should be chosen in such a Manner that each Representation shall make the same agreeable Figure to the Eye, as the Originals themselves would do were they seen under the same Angle.

Fig. 105. To explain the Sense of this more fully, let ADFK be a Picture, C its Center, NL the horizontal Line, AB one Side of a geometrical Square parallel to the Picture; and let it be required to find the Representation of that Square as seen at the several Distances CG, CI, CE.

From A and B draw Lines to C, the vanishing Point of the oblique Sides; and from C set off the several Distances of the Eye upon the horizontal Line in the Points O, N, H; then from these Points draw Lines to B, cutting AC in the Points a, d, e; and from a, d, e, draw Lines parallel to AB: Then shall we have the Representation ABab as seen at the Distance CE, the Representation ABcd as seen at the Distance CI, and the Representation ABfe as seen at the Distance CG.

Now,

Now, by inſpecting the Figure, we ſhall find that the apparent Depth Ae, of the Repreſentation Abfe, which ought to be foreſhorten'd, is longer than the parallel Side AB, ſo that the Figure which ſhould repreſent a Square, is a Parallelogram; and therefore this Repreſentation will not appear to be true: And if the Diſtance be at I, then the Depth will be longer than it ought, becauſe the Figure ABcd will ſtill look like a Parallelogram: But if the Diſtance be taken at E, then the Repreſentation will appear of a more proper Depth; and therefore the Diſtance CE is properer for a Picture of this Dimenſion. And if Lines are drawn from the ſeveral Points of View G, I, E, to the Extremities N and L of the Picture, then theſe Lines will ſhow the Angles under which the Picture is ſeen at thoſe Diſtances; *viz.* that at G will be an obtuſe one, that at I a right one, and that at E an acute one: And therefore from hence we may conclude, that the Angle under which any Picture is to be ſeen, ought never to be ſo great as a right one; and, by making an Experiment, we ſhall find, that if it is much leſs than an Angle of 50 Degrees, the apparent Depths of ſquare Objects will be too much foreſhorten'd, by which Means thoſe Objects which ſhould repreſent ſquare Bodies, will appear like ſo many Parallelograms: However, in ſome Caſes, ſuch as in painting Deceptions for Gardens, or for Pictures with curvilinear Objects, the Diſtance ſhould be taken as great as poſſible; which is left to the Diſcretion of the Artiſt.

There are ſeveral other Reaſons to be given for chooſing a proper Diſtance for the Eye; but as one Example is ſufficient to ſhew the Abſurdity and Inconveniency of diſregarding, or not knowing, this eſſential Part of Perſpective, it becomes needleſs to produce any others.

2. *Of the* HEIGHT *of the* EYE.

'TIS the Height of the Eye that determines the Height of the horizontal Line from the Bottom of the Picture; and therefore, it is that which gives the whole Space for the Repreſentation of the Ground. And in taking the Height of the Eye, we muſt be careful not to let it be ſo great as the Diſtance of the Eye; ſince the ſame bad Conſequences will follow from thence as in chooſing an improper Diſtance. For let PP be a perpendicular Section of the Picture, AP an original Line perpendicular to it, and HE the Height of the Eye.---Draw AE, and then will Pc be the Repreſentation of PA: But if the Eye be placed at I, ſo as to be equal to its Diſtance IP, then will the Repreſentation PC be too long in the Fig. 106.

the Picture; and the nearer the Eye is brought to P, (suppose at Q) that is, the more the Height QR exceeds the Distance QP, the more preposterous will the Representation Pa appear. Indeed if any
Fig. 107. original Object, as AB, be parallel to the Picture, the Height of the Eye will have no Effect upon this kind of Representations, provided the Eye moves in the same perpendicular HI; for the Representation ab, is equal to the Representation CP.

3. *The Consequences of viewing Pictures from any other than the true Point of Sight.*

FROM what has been said upon the Distance and Height of the Eye, it must be manifest, that no Perspective Representations will appear so natural as when viewed from the true Point of Sight; because, at that Point, all the Rays which are supposed to come from the original Objects, and produce their several Projections upon the Picture, will concur at the Eye in their proper Point, and thereby exhibit a Picture upon the Retina exactly similar to that of their Originals.

But again, If the Eye is not placed in the true Point of Sight, the Projection of all Objects which are not parallel to the Picture, will not seem to tend to their proper vanishing Points; and for that Reason such Representations will seem to start out of their proper Places, will lose their just Proportions, and consequently, will convey a jumble of confused Appearances to the Eye: And to this we may add also, the shocking Effect it will have upon the horizontal Line in particular, which is always governed by the Place of the Eye.

What has been said upon this Head, relates principally to Pictures painted upon uneven Grounds, such as Domes, vaulted Roofs, irregular Walls, *&c.* where the least Variation from the true Point of Sight, will be productive of the above, and other bad Consequences: For as to flat Pictures, the Fancy will be ready to give some Assistance towards correcting what is not strictly right in them; and therefore, a little Variation of the Eye from the true Point of Sight, is allowable in such Cases: For no great Inconveniency will appear, so long as the Eye keeps upon a Level with the horizontal Line.

4. *Of the* SIZE *of the* PICTURE.

THE Size of the Picture is to be governed by the Distance and
Fig. 105. Height of the Eye.----Thus, let CE be the Distance of the Eye, and CP its Height.

With

With the Diſtance CE deſcribe the Circle FKAD, and make CI equal to CP; through P and I draw AK, DF, parallel to the horizontal Line, cutting the Circle in A, K, D, F; from which Points draw the Lines AD, FK: Then ſhall we have a Square, which will give the utmoſt Size a Picture ſhould be of if ſeen from no greater Diſtance than CE. But if the Height of the Eye be leſs than CP, then the Picture will be a Parallelogram, which is the moſt general Shape given to Pictures.---This Method of limiting the Size of the Picture to the Diſtance and Height of the Eye, will be of great Uſe in ſeveral Operations.

5. *Some Conſiderations upon the Appearance of round Objects upon the Picture.*

FROM what has been ſaid upon the Diſtance of the Eye, *&c.* it may ſeem very improbable that any perſpective Repreſentation ſhould have a diſagreeable Effect, if the Rules we have laid down be nicely obſerved: Yet there are ſome Caſes, perhaps, in which the Artiſt will think it better to be guided by his own Judgment, than to follow the ſtrict Rules of Perſpective. This ſeems to have been the Opinion of Monſieur *Freſnoy*: For in his excellent Poem upon Painting, tranſlated by Mr. *Dryden*, he ſays, "Though "Perſpective cannot be called a perfect Rule for Deſigning, yet it "is a great Succour to Art, and facilitates the Diſpatch of the "Work; tho, frequently falling into Error, it makes us behold "Things under a falſe Aſpect; for Bodies are not always repre- "ſented according to the Geometrical Plane, but ſuch as they ap- "pear to the Sight." But as there are different Opinions upon this Subject, I ſhall beg Leave to offer my Thoughts upon it.

Suppoſe it was required to draw the Repreſentation of a Range of Columns parallel to the Picture; if they are drawn according to the ſtrict Rules of Perſpective, then that Column which is in the Center of the Picture will be the leaſt, and conſequently, thoſe on each Side of it will be larger and larger continually, the farther they are removed from the Center of the Picture. But to explain this more fully: Let KLMN be a Plane which paſſes through the Eye Fig. 108.
parallel to the Ground; then will PP be the horizontal Line, and C the Center of the Picture: And let AB, H, I, be three Columns cut by this Plane; then let Lines be drawn from the Extremity of each Circle to the Eye; and the Sections ab, cd, ef, with the

the Picture, are the Projections of thoſe Circles upon the Picture; and by meaſuring the ſeveral Repreſentations we ſhall find, that cd, and ef, are much longer than ab. From whence we may conceive, that the farther any Column is removed from the Center of the Picture, the larger will be its Repreſentation; and we may moreover conceive, that this Increaſe of the apparent Magnitude of the Columns, is owing to the Obliquity of the Lines gh, ik, with the Picture, which Lines meaſure their apparent Widths. Now the Queſtion is, Whether Columns ſituated in this Manner are to be thus repreſented upon the Picture, or not?

The Definition I have given of the Word Perſpective, is this; *viz.* To draw the Repreſentations of Objects as they appear to the Eye, *&c.* and I have avoided the more general Definition, *viz.* of drawing the Repreſentation of Objects by the Rules of Geometry, *&c.* as the former appeared to be more ſignificant of what I intended to expreſs by the Term Perſpective. For ſince the Fallaces of Viſion are ſo many and great*, and ſince we form our common Judgment and Eſtimation of the Appearance of Objects from Cuſtom and Experience†, and not from mathematical Reaſoning; therefore it ſeems reaſon-

* The ingenious Dr. *Smith*, in his Treatiſe upon Opticks, has given us ſeveral Inſtances of the Fallacies in Viſion, amongſt which, he ſays, "We are frequently deceived in our Eſti-"mates of Diſtance by any extraordinary Magnitude of Objects ſeen at the End of it: As in "travelling towards a large City or a Caſtle, or a Cathedral Church, or a Mountain larger "than ordinary, we think they are much nearer than we find them to be upon Trial. For "ſince by Experience the Ideas of certain Quantities of known Diſtances are uſually annexed "to the apparent Magnitudes of known Objects of a common Size; and ſince the apparent "Magnitudes of thoſe larger Objects at a greater Diſtance are the ſame as of the ſmaller at "a ſmaller Diſtance, it is no Wonder they ſuggeſt the uſual Idea of ſmaller Diſtance annext "to more common Objects. This is further evident, becauſe we are ignorant of the Coun-"try, and of the Inequalities in the Ground interpoſed." Again, he obſerves, "the Part of "the Monument extant above the Tops of the adjoining Houſes, I am told, is five times "longer than the Height of the Houſes, and yet from below that Part appears but two or "three times longer at moſt; becauſe of its unuſual Magnitude and Obliquity to the Sight." And the ſame curious Gentleman adds, "I remember a red Coat of Arms, upon the Top of "an Iron Gate at the End of a Walk, was taken for a Brick Houſe in the Fields beyond "it". *Vide Smith's Opticks, Book* I. *p.* 61, 62.

† In regard to Perception, that acute and judicious Reaſoner Mr. *Locke*, obſerves, "We "are to conſider concerning Perception, that the Ideas we receive by Senſation are often in "grown People alter'd by the Judgment, without our taking Notice of it. When we ſet "before our Eyes a round Globe, of any uniform Colour, *v. g.* Gold, Alabaſter, or Jet, 'tis "certain, that the Idea thereby imprinted in our Mind, is of a flat Circle variouſly ſhadow'd, "with ſeveral Degrees of Light and Brightneſs coming to our Eyes. But we having by uſe "been accuſtom'd to perceive, what kind of Appearances convex Bodies are wont to make in "us; what Alterations are made in the Reflections of Light, by the Difference of the ſenſible "Figures of Bodies, the Judgment preſently, by an habitual Cuſtom, alters the Appearances "into their Cauſes: So that from that, which truly is Variety of Shadow or Colour, collect-"ing the Figure, it makes it paſs for a Mark of Figure, and frames to itſelf the Perception "of

reasonable not to comply with the strict Rules of Mathematical Perspective in some particular Cases (as in this before us) but to draw the Representation of Objects as they appear to the Eye; and therefore, I presume, a Painter should represent those few Objects which are an Exception to the General Rules of Perspective, in such a Manner as may not offend the Eye of any common Spectator. For if the above Columns are to be represented according to the strict Rules of this Art; then the Columns as they recede from the Center of the Picture will grow thick and clumsy, their Intercolumnations will be continually growing less and less, and the whole Beauty of the Building will be intirely destroyed. *

" of a convex Figure, and an uniform Colour; when the Idea we receive from thence, is " only a Plane variously colour'd, as is evident in Painting. To which Purpose I shall here " insert a Problem of that very ingenious and studious Promoter of real Knowledge, the lear- " ned and worthy Mr. *Molineux*; and it is this: Suppose a Man born blind, and now adult, " and taught by his Touch to distinguish between a Cube and a Sphere of the same Metal, " and nearly of the same Bigness, so as to tell when he felt one and t'other, which is the " Cube, which the Sphere. Suppose then the Cube and Sphere placed on a Table, and the " blind Man be made to see: *Quære*, Whether by his Sight, before he touched them, he " could now distinguish, and tell, which was the Globe, which the Cube. To which the " acute and judicious Proposer answers: Not. For though he has obtained the Experience " of, how a Globe, how a Cube, affects his Touch; yet he has not yet attained the Ex- " perience, that what affects his Touch so or so, must affect his Sight so or so: Or that a " protuberant Angle in the Cube, that pressed his Hand unequally, shall appear to his Eye as " it does in the Cube. I agree with this thinking Gentleman, whom I am proud to call my " Friend, in his Answer to this his Problem; and am of Opinion, that the blind Man, at " first Sight, would not be able with Certainty to say, which was the Globe, which the Cube, " whilst he only saw them, though he could unerringly name them by his Touch, and cer- " tainly distinguish them by the Difference of their Figures felt. This I have set down, and " leave with my Reader, as an Occasion for him to consider how much he may be beholden " to Experience, Improvement, and acquired Notions, where, he thinks, he has not the " least Use of, or Help from them." *Vide Locke's Essay upon Human Understanding, Vol.* I, *Ch.* 9.

But this is no new Opinion; for so old an Author as *Lucretius*, takes particular Notice of it; for he, after having given innumerable Instances of the Errors in our Judgment, in regard to Sight, sums them up in the following Lines.

Cætera de genere hoc mirando multa videmus,
Quæ violare fidem quasi Sensibus omnia quærunt:
Nequicquam. Quoniam pars horum maxima fallit
Propter opinatus Animi, quos addimus ipsi,
Pro visis ut sint, quæ non sunt sensibu' visa. LUCRET. Lib. 4.

Or, as Mr. CREECH has translated it:

" Ten thousand such appear, ten thousand Foes
" To Certainty of Sense, and all oppose:
" In vain, 'tis Judgment, not the Sense mistakes,
" Which fancy'd Things for real Objects takes." *Vide Creech's Lucret. B*4.

* Of this we have several Instances in *Pozzo*'s first Book upon Perspective, particularly in Fig. 45, 46, 50, and 51; in which, those Columns that are farthest from the Point of Sight, are so prodigiously increased in their apparent Widths, as to lose very near one Diameter in Height; and, I think, the Disproportion is too visible to be disputed, especially in the 45th and 46th Figures.

What

What has been said upon this Subject, relates principally to round or cylindrical Bodies, such as Globes, Columns, or the like; but as to angular ones, (especially those that are Square) since their apparent Widths are perpetually increased the more diagonally they are seen by the Eye, therefore, the Representations of such Objects upon the Picture should continually grow larger and larger in Width the more they are removed from the Center of the Picture. Thus the Representation of the Square Q, which is seen only in Front, cannot appear so large as the Representation of the Square R, which is viewed as a Triangle. I say, that the apparent Magnitude of Objects that are Square or Triangular, will be greater when view'd Angle-wise, than when seen in Front: But the apparent Magnitude of Columns, or any other round Objects, will always be the same at the same Distance; because, in the first Case, the Diagonal of a Square (which in some Views measures its apparent Width) is longer than its Sides; but in the latter Case, the Diameter of a Circle (which constantly measures its apparent Width) is always of the same Length; and therefore to represent Columns, *&c.* larger and larger, when they are at a greater and greater Distance, is, I presume, false in Theory, (I mean in an optical Sense only) and cannot be true in Practice. To this it may be said; Why then should they not be represented less and less in proportion to their several Distances, since in fact they are so? To which I answer again, that by a Habit of judging, and from the prevailing force of Experience, we are taught to think, they are all of the same Size, because they are upon the same Parallel with the Eye. Thus, for Instance; when we stand before the Middle of a Building of any considerable Length, we apprehend the Ends to appear exactly as high as the Middle of it, though in fact they cannot, because the Angle subtended at the Eye from the Middle, is greater than those subtended at the Corners. Again, suppose it was required to draw the Representation of round Balls, or Globes, which are supposed to be at the same Distance from the Picture, according to the strict Rules of Mathematical Projection: Then the Projection of that Ball only which is in the Eye's Axis will be a Circle, and, being properly shaded, will appear like a Globe; but all the other Projections, which are not in the Eye's Axis, will be Elliptical, and, shade them how you will, they can never appear like Globes to any common Spectator: I say to any common Spectator, because such Appearances contradict the common Idea which Men in general have form'd to themselves of Rotundity. In short, Perspective, in in a strictly Mathematical or Optical Sense, is one Thing; and Perspective, according to the Acceptation of that Word among Painters, is another: The First teaches how to describe on a Plane, to a mathematical Exactness, the Projections of any Objects; but the Second, like a modest and judicious Master, teaches the most simple and general Principles of Art; and instead of leading us into the Mazes of Lines and Angles, and losing us in the Labyrinths of mathematical Reasoning, directs us only to the Study of SIMPLICITY, which is the Foundation of Grace and Beauty.

I know it may be said, that if we make choice of a proper Distance, all Inconveniencies of this Kind may be avoided: But let the Distance be ever so proper, yet still the Projections of Columns, *&c.* as they are removed farther and farther from the Center of the Picture, will grow larger and larger continually; which surely ought not to be admitted.

These are the Reasons which induced me to consider this Subject in a particular Manner; but whether they are sufficient, or not, to answer the intended Purpose, is submitted to the Candour of every ingenuous Reader.

CHAP. VII.

Of Aerial Perspective, Chiara Oscuro, *and* Keeping *in Pictures.*

From Mr. Hamilton.

" BY Aerial Perspective is meant, the Art of giving a " due Diminution or Degradation to the Strengh of Light, " Shade, and Colours of Objects, according to their diffe- " rent Distances, the Quantity of Light which falls upon them, " and the Medium through which they are seen.

" The Chiara Oscuro consists more particularly in * ex- " pressing the different Degrees of Light, Shade, and Colour of " Bodies, arising from their own Shape, and the Positon of their " Parts with respect to the Eye and neighbouring Objects, where- " by their Light or Colours are affected.

" And Keeping, is the Observance of a due Proportion in " the general Light and Colouring of the whole Picture; that no " Light or Colour in one Part, may be too bright or strong for " another; but that a proper Harmony amongst them all together " may be preserved.

" All these are necessary Requisites to a good Picture, and may " be properly enough included within the general Name of Aerial " Perspective, as they all relate to the different Degrees of Strength " of the Light and Colouring, according to the Circumstances of " the Shape and Position of the Objects with regard to each other, " the Eye, and the Light which illuminates them.

" The Eye does not judge of the Distance of Objects barely by " their apparent Size, but also by their Strength of Colour and " Distinction of Parts; it is not, therefore, sufficient to give an " Object its due apparent Bulk, according to the Rules of Perspec- " tive, unless at the same Time it be expressed with that proper " Faintness and Degradation of Colour which that Distance " requires.

" Thus, if the Figure of a Man at a Distance were painted of " a due Size for the Place, but with too great a Distinction of

* But it is the Opinion of some very eminent Painters, that the Words *Chiara Oscuro*, more properly signify a Clearness of Shadow.

" Parts,

" Parts, or too strong Colours, it will appear to stand forward, " and seem proportionably less, so as to represent a Dwarf situated " nearer the Eye, and out of the Plane on which the Painter in" tended he should stand.

" By the ORIGINAL COLOUR of an Object, is meant that Colour " which it exhibits to the Eye when directly exposed to it in a full, " open, uniform Light, and at such a moderate small Distance as " to be clearly and distinctly seen.

" This Colour receives an Alteration from many Causes, the " principal of which are these:

" 1. From the Object's being removed to a greater Distance from " the Eye, whereby the Rays of Light which it reflects are less vivid, " and the Colour becomes more diluted, and tinged in some mea" sure with the faint blueish Cast, or with the Dimness or Hazi" ness of the Body of Air through which the Rays pass.

" 2. From the greater or less Degree of Light with which the " Object is enlightened: The same Original Colour having a dif" ferent Appearance in the Shade from what it has in the Light, " although at an equal Distance from the Eye, and so in Propor" tion as the Light or Shade is stronger.

" 3. From the Colour of the Light itself which falls upon it, " whether it be by the Reflection of coloured Light from any neigh" bouring Object, or by its Passage through a coloured Medium; " which will exhibit a Colour compounded of the Original Colour " of the Object, and the other accidental Colours which the Light " brings with it.

" 4. From the Position of the Surface of the Object, or of its " several Parts with respect to the Eye; such Parts of it as are " directly exposed to the Eye appearing more lively and distinct " than those which are seen slanting.

" 5. From the Closeness or Openness of the Place where the Ob" ject is situated, the Light being much more variously directed " and reflected within a Room, than abroad in the open Air; " every Aperture in a Room giving an Inlet to a different Stream " of Light with its own peculiar Direction, whereby Bodies in such " a Situation will be very differently affected with respect to their " Light, Shade, and Colours, from what they would be in an " open Place.

" 6. Some Original Colours naturally reflect Light in a greater " Proportion than others, though equally exposed to the same

"Degrees of it; whereby their Degradation at severa Distances "will be different from that of other Colours which reflect less "Light.

"From these several Causes it arises, that the Colours of Ob-"jects are seldom seen pure and unmixed, but generally arrive at "the Eye broken and softened by each other; and therefore, in "Painting, where the natural Appearances of Object are to be "described, all hard or sharp Colouring ought to be avoided.

"A Painter, therefore, who would succeed in Aeral Perspec-"tive, ought carefully to study the Effects which Distance, or "different Degrees or Colours of Light, have on each particular "Original Colour, to know how its Hew or Strength is changed "in the several Circumstances above-mentioned, and to represent "it accordingly; so that in a Picture of various-coloured Objects, "he may be able to give each Original Colour its own proper Di-"minution or Degradation according to its Place.

"Now, as all Objects in a Picture take their Measures in Pro-"portion to those placed in the Front, so, in Aerial Perspective, "the Strength of Light, and the Brightness of the Colours of Ob-"jects close to the Picture, must serve as a Measure, with respect "to which, all the same Colours at several Distances, must have "a proportional Degradation in like Circumstances. But, as in "Musick, it is not necessary to the Harmony, that the Instru-"ments should be tuned to the Concert Pitch, but they may be "set above or below it, so long as they are in tune to each other; "so in Painting, it is not requisite that the Measures on the in-"tersecting Line of the Picture, or the Brightness of the Light "there, should be equal to the Life; but they may be taken "greater or less, so long as every Thing else in the Picture bears "a true Proportion to that which is chosen as the first Standard.

"Hence, almost any Degree of Light may be taken for the "greater Light in a Picture, when the lesser Degrees of Light are "expressed with darker or weaker Colours; for any Degree of "Light may either represent a Light in respect of a darker, or it "may serve as a Shade to a lighter; and it matters not in Point "of Keeping how light or how dark a Picture is in general, so "that its several Parts have proportionable Degrees of Light and "Shade given them.

"In order, therefore, to the giving any Colour its due Dimi-"nution in Proportion to its Distance, it ought to be known, what

" the Appearance of that Colour would be, were it close to the " Picture, Regard being had to that Degree of Light which is " chosen as the principal Light of the Picture; as in order to the " giving any Object its due apparent Size, its true Size must be " reduced to the same Scale with the Measure on the Bottom of " the Picture.

" For if any Colour should be made too bright for another, or " for the general Colours employed in the rest of the Picture, it " will appear too glaring, and seem to start out of its Place, and " throw a Flatness and Damp on the rest of the Work; or, as the " Painters express it, the Brightness of that Colour will kill the " rest.

" No Painting can express the dazzling Brightness of the Sun, " or even its reflected Light coming from polished Metals, with " that sparkling Vivacity as it appears in the *Camera Obscura*, in " the Images of polished Surfaces on which the Sun shines; or if " it could in some Sort be imitated in a Picture, by the Assistance " of Gilding, it would not have a good Effect with regard to the " other Colours, which it would too much outshine; and thereby " hurt the Keeping: And this is one Defect which the Represen- " tation of Objects in the *Camera Obscura* is liable to; for by " reason of the Refraction of the Rays by the Glass, those Objects " which naturally reflect less Light, lose a greater Proportion of " it than those which reflect Light more plentifully; whereby the " due Keeping in the whole, is not so exactly preserved as in " direct Vision, the Lights and Shades appearing generally too " strong for each other."

Thus far Mr. *Hamilton*. And I have thought proper to add the following Figure, with a Design of fixing what he has said upon the Subject more strongly in the Memory.

Let E be the Eye, PP the Picture, RS, AB, CD, EF, and HL, the same Object seen by the Eye at different Distances; now, the farther they are removed from the Eye, the larger will be the Space of Air through which they are seen, and the more they will be tinged with its Hew; therefore, in Proportion as the Representations Ps, Pb, &c. are more and more diminished upon the Picture, so likewise, in the same Proportion, must the Original Colour of those Objects be more and more broken and diluted with the Colour of the Air. Thus, suppose the Representation Ps of RS, to be painted of the Original Colour; then, because the Representations Pb, Pd, Pf, and Pl, are perpetually diminished in propor-

proportion to the Diſtance of their reſpective Originals; therefore in colouring thoſe ſeveral Repreſentations, Care muſt be taken to diminiſh that alſo in the ſame Proportion.

There may be ſome Exceptions made to this general Rule by a nice Obſerver of Nature, for there are ſome Incidents will happen which ſeem to contradict it; ſuch as a white Houſe, or any other very light Object directly oppoſed to the Sun at a great Diſtance; yet notwithſtanding, what has been advanced will be of great Service in fixing right Ideas of theſe eſſential Requiſities: And I may venture to affirm, that without a general Obſervance thereof, every Picture will be at beſt but a flat and lifeleſs Performance.

I might now proceed to the Conſideration of ſome other Things relative to Perſpective; but ſince they are not at all eſſential in the Theoretical Part, and as I muſt take Notice of them in another Place, I ſhall therefore put an End to this Book.

END of the FIRST BOOK.

107.

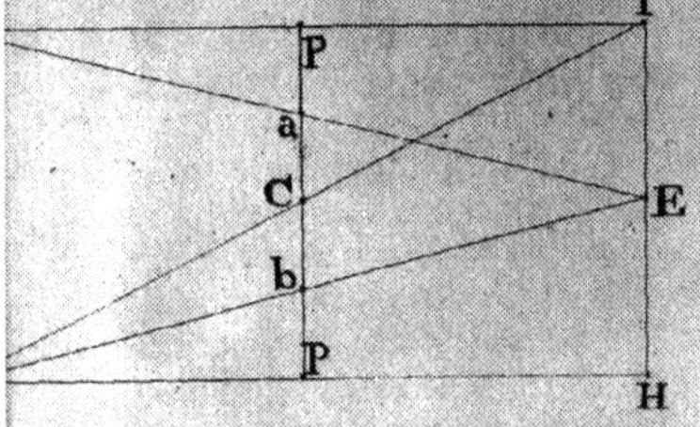

106.

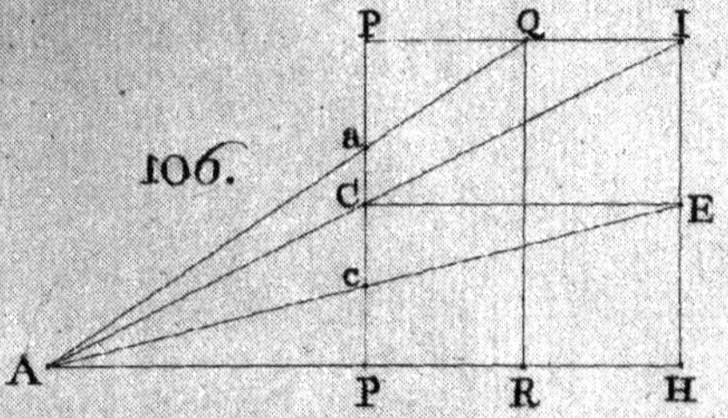

108.

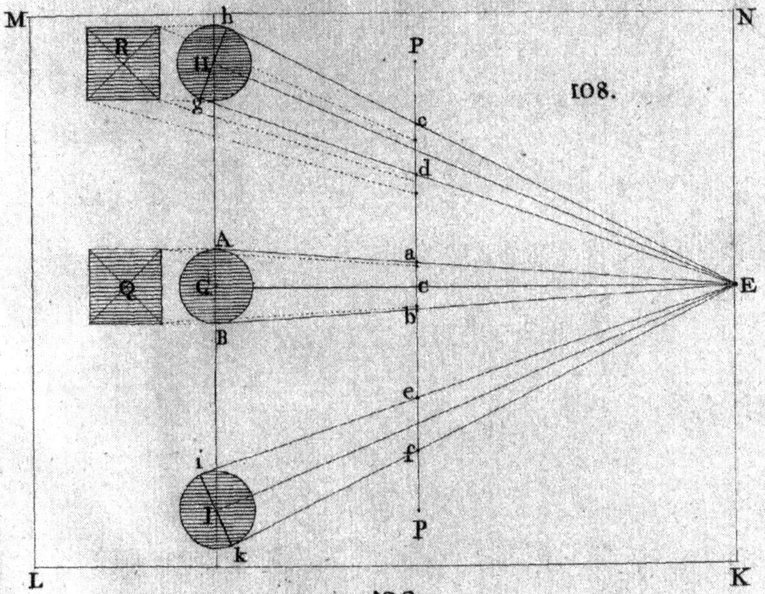

109.

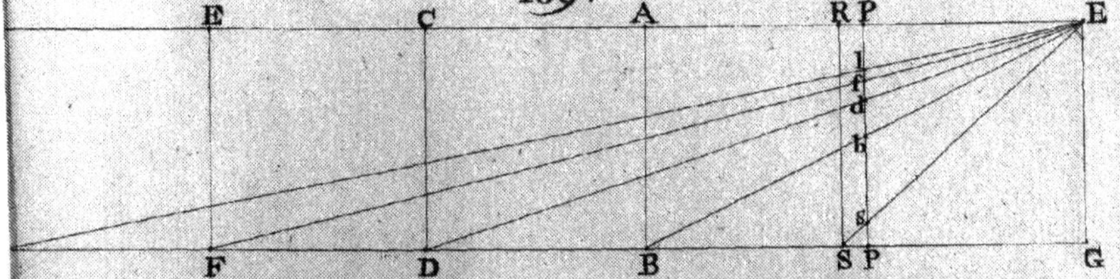

THE

PRACTICE

OF

PERSPECTIVE:

Being

The SECOND BOOK

OF

DR. BROOK TAYLOR's METHOD *of* PERSPECTIVE *made easy, &c.*

By JOSHUA KIRBY, Painter.

The Practice [*of* Painting] *ought always to be built on a rational Theory, of which* PERSPECTIVE *is both the Guide and the Gate, and without which it is impossible to succeed either in Designing, or in any of the Arts depending thereon.*

Leonardo da Vinci upon Painting, p. 36

The SECOND EDITION.

IPSWICH:
Printed by W. CRAIGHTON. MDCCLV.

TO THE

ACADEMY

OF

PAINTING, SCULPTURE, ARCHITECTURE, &c. in LONDON.

GENTLEMEN,

AS PERSPECTIVE is absolutely necessary to a JUST DESIGN, give me Leave to dedicate this Book to You on the Subject. It is the Product of many Years Application and Study, and wrote with an Intention to render that hitherto perplexed, but useful Art, easy and familiar. How I have succeeded in the Attempt, is submitted to your Candour and Judgment; and I hope that this Dedication will be received as an Instance of my Gratitude, for the Favour of that Encouragement and Recommendation, which you have been pleased to give to the Work.

I do not presume to offer any Thing *new* to the Principal Members of the Society; for I am not ſo vain as to think I can give any Inſtructions to Perſons of ſuch ſuperior Abilities: But if I can contribute a little towards inſtructing the PUPILS in the *firſt Rudiments of Deſign*, it may ſpare ſome Time and Trouble, and I hope will be accepted as a Token of my Regard for You, and Affection for thoſe ARTS.-----I ſhall only add, that it is my ſincereſt Wiſh, that every Encouragement may be given to your indefatigable Endeavours, in promoting the ARTS of PAINTING, SCULPTURE, ARCHITECTURE, *&c.* That the Pupils may do Honour to their ſeveral MASTERS, and become Ornaments to their Country; and that every other Advantage may concur to raiſe the Glory of the ENGLISH ACADEMY to the higheſt Pitch.

I am,

GENTLEMEN,

Your moſt Obliged,

Humble Servant,

JOSHUA KIRBY.

P R E F A C E.

IN this Practical Book upon PERSPECTIVE *I shall endeavour to give some general Methods for finding the Representations of all Kinds of Objects, however they are situated in regard to the Eye or the Picture, or however irregular they are amongst themselves. And since great Care has been taken to adapt every Example in this Part to the Theory, the Reader may be satisfied that every Figure is strictly true, and capable of a Mathematical Demonstration; so that those whom Curiosity will not invite, or Leisure permit, to go regularly through the preceeding Theory, need not trouble themselves about it, because what follows will be sufficient for their Purpose. But let them consider, that it is in this as in all other Studies, with which, if a Person desires either to be thoroughly acquainted, or to profit by his Study, he must* read *with* Attention, draw out *every* Figure *as he proceeds, and be* well acquainted *with one* Example *before he begins with another.*

And since it is presumed that every Example in the following Work, may be as easily understood and applied to Practice by every Student in the Arts of Design, as are the common Principles of Arithmetick by every ordinary Mechanick; therefore it is hoped that PERSPECTIVE *will be no longer thought an abstruse and difficult Study, nor be disregarded as trifling and insignificant; but that the young* Tyroes *in the above Arts will first make* PERSPECTIVE *familiar to them, and treat her with the Respect which she deserves, as the* PARENT *of the noble Art of* PAINTING; *and upon whose general, though not rigid Precepts, every Design must be regulated, if the Artist intends it shall appear a* true Representation of NATURE.

THE

PRACTICE of PERSPECTIVE made EASY, &c.

BOOK II. CHAP. I.

An INTRODUCTION *to the* PRACTICE *of Perspective.*

IN order to convey a general Idea of PERSPECTIVE with as much Ease as the Nature of the Thing will admit, let ABCD represent a square Board standing perpendicularly upon the Ground, which is represented by H M, and suppose the Figure EH to be looking at it; then it will be evident, that he must see it by means of an infinite Number of Rays of Light, which are continually reflected from every Point of the said Object to his Eye. But since the Rays which come from the four Corners only will be sufficient for our Purpose, we will suppose that he sees it by means of the four Lines AE, BE, CE and DE, which represent those four Rays of Light: And, if we suppose a transparent Plane, like a large Piece of Glass, to be placed between the Object ABCD and the Spectator's Eye, it must be obvious, that this Plane will cut the Rays of Light in their Passage to his Eye. Now, the Shape a b c d, which that cutting of the Picture makes with the Rays, is called *the Projection of the real Object* ABCD, upon the Glass. And if instead of this transparent Plane, we suppose GLOP to be a Canvas, and the above Projection to be drawn upon it in the very same Manner as it was projected upon the Glass, then the Figure so described is called *the Perspective Appearance of the real Object* ABCD; for the Rays of Light coming to the Eye from the Points a. b, c, d, which are drawn upon the Picture, in the very same Manner as they do from the corresponding original Points A, B, C, D, of the real Figure; therefore, if they are painted with the Fig. 1.

the ſame Strength of Colour, *&c.* they will to the Spectator EH, appear like that original Object: So that the whole Art of Perſpective conſiſts, in determining theſe, and the like Appearances, upon the Picture, and in giving them their proper Force and Colour.

Now let us obſerve, *Firſt*, If the original Figure be parallel to the Picture, then its Repreſentation will be exactly like it; thus, ABCD is parallel to the Picture, therefore, a b c d, its Repreſentation, is exactly like it. For which Reaſon, the Repreſentations of the Sides of all Objects that are parallel to the Picture, will not tend to any Points upon the Picture, but will be parallel amongſt themſelves, and only proportionally diminiſhed as their Diſtance from the Eye is greater or leſs: But the Repreſentations of the Sides of all Objects that are not parallel to the Picture, will vaniſh into various Points upon the Picture, which, are therefore called, *the vaniſhing Points of ſuch Objects*.

Fig. 2. *Secondly*, The Projections A B c d and e f g h, of the Squares A B C D, E F G H, which lie flat upon the Ground, HM, will to the Spectator, EH, be the perſpective Appearance of thoſe Objects: And the Repreſentations of the Sides AB, cd, e h and f g, will be parallel to the Bottom of the Picture, but will be ſeverally diminiſhed in proportion to their Diſtance from the Picture. Thus AB is even with the Bottom of the Picture, and therefore its Repreſentation is the ſame as the original Line A B, and conſequently equal to it: But the Repreſentations cd, eh, and f g, will be perpetually diminiſhed in the Degree of Diſtance they are from the Picture; as is evident by inſpecting the Figure. For which Reaſon, the Repreſentations A d, Bc, e f, and g h, of Lines AD, BC, EF, and GH, which lie flat upon the Ground, and are parallel amongſt themſelves, but not parallel to the Picture, will continually approach towards each other, 'till they vaniſh into a Point C, exactly as high above the Bottom GL of the Picture, as the Eye is removed above the Ground HM. Thus, FC is equal to the Height of the Eye E H, and the Sides Ad, Bc, *&c.* will vaniſh into the Point C. From hence then, we ſee the Reaſon why the Repreſentations of Objects are more and more diminiſhed upon the Picture, the farther thoſe Objects are ſuppoſed to be from it.

Thirdly, We have obſerved that the Repreſentations Ad and Bc, of the oblique Sides AD and BC of the real Object, will vaniſh into the Point C upon the Picture; and therefore the Point C may very properly be called the vaniſhing Point of the Lines A D and BC,

BC.----Now, in order to determine the vaniſhing Point of any Line, we muſt always draw a Line from the Eye parallel to that Line: Thus EC is parallel to AD, or BC, and therefore, C, where EC cuts the Picture, is the vaniſhing Point of AB, or BC.

And in like Manner, EJ being drawn parallel to the Line BK, which is oblique with the Ground, will give J for its vaniſhing Point upon the Picture. For, from K draw the Ray KE to the Eye, which will cut the Picture in k; then is k the Repreſentation of K, and b is the Repreſentation of B; therefore, kb is the Repreſentation of KB: And, if kb was continued upwards upon the Picture, it would cut EJ in the Point J, and therefore J is its vaniſhing Point. Fig. 1.

Fourthly, If thro' the vaniſhing Point C, a Line HL be drawn parallel to the Bottom of the Picture, then that Line will be the vaniſhing Line of all Objects that lie flat upon the Ground, or are parallel to it. Now this Line, HL, hath always been called the Horizontal Line, and therefore, I ſhall call it by that Name in the following Work. Indeed, it is the moſt uſeful of all vaniſhing Lines; but nevertheleſs, too much Streſs hath been laid upon it by almoſt all Writers upon this Subject; who have paid no Sort of Regard to any other vaniſhing Lines. But had they conſider'd, that there are ſeveral Objects whoſe Repreſentations cannot be correctly determined upon the Picture, without a general Knowledge of all Kinds of vaniſhing Lines and vaniſhing Points, they would not have confined themſelves to the Horizontal Line only; and had they built their ſeveral Syſtems of Perſpective upon as ſolid Principles as Dr. *Taylor* or Mr. *Hamilton*, their Works would not have been crouded with ſuch a Confuſion of Lines, nor with ſuch a Number of uſeleſs Examples; but they would have been more *true*, *ſimple*, and of more *general Uſe*. But to return from this Digreſſion.

Fifthly, Since the Horizontal Line is level with the Eye and parallel to the Ground, and, for that Reaſon, the vaniſhing Line of all Objects which lie flat upon the Ground, or are parallel to it; ſo, for the very ſame Reaſon, the vaniſhing Line of any other Object will be parallel to that Object. Thus, ſuppoſe ABK to be a triangular Plane, which ſtands upon the Edge AK, perpendicular to the Ground: Then the vaniſhing Line of this perpendicular Plane will be perpendicular to the Horizontal Line; and if this Plane be perpendicular to the Picture alſo, then its vaniſhing Line will paſs through the Center of the Picture; thus JE is the vaniſhing Line of ABK. Fig. 1.

Thus

Thus much, I presume, may suffice to give the unlearned Reader a tolerable Idea of Perspective.---We will now give an Explanation of a few Terms made use of in the following Work, and then proceed to the Mechanical Part of Perspective.

DEFINITIONS.

Fig. 1. 1. THE *Point of Sight*, is that Point where the Spectator's Eye is placed to look at the Picture.---Thus E is the Point of Sight.

2. If from the Point of Sight E, a Line EC is drawn from the Eye perpendicular to the Picture, then the Point C, where that Line cuts the Picture, is called *the Center of the Picture.*

3. *The Distance of the Picture*, is the Length of the Line E C, which is drawn from the Eye perpendicular to the Picture.

4. If from the Point of Sight E, a Line EC be drawn perpendicular to any vanishing Line HL, or JF, then the Point C, where that Line cuts the vanishing Line, is called *the Center of that vanishing Line.*

5. *The Distance of a vanishing Line*, is the Length of the Line EC, which is drawn from the Eye perpendicular to the said Line: And if PO was a vanishing Line, then EJ will be the Distance of that Line.

6. *The Distance of a vanishing Point*, is the Length of a Line drawn from the Eye to that Point: Thus, EC is the Distance of the vanishing Point C, and EJ is the Distance of the vanishing Point J.

7. By *Original Object*, is meant the real Object whose Representation is sought: And by *Original Plane*, is meant that Plane upon which the real Object is situated: Thus, the Ground HM is the Original Plane of ABCD, &c. Fig. 1, 2.

AXIOMS.

Fig. 2. 1. The Representations of all Lines that are parallel to each other, but not parallel to the Picture, will have the same vanishing Point: Thus, the Representations Ad, Bc, of the parallel Lines AD, BC, have the same vanishing Point C.

2. The Representations of all Lines that are parallel to each other, and parallel to the Picture also, will not vanish into any Point upon the Picture, but will be parallel to each other: Thus, AB, cd, eh, and fg, are parallel to each other, because the Originals AB, CD, EH, and FG, of those Lines, are parallel to each other.

CHAP.

B.2.

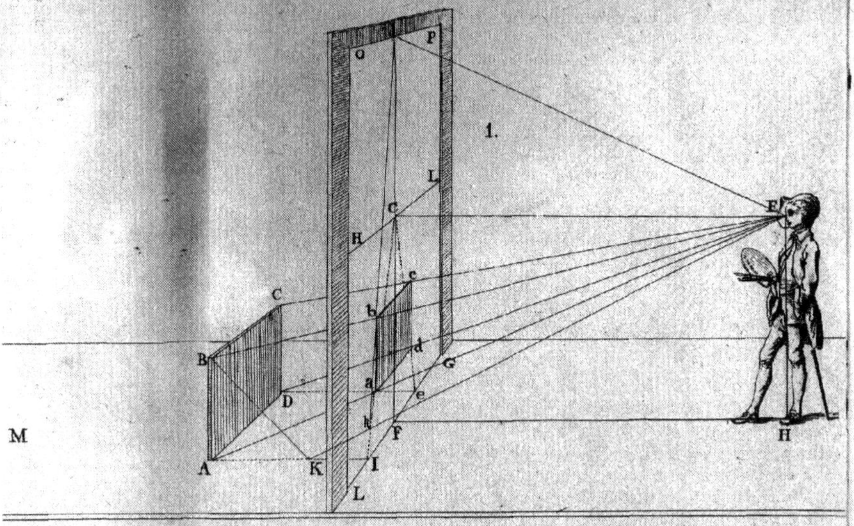

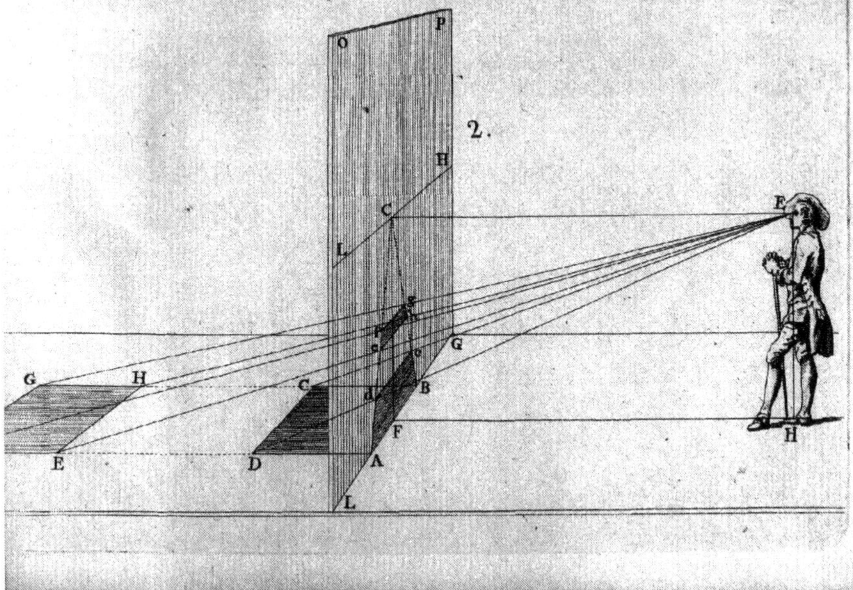

CHAP. II.

PRACTICAL PERSPECTIVE.

SECT. I.

To prepare the PICTURE.----1. *Of the* SIZE *of the* PICTURE. 2. *Of the* HEIGHT *of the* EYE. 3. *Of the* DISTANCE *of the* EYE.

1. THE Size of the Picture must be adapted to the Distance of the Eye, if it be an immoveable Picture, like the Side of a Room, Ceiling, or the like; which may very easily be done by means of Frames, or other Compartments: But, if the Picture be an Easel-Piece,* then the Bigness of it may be left to the Artist's Discretion. The Height of the Eye, must always govern the Height of the Horizontal Line from the Bottom of the Picture; and particular Care must be taken not to let it be so great as the Distance of the Eye, since it will be productive of very bad Consequences. And great Regard must be had to the choosing a proper Distance to be worked with; for otherwise, every Perspective Representation will have a very bad Effect.

2. *Of the* HEIGHT *of the* EYE.

Suppose GLTP to be a Canvas, representing the Size of the Fig. 5.
Picture.----Divide the Bottom of it, GL, into two equal Parts in F, and draw FI perpendicular to the Bottom GL; then from F set off FC, equal to the Height of the Eye from the Ground, and draw HL, through the Point C, parallel to the Bottom GL: And then will HL be the Horizontal Line, and C the Center of the Picture. Now, though the Height of the Eye in Easel-Pictures is left intirely to the Discretion of the Artist; yet, in general, low Horizons have a much better Effect than high ones; for which Reason, the Height of the Horizontal Line should never exceed one half of the Height of the Picture; and, I believe, a little Experience will teach any one, that if it is made equal only to one third Part of the Height of the Picture, it will be the most proper Height of any: I mean only in regard to Easel-Pieces; for if the

* The Instrument upon which a Picture is placed to be painted, is called an *Easel*; and therefore, every Picture which is moveable, is called an *Easel-Piece*.

Picture be a fixed one, then the Height of the Horizontal Line must be exactly level with the Spectator's Eye.

3. Of the DISTANCE of the EYE.

The choosing a proper Distance for the Eye is such an essential Requisite, that without a nice Observance thereof, every Perspective Representation will appear a shocking Deformity; therefore, we shall be the more particular in settling a proper Distance for the Eye; the Necessity of which will appear by the following Example.

In the 4th Figure I suppose ABED a real Square upon the Ground, and CE one Distance of the Eye, and CI another. Now, by putting this Square into Perspective, agreeable to those different Distances, we shall have abED for the Representation of the Square as seen at the Distance CE, and EDcd for the Representation of the Square as seen at the Distance CI; and by inspecting the Figure, we may perceive, that the Representation EDcd, which is seen by the Eye at the Distance CI, does not appear like a Square, but looks much longer than 'tis wide, and therefore, it is a false Representation; but the Representation abED, which is seen by the Eye at the Distance CE, has a more agreeable Appearance, and looks like a Square seen in Perspective, and therefore is a more just Representation. Now, that this Difference between the two Representations of the same Object is wholly owing to the different Distances of the Eye, is apparent from the Figure; and therefore, this one Instance, out of many, may suffice to shew the Necessity of choosing a proper Distance to be worked with; In order to do which, the following Method seems the most easy, and the most useful, of any I can think of.

Fig. 3. Having drawn the horizontal Line HL, and fixed the Center C, of the Picture; draw a Line (as CP) from the Center C, to one of the farthest Corners (as P) of the Picture; draw also the Perpendicular CD, and continue it at pleasure; then from C, set off the Length CP, upon CE, and call CE the least Distance: Again, from C, set off CD, upon the Line CD, equal to the longest Dimensions of the Picture, and call CD the greatest Distance. That is, never let the Distance you work with be greater than CD, nor less than CP; because, as was observed before, if the Distance be less than CE, the Representations will be too deep; and if it be more than CD, the Representations will not be deep enough; and, I think, if a Medium between those two Distances be taken as a general

general Rule, it will produce the most agreeable Shape of any Distance whatsoever. Thus, the Representation EDmn, (Fig. 4.) is determined by such a Distance.

In this Place it may not be improper to take Notice, that the Distance of the Picture is sometimes placed upon a Line as CD, perpendicular to the horizontal Line, and sometimes upon the horizontal Line itself; as the Nature of the Work may require. And I will also observe, that the Distance generally made use of in this Work, is the least Distance, for the Conveniency of having as many Figures upon each Plate as was possible. And the Reader is desired to remember, that the Letters CE will always stand for the Distance of the Eye, E for the Eye, or Point of Sight, C for the Center of the Picture, HL for the horizontal Line, and GL for the Ground Line, or Bottom of the Picture. For, to avoid Prolixity, I shall not mention either of those Terms but upon some particular Occasion. And that he may fix them the easier in his Memory, I have made every Letter as significant as possible: Thus E is the Eye, C the Center, HL the horizontal Line, &c. And I shall, moreover, always suppose a Picture, as GLTP, (which may be considered as a large Picture in Miniature) to be laid flat, and that we are actually at work upon it, in determining the Representation of the following Figures. Fig. 3.

SECT. II.

Of OBJECTS *which lie flat upon the* GROUND, *or that are in Planes perpendicular to the Picture.*

I. *To find the Representation of a Point upon the Picture, after having prepared the Picture as above directed.*

METHOD 1. *By one vanishing Point only.*

LET A be the Point upon the Ground.----From A draw any Line at Pleasure, as A 1, cutting the Bottom of the Picture in 1; and from the Eye E, draw EL parallel to A 1, cutting the horizontal Line in L; then is L the vanishing Point of A 1; therefore, draw the Line L 1, then from the Point A, draw a Line to E, cutting L 1, in a; and then is a, the Representation of the original Point A. Fig. 5.

METHOD 2. *By two vanishing Points.*

Draw A 1, A 2, at pleasure, cutting the Bottom of the Picture in 1 and 2; and from the Eye E, draw EL parallel to A 1, and

EH parallel to A 2; then draw L 1 and H 2, which will cut each other in a, and so give a, for the Representation of A.

Fig. 6. II. *To find the Representation of a Line* AB, *which is perpendicular to the Bottom of the Picture.*

METHOD 1. *By one vanishing Point.*

Let AB be the real Line upon the Ground.----Now since AB is perpendicular to the Bottom of the Picture, therefore EC is parallel to it; and therefore C, where EC cuts the horizontal Line, is the vanishing Point of AB.---Draw AC, and from B draw BE, cutting AC in b; and then is Ab the Representation of AB.

METHOD 2. *By two vanishing Points.*

From B draw B 1 at pleasure, cutting the Bottom of the Picture in 1; and from the Eye E, draw EH parallel to B 1, cutting the horizontal Line in H; then is H the vanishing Point of B1; therefore draw 1 H, cutting AC in b; which will determine the Representation proposed.

In like manner, the Representation Fd, of FD, which lies directly against the Middle of the Picture, is to be determined. For C is the vanishing Point of FD, and H is the vanishing Point of D2.

From hence then we may conceive, that if there were ever so many Lines parallel to AB, they would all vanish into the Center of the Picture; and that the Representation Fd, of any Line that lies directly against the Middle of the Picture, will be perpendicular to the Bottom of the Picture; that is, will be Part of the Perpendicular FC, which is drawn from F to the Center C; but in proportion as any other perpendicular Lines (as AB) are more and more removed from the Middle F, the Representations Ab of such Lines will be more and more oblique with the Bottom of the Picture.

III. *Of a Line parallel to the Bottom of the Picture.*

METHOD 1. *By one vanishing Point.*

Fig. 7. Let AB be the Original Line.---Draw A 1, B 3, perpendicular to the Bottom of the Picture; then is C their vanishing Point; therefore draw 1C, 3C; and from the Extremities of the Line AB draw Lines (as AE) to the Eye, cutting 1C, 3C, in a and b; then draw a b, which will be the Representation of AB.---Or it may be done by finding one End only of the Representation (as a) and then drawing a b parallel to the horizontal Line, 'till it cuts 3C.

METHOD.

METHOD 2. *By two vanishing Points.*

Draw A 2, B 4, at pleasure, (but parallel to each other) cutting the Bottom of the Picture, as before: Then draw EH parallel to A 2; and then is H the vanishing Point of A 2 and B 4; therefore draw 2 H, 4 H cutting 1 C and 3 C in a and b; finally, draw, the Line a b, which is the Representation proposed.---Or, finding one Point only (as a) and then drawing a b parallel to the horizontal Line, as before, will be sufficient.

IV. *Of a Line* AB *oblique with the Bottom of the Picture.* Fig. 8.

METHOD 1. *By one vanishing Point.*

Continue AB to the Bottom of the Picture, and draw EH parallel thereto; and from 3 draw 3 H; then from the Extremities A and B draw Lines to E, which will cut 3 H in a and b; and then is a b the Representation of AB.

METHOD 2. *By two vanishing Points.*

From the Extremities AB draw A 1, B 2, parallel to each other; and from E draw EL, parallel to A 1, B 2; then draw 1 L, 2 L, cutting 3 H in a and b; and then is a b the Representation of AB.

Here let us observe, that since Lines must be either perpendicular to the Picture, parallel to the Picture, or oblique with the Picture, the three last Examples may serve as universal Rules for the Situation of all Objects that are supposed to lie upon the Ground; which is fully explained in the following Figure.

V. *Of an equilateral Triangle,* one of whose Sides is parallel to the Picture.*

METHOD 1. *By having the Original Figure* ABD *drawn out upon the Ground.* Fig. 9.

Continue BA and BD to the Bottom of the Picture, and draw EL parallel to AB, and EH parallel to BD; then draw 1 L and 4 H, cutting each other in b; and then is b the Representation of the Angle B. Again, from D draw D 3 parallel to B 1; then is L its vanishing Point; therefore draw 3 L, cutting 4 H in the Point d; and then is d the Representation of the Angle D: And since AD is parallel to the Bottom of the Picture, therefore, if from the Point d, the Line a d be drawn parallel to the Bottom of the Picture, it will compleat the Representation proposed.---Or, it may be

* An Equilateral Triangle is that whose Sides and Angles are all equal.

be done by drawing A2 perpendicular to GL, and then drawing 2C, cutting 1L in the Point a.

METHOD 2. *By making an Angle at the Eye* E, *equal to the given Angle* ABD.

Let ab be one Side of the Representation given upon the Picture.---Continue ab to the horizontal Line; then is L its vanishing Point: From L draw LE to the Eye; and any where a-cross the Line CE, draw ef parallel to the horizontal Line, and then make ef equal to fE: Again, draw EH through the Point e, and then is H the vanishing Point of the Side bd; therefore, thro' b draw bd, and from a, draw ad parallel to the horizontal Line; which will compleat the Representation.---Or it may be done thus: Having continued ab to its vanishing Point L, and having drawn LE, make an Angle at the Eye E equal to 60 Degrees*, and draw EH, which will cut the horizontal Line in the vanishing Point of the other Side bd.

METHOD 3. *Without having any Original Figure drawn out, but by having one Side given only.*

Let ab be the Side given.---Continue ab to its vanishing Point L, and draw LE; then at L, with the Distance LE, describe the Arc EH, cutting the horizontal Line in H; then is H the vanishing Point of the other Side bd; and by drawing ad parallel to the horizontal Line, the Representation will be compleated.

Here let the Reader observe again, that if the Distance LE, of any vanishing Point L, be transferred unto the horizontal Line, as LH, it will cut off one Line equal to another Line given. Thus, let ba be a given Line.---From a, draw ad parallel to the horizontal Line; and from H (the Distance of L from the Eye E) draw Hd through the Point b, cutting ad in d; then is ad equal to ab; for they are both the Representations of two Sides AB, AD, of a Triangle ABC, whose Sides are all equal.---In like Manner, if ad was a Line given, and L the vanishing Point of a Line ab, which is required to be cut off equal to ad: Then make LH equal to LE; and from d, draw dH, cutting aL in b; and then is ab equal to ad.†

* This Angle may be set off with an Instrument called a Protractor, which is a Semi-Circle divided into 180 equal Parts, called Degrees.

† The Learner cannot make this Figure too familiar too him, as 'tis of prodigious Use.

VI. *Of*

VI. *Of an Equilateral Triangle* ABC, *whose Sides are all oblique with the Picture.* Fig. 10.

METHOD 1. *By having the Original Figure drawn out upon the Ground.*

Continue the Sides of the Triangle to the Bottom of the Picture, as 1, 2, 3, and draw EI parallel to AC, EF parallel to AB, and EK parallel to BC, which will severally cut the horizontal Line in the vanishing Points of AB, AC, and BC; therefore, from those vanishing Points draw Lines to 1, 2, 3, and their mutual Intersections a, b, c, with each other, will give the Representation a b c of the original Triangle ABC.

METHOD 2. *By making Triangles at the Eye, as before.*

Let a b be one Side of the Representation given.----Continue it to its vanishing Point F, and draw FE; then at E, upon the Line EF, make the equilateral Triangles MEN, MEO; continue EN and EO 'till they cut the horizontal Line, which will give the vanishing Points required; therefore from a, draw aI, and thro' b draw K c, which will compleat the Representation a b c.

METHOD 3. *By giving one Corner* a, *of the Triangle, and from thence finding the whole Representation* a b c.

From a, draw a F, and call F one vanishing Point; then from F draw FE, and at E make an Angle of 60 Degrees, and draw EI; then draw Ia, and through a, draw f e, parallel to the horizontal Line, at pleasure, and make a f, a e, each equal to one Side of the supposed Representation; then from the vanishing Point I, set off the Distance IE to D; and from e, draw eD cutting aI in c; then is a c equal to a e. Again, from F set off the Distance FE, (as FP) and draw f P, cutting aF in b; then is a b equal to a f; finally, draw b c, which will compleat the Representation a bc.

VII. *Of a Geometrical Square* ABCD, *having one Side* AB *parallel to the Picture.* Fig. 11.

METHOD 1. *By a Plan; that is, by having the Original Square drawn out upon the Ground.*

Draw AC, BC, to the vanishing Point C, of the perpendicular Sides AD, BC; and from the Eye E, draw EH and EL parallel to the Diagonals BD and AC; then from A and B draw Lines to L and H, cutting AC in d, and BC in c; then draw d c, which compleats the Representation.----Having found the Representation of of one Square, any other Square, as i k, may be found also. For let i k be one Side of the Representation given.----From i and k draw i C and k C; then from i draw i L, and from k draw k H; which will give the Depth of the Square, as in the Figure.----Or, one Diagonal only will be sufficient. Thus, A L cuts B C in c; therefore draw c d parallel to the horizontal Line.

From hence we may observe, that when original Squares are thus situated, the vanishing Points H and L of their Diagonals, are exactly as far from the Center of the Picture, as the Eye is from the Center of the Picture. Thus HC and LC are each equal to the Distance CE; and therefore, by setting off CH, or CL, equal to CE, the Lines EH and EL may be omitted.

METHOD 2. *By having only the Depth* F I *of the Square* F I L *given.*

Set off IL and I 1, equal to the Depth F I.------From L and L draw Lines to C, and make C L equal to C E; then draw 1 L, cutting 1 C in f; then is I f cut off equal to I 1; therefore draw f e parallel to the horizontal Line, and the Representation will be compleated.

METHOD 3. *By having only one Side, as* G K, *given.*

From G and K, draw Lines to C; continue G K, and make K 2 equal to G K; then make C H equal to C E, and draw H 2, cutting K C in b; finally from b, draw a b parallel to the horizontal Line, and the Thing proposed is done. In like manner any other Square, m n o, may be found.

VIII. *Of a Geometrical Square, when its Sides are oblique with the Picture.*

Fig. 12. METHOD 1. *By a Plan* ABCD.

Parallel to the Sides AB, CD, AD, BC, draw E L and E H; then are L and H the vanishing Points of those Sides; for continue the Sides of the Square 'till they cut the Bottom of the Picture in 1, 2, 3, 4; then from 1 and 2, draw Lines to H, and from 3 and 4, draw Lines to L, and their mutual Intersections a, b, c, d, will give the Representation proposed.-----Or the original Square may be made at the Eye, as in the Figure.

METHOD

METHOD 2. *By having only one Side, as* G i, *given upon the Picture.*

Continue G i till it cuts the horizontal Line in H, and from H draw HE; then at E, made a right Angle * with the Line HE, and draw EL; then is H the vaniſhing Point of the Sides G i, l k, and L is the vaniſhing Point of the Sides G l and i k; therefore, from G and i draw GL and i L, then from G draw GC, cutting L i in k; finally, from H draw a Line through k, cutting GL in l, and then is G i k l the Repreſentation propoſed.

METHOD 3. *By having only the Length of the Diagonal* e L *given upon the Bottom of the Picture, as* LP.

From L draw LC; then from P draw PH, cutting LC in e; then is L e the Repreſentation of the Line LP: Again, from L draw LL, cutting PH in f, and from L draw LH, then thro' e draw L h, cutting LH in h; and then ſhall we have the Repreſentation L f e h.

IX. *To find the Repreſentation of a Square,* a b c d, *of any determinate Width; ſuppoſe three Feet.* Fig. 13.

Let a be one Corner given, and K the vaniſhing Point of the Side a d.---Make KD equal to KE, and from D draw a Line thro' a, cutting the Bottom of the Picture in f; then from f, on the Side of a d, ſet off three Feet upon the Bottom of the Picture, and from e draw eD, cutting aK in d; then is a d equal to three Feet: Again, from K draw KE, and make a right Angle at E, then draw EL; and then is L the vaniſhing Point of the Side a b; therefore draw aL, and biſect † the Angle KEL, and draw EB cutting the horizontal Line in B; then is B the vaniſhing Point of the Diagonal of the Square; by which means the whole Figure may be compleated. For draw aB and dL, cutting it in c, then draw K b through the Point c; and then is a b c d the Square propoſed.

* A right Angle is one Corner of a Square, or 90 Degrees.

† Biſect, is to divide any thing into two equal Parts: Thus, on E deſcribe any Arc, OQP, then divide that Arc, in Q, into two equal Parts, and draw EB, and then is the Angle KEL biſected.

X. *Of a regular Hexagon* *, *having one of its Sides parallel to the Picture.*

Fig. 14. METHOD I. *By a Plan* ABCDEF.

Continue the several oblique Sides 'till they cut the Bottom of the Picture, and draw EH and EL parallel thereto; then will L be the vanishing Point of AB and DE, and H will be the vanishing Point of BC and EF: Therefore, through the Corners A, D, and F, C, drawn D 2, C 5, which being parallel to the Sides AB, EF, will have H and L for their vanishing Points; and therefore, from 1 draw 1 H, and from 3 draw 3 L, cutting each other in b; then is b the Representation of the Corner B. Again, from 2 draw 2 H, cutting 3 L in a; then is a the Representation of the Corner A, and a b is the Representation of the Side A b; therefore, draw 4 H and 5 L, and then is f the Representation of F; then draw a f, which will be the Representation of A F; finally, draw 6 L, which will cut 4 H in e, and give the Representation of E F; and so on.---Here the Learner may take Notice, that this whole Representation is found in the same Manner as the single Point A, Fig. 5; only the Operation in this Figure is repeated six times, because here are six Points, which represent six Corners, instead of one.

METHOD 2. *By having one Side* a b, *in the Representation given.*

Through the Corner a, draw a Line f h, parallel to the horizontal Line, and continue a b to its vanishing Point L; and from L draw L E, and make L H equal to L E; then from H draw a Line through b, cutting a h in h; then is a h equal to a b; therefore make a f equal to a h; and then is a f the Representation of the parallel Side A F: From f draw f L, and from a, draw a C, cutting f L in c; then is c another Corner; therefore draw b c, which represents another Side; then from c draw c d, parallel to the horizontal Line, and draw f C cutting it in d; then is d another Corner, and c d another Side; finally, through d draw L e, and from f draw f H, which compleats the Representation.

Fig. 15. In like Manner the Representation of an Octagon (or eight-sided Figure) ABCDEFGH, is to be determined.----I have put every

* A Hexagon is a six-sided Figure; and when its Sides are all equal, it is called a regular Hexagon.

Line

Line and Point used in the Operation, which, it is presumed, is now sufficient, without any further Explanation.

XI. *To find the Representation of the Circle* ABC. Fig. 16.

METHOD 1. *By finding the Representation of several Points, as* A, B, C, *&c.*

From these Points draw any Lines at pleasure, but parallel to each other, as C 1, C 2, B 3, B 4, *&c.* cutting the Bottom of the Picture; then find their vanishing Points, as H, L, and from each original Section at the Bottom of the Picture, draw Lines to their respective vanishing Points, and their several Intersections will give the Representations of the original Points; from whence the Representation of the Circle may be drawn by hand: Thus a, b, c, are the Representations of A, B, C, *&c.* This also is a Repetition of Fig. 5.

METHOD 2. *Or the Representation of a Circle may be found by means of a Geometrical Square; which is the most useful Method of any.*

Thus, let O be a Circle, and ABCD a Square described about it, as in the Figure.---Find the Representation of that Square; which will be a sufficient Guide for drawing the Representation of the Circle, to any one who has but the least Notion of Drawing. But if the Circle is very large, or if this Method should not be thought correct enough, then divide the Circle into any Number of Parts, and draw Lines through those Divisions parallel to the several Sides of the Square, as in the Figure; then by finding the Representation of those Lines, the Appearance of the Circle may be determined with great Exactness. Fig. 17.

METHOD 3. *To find the Representation of a Circle by having only the Diameter given upon the Picture.*

Let ef be the Diameter given.----Divide ef into two equal Parts; then is n the Center of that Circle. From C, and through the Points e and f, draw Cg and Ch, at pleasure, and make CL equal to the Distance CE; then through n draw Lg, cutting gC and hC in g and k; finally, from the Points g and k draw two Lines, gh, ki, parallel to the horizontal Line; and then is ghik the Representation of a Square equal to the Diameter of the proposed Circle; and consequently, will be a sufficient Guide for drawing its Representation.

From hence then it is evident, that the Representations of Circles are as easily to be determined upon the Picture, as any other Representations whatsoever; and, that after having fixed upon the Diameter of any Circle, and the Place that Circle is to possess upon the Picture, then such a Representation may be determined with the greatest Exactness, without the tedious Method of Plans, and that Infinity of occult Lines, which have hitherto been made use of.

What hath been said in regard to finding the Representations of Circles without a Plan, or having the original Object drawn upon the Ground, is equally applicable to any of the preceding Figures, as I have shewn in the Course of this Work; and therefore, though I have put the Plans at the Bottom of each Figure, it was for no other Reason than to explain the Truth of the Operation; and therefore the Reader will do well to exercise himself with several Examples of the like Nature, before he proceeds to the next Section.

And here let us take Notice, that the Figures I have been putting into Perspective, though few in Number, and the most simple in Nature, yet they are such as comprehend Forms in general.* I say, the Forms or Shapes of Objects in general are compounded of such Figures as I have been reducing into Perspective; that is, they must be either Square, Triangular, or Circular, or else compounded of some, or all of these put together. Thus, a Cube is composed of six Squares joined together at right Angles; a Pyramid, of several Triangles meeting in a Point; and a Column, of a Number of round Superficies laid upon each other exactly even, and perpendicular to the Ground. These, and the like, may therefore be called simple Objects; but when they are joined together, so as to make but one Object, then that Object may be called a Compound one: Thus a Building may be called a Compound Object; the Body of which is either a Cube or Parallelopiped; the Roof and Pediments several Triangles, and the Arches, Domes, Columns, *&c.* are nothing else but Circles, or Parts of Circles, put together. And therefore, it follows from hence, that whoever is able to put a Square, a Triangle, or a Circle, rightly into Perspective, has got all the Materials that are necessary for drawing the Representation

* I mean such Forms only as are proper Subjects for Perspective; for as to Objects which are composed of an infinite Variety of Curve-Lines, I will not pretend to give any Rules for determining their Appearances according to the strict Rules of this Art; and was I able to do it, I should think it unnecessary; since a good Eye, in such Cases, will direct the Hand with more Ease, if not with as much Certainty, as any Rules whatsoever; especially if the Person has a general Notion of Perspective.

of

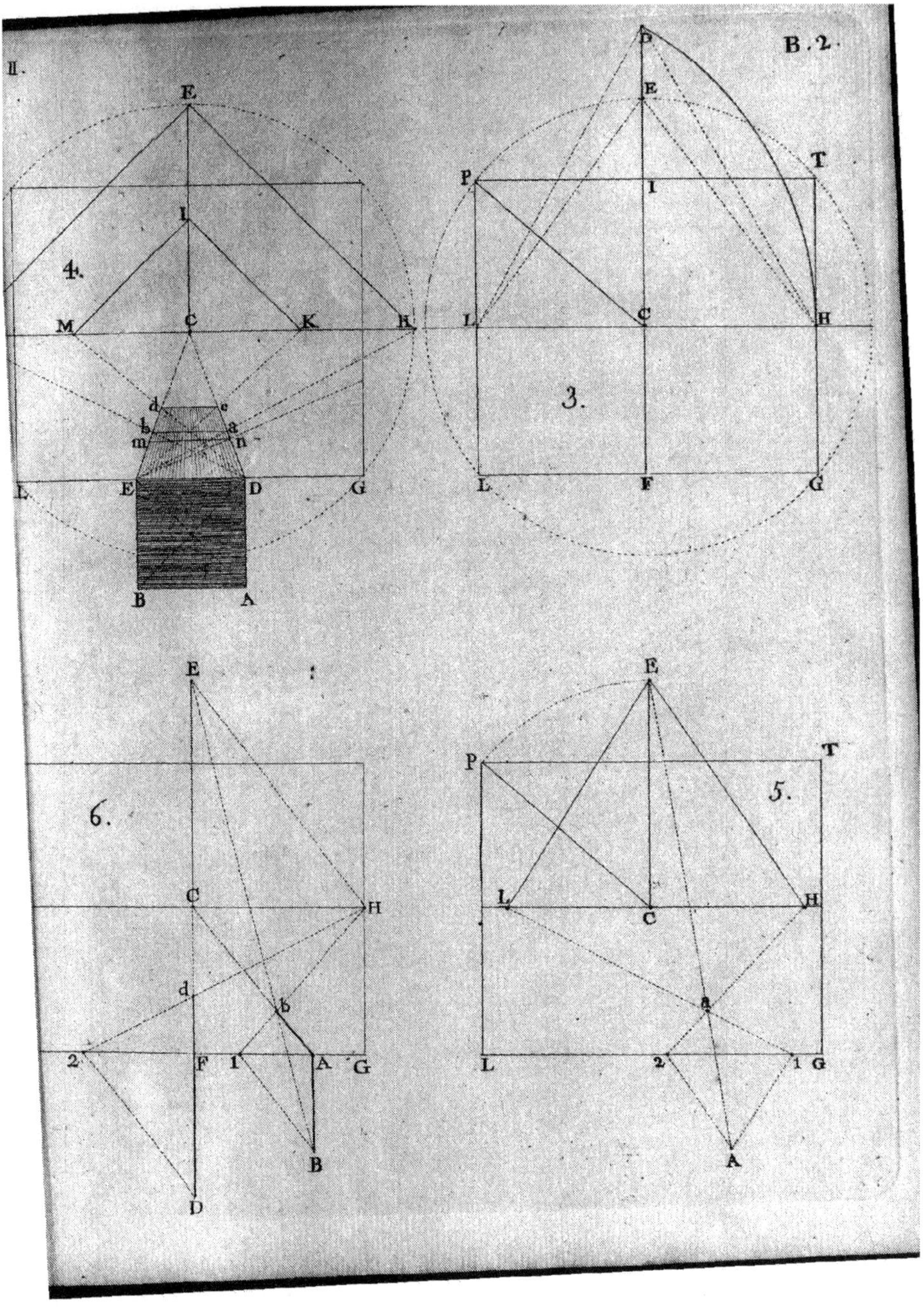
II.
B. 2.
4.
3.
6.
5.

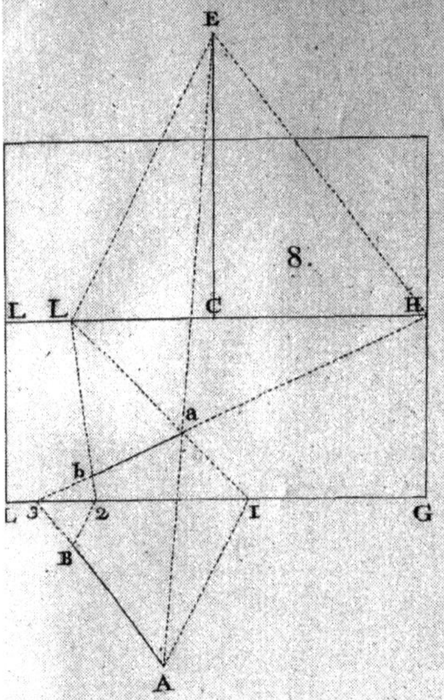
E
8.
L L C H
a
b
L 3 2 I G
B
A

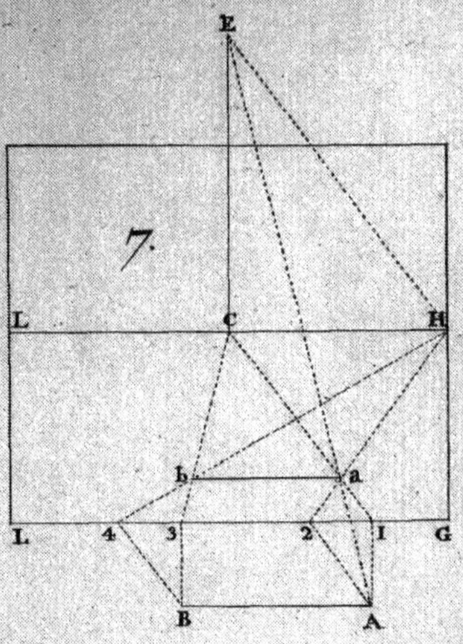
E
7.
L C H
b a
L 4 3 2 I G
B A

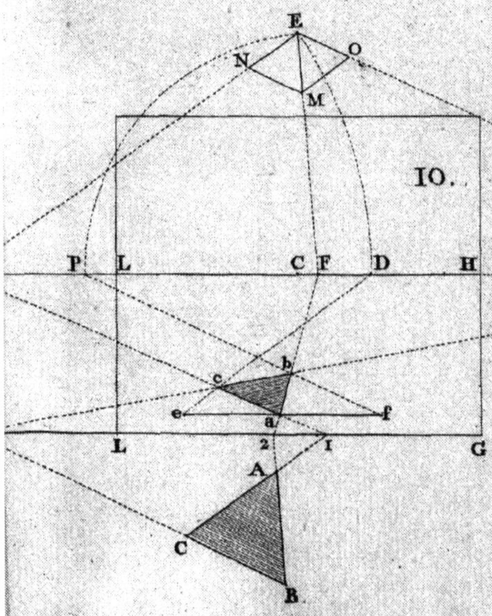
E
N O
M
IO.
P L C F D H
c b
e a f
L 2 I G
A
C
B

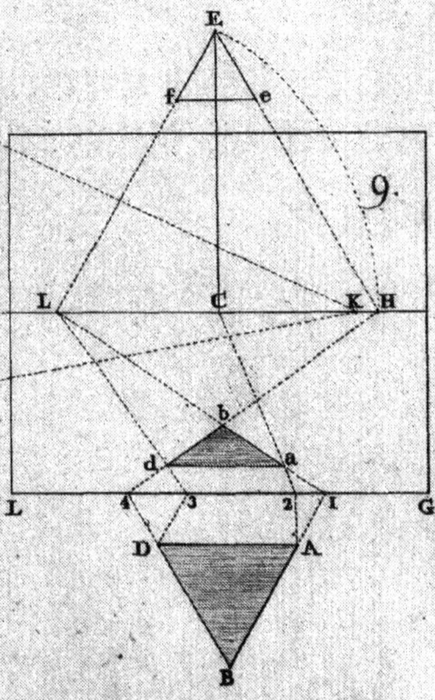
E
f e
9.
L C K H
b
d a
L 4 3 2 I G
D A
B

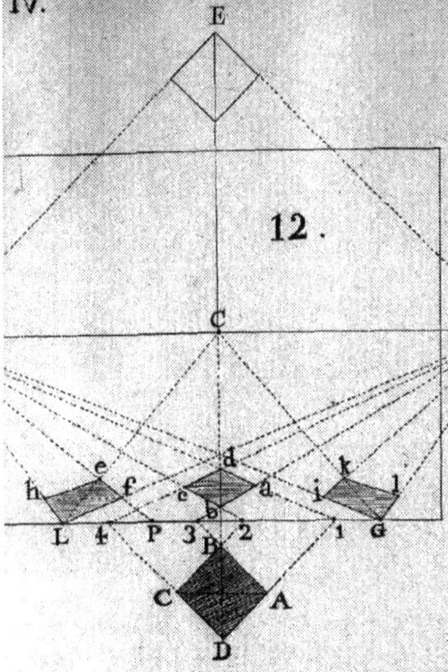
12.
E
C
L
h e f
e d a
b
i k l
L 4 P 3 B 2 1 G
C A
D

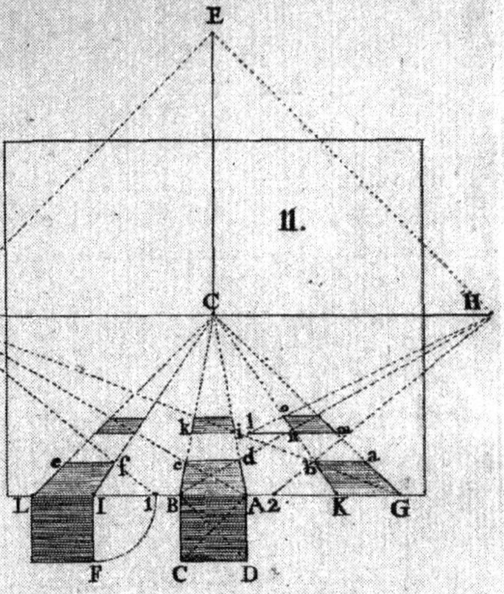
11.
E
C
H
k i l
o n m
e f c d
b a
L I 1 B A 2 K G
F C D

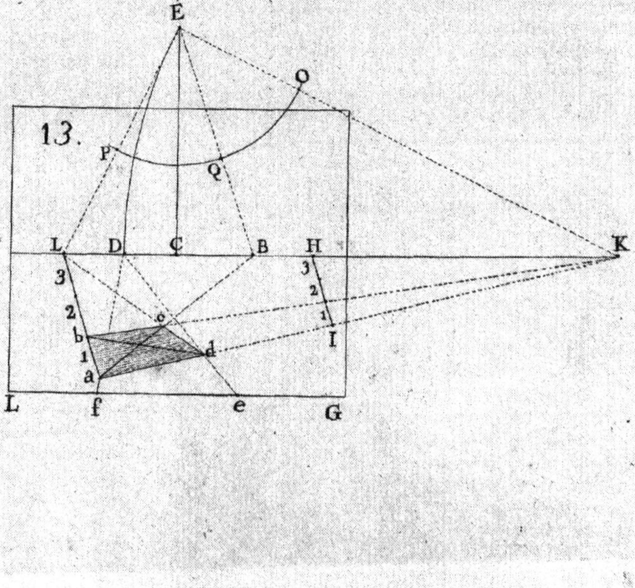
13.
E
O
P
Q
L D C B H K
3 2 b 1 a
c d
3 2 1 I
L f e G

B. 2.

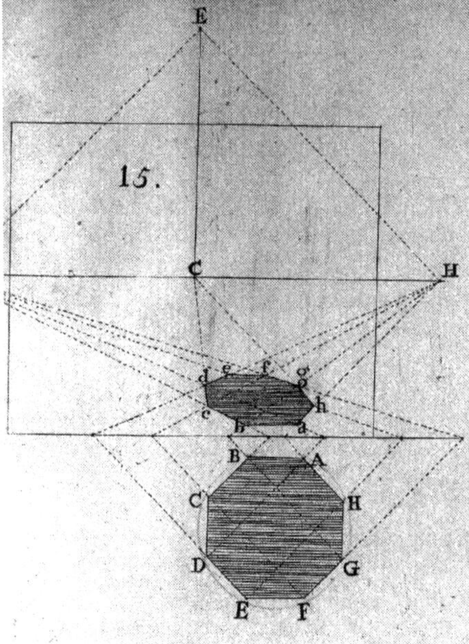
15.
E
C
H
d e f g
c h
b a
B A
C H
D G
E F

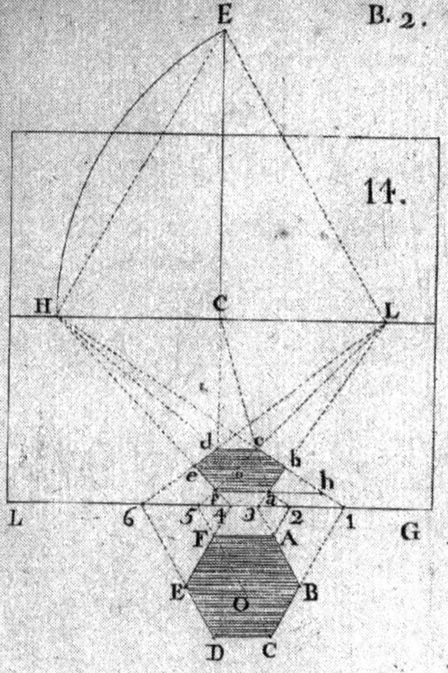
14.
E
H C L
d c b
e h
f a
L 6 5 4 3 2 1 G
F A
E O B
D C

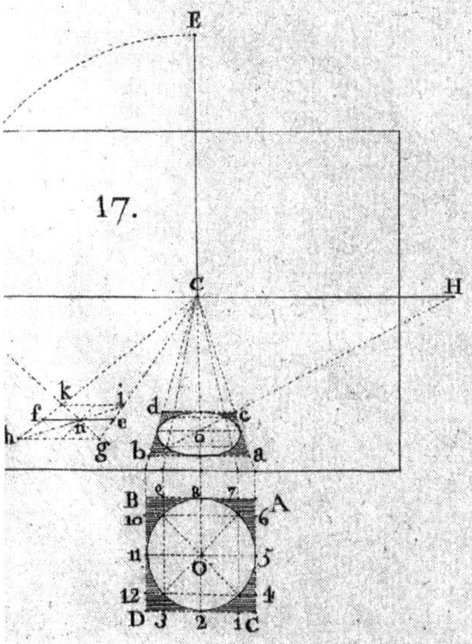
17.
E
C H
k i
f e
h n g
d c
b a
B e 8 7 A
10 6
11 O 5
12 4
D 3 2 1 C

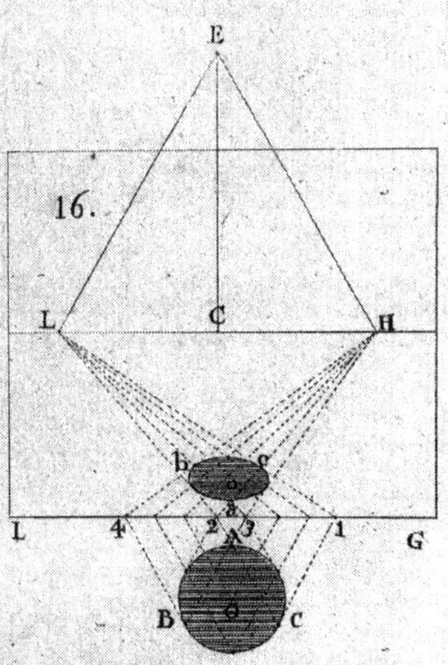
16.
E
L C H
b c
L 4 2 3 1 G
A
B O C

of any Object upon the Picture. I shall therefore follow this simple Method throughout this Work, and will now proceed to shew, how to determine the Representation of Objects when they stand perpendicular to the Ground; which is the Subject of the next Section.

SECT. III.

Of OBJECTS *that are perpendicular to the* GROUND.

I. *To find the Representation of Planes when their Bases are perpendicular to the Bottom of the Picture, like* AB, *Fig.* 6. Fig. 18.

CASE 1. *When one Corner* A, *of the Plane* ABCD, *is at the Bottom of the Picture :----And let it be required to draw the Representation of a Plane six Feet high and four Feet wide.*

FRom A, upon the Bottom of the Picture, make a Scale of Feet*, at pleasure, as in the Figure; and from the Point A draw AD, perpendicular to the Bottom of the Picture, and continue it at pleasure; then upon the Line AD set six Feet from A, and draw DC to the Center C, and from A draw AC; then make CH equal to CE, and draw H 4 cutting AC in B; and then is AB equal to four Feet; therefore, from B draw BC, parallel to AD; and so will ABCD represent a Plane four Feet wide and six Feet high.

CASE 2. *Let it be required to draw the Representation of a Plane* GHIK, *three Feet Square; and let the nearest Corner* G, *be one Foot from the Bottom of the Picture.*

Draw any Line at pleasure, as C 9, and make CL equal to CE; then set off one Foot from 9 to 8, and draw L 8 cutting C 9 in G; then is G one Foot from the Bottom. Again, take three Feet more, as 8 5, and draw 5 L cutting GC in K; then is GK equal to three Feet; therefore, draw GH and IK perpendicular to the Bottom of the Picture, and continue them at pleasure; and from G draw GF, parallel to the Bottom of the Picture; then is GF equal to three Feet; finally, make GH equal to GF, and draw HC; which will compleat the Representation proposed.--Or it may be done thus: From 9, draw 9 N perpendicular to the Bottom of

* What I here mean by a Scale of Feet, is not to make a Scale of so many Feet long, but only to divide the Bottom of the Picture into such a Number of equal Parts, which are to be considered as so many Feet: A Thing very common amongst Workmen.

the

the Picture, and make it equal to three Feet; then draw 9C and NC, and from 8 draw 8L, which will give the Point, or Corner, G; then draw 5L, which will give three Feet for GK; therefore, by drawing GH and IK parallel to 9N, the Thing proposed is done.---In like Manner, suppose a Plane abcd, four Feet square, was removed five Feet into the Picture, and suppose the lower Edge, or Plan, to be somewhere in the Line AC.---From A, where it cuts the Bottom of the Picture, set off five Feet for its Distance, (as A 5) and four Feet for its Width (as 5 9;) then draw H 5 and H 9, cutting AC in a and b; then is ab the Representation of its Depth; therefore, draw AD, ad, bc, perpendicular to the Bottom of the Picture, and make AO equal to four Feet; and then draw OC, cutting ad and cb, which will compleat the proposed Representation.

II. *To find the Representations of Planes that are parallel to the Picture.*

Fig. 19. CASE 1. *For a Plane* ABDE, *four Feet square, which, we suppose, is removed two Feet from the Bottom of the Picture.*

Divide the Bottom of the Picture into any Number of Parts, which call so many Feet; then from G and 4, draw GC and 4C, and make CL equal to CE, and draw 6L cutting 4C in E; then is 4E equal to 4 6, that is, equal to two Feet; therefore, draw EA parallel to the Bottom of the Picture, which will cut GC in A, and give the Length of one Side, upon which make the Square ABDE, which will be the Representation proposed.

CASE 2. *For a Plane six Feet high and three Feet wide, which is to be five Feet from the Bottom of the Picture.*

Any where, at pleasure, draw C4, and set off three Feet, (as 4 7) then draw 7C, and from 4 set off five Feet, (as 4 9) and draw 9L, which will cut 4C in e; then will e4 be equal to 4 9, that is, to five Feet. Again, from e, draw ef parallel to the horizontal Line, which will give ef equal to three Feet; that is, equal to 4 7; therefore, continue ef at pleasure, and call a, one Corner of the intended Plane; make ab equal to ef, and draw ad, bc, perpendicular thereto; then make ad equal to twice ab, and draw dc parallel to the horizontal Line, and then will the Representation be compleated.

III. *To find the Representation of Planes, when their Plans or Bases are oblique with the Bottom of the Picture, like* AB, Fig. 8.

Let ABDF be the Representation sought, which let be six Feet high, four Feet and a Half wide, and one Foot and a Half from the Bottom of the Picture; and let L be its vanishing Point, and LG the Line in which the Plane is to stand.---Draw GI perpendicular to the Bottom of the Picture, and set six Feet upon it (as in the Figure) and draw IL; then from G set off Ga equal to one Foot and a Half, and draw aH cutting GL in A; then is GA equal to Ga; that is, equal to one Foot and a Half. Again, from a, set off four Feet and a Half, (as a6) and draw 6H cutting GL in B; then is AB equal to a6, that is, equal to four Feet and a Half; therefore by drawing AF and BD perpendicular to the Bottom of the Picture, we shall have the Representation of a Plane, six Feet high, and four Feet and a Half wide. Fig. 20.

If the vanishing Point L is out of the Picture, the Figure may be draw thus.---Let BA be the Representation of one Side given, and AD its Height.---Continue AB at pleasure, and any where upon it draw ab perpendicular to the Bottom of the Picture; then make cb to ca, as FD is to FA, and draw Db; which will give the Length of BC; for if DC be continued it will vanish into L*. Fig. 21.

From hence then it is evident, that the Representation of any perpendicular Plane may be immediately determined upon the Picture, without having Recourse to the tedious Methods of Plans, Elevations, &c. and but very few Lines are required, even when the Representation is to be of any given Dimension, or however it is to be situated upon the Picture: But, if the Representation is not to be of any particular Dimension, being left to the Discretion of the Artist, then nothing can be more simple than the Operation. For let AB be one Side given, and AD its Height; then from A and B draw AD, BC, perpendicular to the Bottom of the Picture; and from C, draw CD; which will compleat the Figure. Fig. 18.

Here let us observe again, that the vanishing Point C of the Line AB, is the vanishing Point of every Line DC, NM, &c. that is parallel to AB; agreeable to the second Axiom.

Having shewn how to find the Representation of Square Planes perpendicular to the Ground; let us now proceed to join them together, which begins the Perspective of solid Figures.

* Suppose FD is equal to FA, then cb must be made equal to ca.

IV. *To*

IV. *To find the Representation of Triangular Pieces of Wood, &c. when they are either above or below the Horizontal Line.*

Fig. 22. CASE 1. *When they are below the Horizontal Line, and have one Side,* a b e d, *parallel to the Picture.*

Find the vanishing Points H and L, of the oblique Sides, as taught in Figure 9; then from b and d, draw bL, dH, cutting each other in c; then is b c d the Top; which compleats the Figure. In this Figure the Front Side a b d e, is parallel to the Picture, but in the Figure n o p q r m, the back Side n p m q is parallel to the Picture; therefore let us find the Appearance of that also:---Here let m q p n be the parallel Side given.---Through the Points n and m draw Lines from H, and through the Points p and q draw Lines from L, which will cut the Lines Hm, Hn, continued in o and r; therefore draw o r, and the Thing proposed is done.--Or it may be found by giving one Edge m r.---Continue m r to its vanishing Point H, and draw rL; then draw m q parallel to the horizontal Line, cutting r L in q; then is r q the other Side; therefore draw mn, ro, pq, each perpendicular to the horizontal Line, and make any of them the proposed Height, (suppose r o) then draw o H, oL, cutting mn, and qp, in n and p, and then draw n p; which finishes the Figure.

CASE 2. *When they are above the Horizontal Line.*

Let f g be one of the Bottom Edges given.---Draw f i perpendicular to the horizontal Line, and make it equal to the proposed Height; from f draw f L, then draw g l parallel to the horizontal Line, cutting f L in l; and then is f l the Depth of the other Side; therefore, draw g h and l k parallel to f i, and from i draw i H and i L; which compleats the Representation.

V. *To find the Representation of any triangular Figure, when all its Sides are oblique with the Picture.*

Fig. 23. CASE 1. *When it is below the Horizontal Line.*

Let AD be one Edge given, whose vanishing Point is out of the Picture, and let L be the vanishing Point of the other Edge AG.---Make AG equal to AD, by Figure 10; and from A, D, G, draw Lines perpendicular to the Ground; then make AB equal to the Height, and draw BL; which will compleat the Side ABFG: Again, continue AB and DE to the horizontal Line, and make

DE

DE to DH, as AB is to AR*; then draw BE, which compleats the Side ABED; finally, draw EF, which finishes the Representation. For, if AD and BE were continued, they would both vanish into the same Point in the horizontal Line; as was observed in Fig. 21.

CASE 2. *When it is above the Horizontal Line.*

Let HO be one Edge given, whose vanishing Point is out of the Picture, and let L be the vanishing Point of the Edge HN.---- Make HN equal to HO, as before; and from N, H, O, draw Lines perpendicular to the Ground, then make HK equal to the proposed Height, and draw KL, which will give one Side: Again, make PQ (the Part above the horizontal Line) to PO (the Part below the horizontal Line) as IK is to IH (which in this Figure is as 2 is to 3), and draw KQ; which will compleat the Representation proposed. For if HO and KQ were continued, they would meet in a Point upon the horizontal Line.

This Method of determining the Appearance of any Line, when its vanishing Point is out of the Picture, is extremely useful; and therefore, the Reader cannot make it too familiar to him; the general Method for which I have farther explained in Figure 41.

VI. *To find the Representations of Cubes, both above and below the Horizontal Line, when some of their Sides are parallel to the Picture.*

CASE 1. *When below the Horizontal Line.*

Let abeg be one Side given.----Draw bC, eC, and gC, and find the vanishing Point H of the Diagonal ef, by Figure 11; and draw eH cutting Cg in f; then from f, draw fd parallel to the horizontal Line, cutting eC in d; and then draw dc parallel to eb, and the Representation is compleated. And for the Cube E--Make the front-side like the Cube A, and draw Lines from the upper Corners to the Center C; then by continuing eg and fd we may compleat the other also; as in the Figure. And therefore, having got one Representation, That will be sufficient for any Number of the same Kind, provided they stand all in the same Line, an; that is, at the same Distance from the Bottom of the Picture. Fig. 24.

* Suppose AB is four Parts, and BR one Part; then divide DH into five Parts; and then is HE to ED as RB to BA; that is, as one to four.

CASE 2. *When above the Horizontal Line, as* B *and* D.

Here let the Reader observe, that the Rule in either Case is the same; and therefore he is to proceed in the same Manner in finding the Representation of a Cube above the Eye, as we have done in determining the Appearance of a Cube below the Eye; which is sufficiently explained by the Figures.---And so likewise for the Depth m o, of the Parallelopiped F; which is found by drawing a Line from the Corner n, to the vanishing Point of the Diagonal H.

VII. *Of a Cube and Parallelopiped, whose Sides are all oblique with the Picture.*

CASE 1. *Of the Cube.*

Fig. 25. Let a b be given, whose vanishing Point is L; and let H be the vanishing Point of the other Side a g.----From a, draw a 1 parallel to the horizontal Line, and make L A equal to the Distance L E; then through b, draw A 1, cutting A 1 in 1; and then is a 1 equal to a b; and from a and b draw Lines perpendicular to the horizontal Line, and make a e equal to a 1; then from e, draw e L, cutting b c in c; and then we shall have one Side: Again, from c and e, draw Lines to H, and from e, draw a Line to C, (the vanishing Point of the Diagonal) which will cut c H in d; then from L draw a Line through d, cutting e H in f; finally, from f, draw f g parallel to a e; and then will the Representation be compleated.

CASE 2. *Of a Parallelopiped, or oblong Piece of Wood; resting upon one of its longest Faces.*

Let it be required to make it three Feet long, one Foot thick, and one Foot high: And let o be the nearest Corner, and H, L, the vanishing Points of the Sides.----Through o, draw 2 o 3, parallel to the horizontal Line, and set off three Feet upon it; then draw o H and o L, and make H B equal to H E, and draw B 2 cutting o H in i; then is o i equal to three Feet: Again, make L A equal to L E, and from o, set off o 3, equal to one Foot; then draw 3 A, cutting o L in n; and then is o n equal to o 3: Again, from i, o, n, draw Lines perpendicular to the horizontal Line, and make o m equal to o 3; finally, from m, draw m H and m L, cutting i h in h, and n l in l; then from l draw a Line to H, and from h draw a Line to L, which will cut each other in k, and so finish the Representation; which will be three Feet long, one Foot thick, and one Foot high.

VIII. To

VIII. *To find the Representation of an Hexangular Figure, both above and below the Eye.*

CASE 1. *When below the Eye.*

Let ab be one Side given, and let H and L be the vanishing Points of the other Sides.---Continue ab on either Side, at pleasure, and make a1, b2, equal to ab; then cut off ae and bf, equal to 1a and 2b; and from e, a, b, f, draw Perpendiculars to ab; then make ad equal to the proposed Height, and draw cd parallel to ab; then from c and d, draw Lines to L and H, cutting fh and eg in h and g; and from g and h, draw Lines to L and H, and from c and d, draw Lines to C, cutting them in i and k; finally, draw ik, which will be parallel to cd, and will be the Representation proposed. Fig. 26.

CASE 2. *When above the Eye.*

Let mn be one Side given, and H, L, the vanishing Points of the other Sides, as before.---Continue mn, at pleasure, as 3 4, from whence the other Sides may be found, and consequently, the whole Representation; as is evident by the Figure: In which I have put every Line in the Operation, to make it easy to be understood without any further Explanation.

From hence then it follows, that the Appearance of any Objects may be as easily determined above the horizontal Line as below it; since one Rule serves in both Cases; and therefore it matters not whether we begin our Work at the Bottom or at the Top of the Picture. Now, this Method of finding the Representation of Objects is of prodigious Use. For suppose it was required to draw the Representation of the Top of any Building; we need not sketch out any more of it than is to appear upon the Picture; but we may begin in the very Place where that Top is to be, without undergoing the tedious Task of beginning at the Bottom of such a Building, and afterwards rubbing out what is not to appear.

IX. *To put an Octangular Building into Perspective.*

Let ab be one Side given, and let H, C, L, be the vanishing Points of the several Sides.---Find the Representations of the Sides, as ah, bc, and cd, which are visible to the Eye (by Fig. 15.) and from the several Points h, a, b, c, d, draw Perpendiculars to the Bottom of the Picture; then make ak equal to the proposed Height, and draw kg parallel to ab, which compleats one Side; then from k draw Fig. 27.

draw kH, and from g draw gL, which finiſhes two Sides more; finally, from f draw fC, which will compleat the whole Repreſentation.

X. *To find the Repreſentation of Cylindrical, or round Objects, ſuch as Columns, and the like.*

In the 16th and 17th Figures we have ſhewn ſeveral Methods of finding the Appearance of Circles upon the Picture, by which means the Repreſentations of Circles of any Dimenſions may be determined with great Exactneſs; and ſince a Circle is the Baſe of a cylindrical Object, therefore, by finding the Repreſentation of two Circles at any determinate Diſtance, the Appearance of that Object may be determined alſo.

Fig. 28. *Let it be required to find the Repreſentation of a round Object like* D.

CASE 1. *When it ſtands upon one End.*

Let e f be the Diameter given, and n the Center of the Circle. ---Draw n b perpendicular to the Bottom of the Picture, and make it equal to the Height you intend for the Repreſentation; then, by Method 3, Fig. 17, find the Repreſentation of the Square g h f k i e; which will be a ſufficient Guide for drawing the Appearance of the Circle, as in the Figure. Again, through b, draw c d parallel to e f, and, by the ſame Method, find the Repreſentation of the Square a l, which will be a Guide for the upper Circle; finally, from the Extremities of both Circles, draw ec, fd, parallel to n b, which will exhibit the viſible Appearance of the round Object, as in Figure D.

From hence then it is manifeſt, that any Number of round Objects, (ſuch as Columns, &c.) may be found upon the Picture, by having only their Diameters and perpendicular Heights, as we have further ſhewn in Figure 63, &c.

Fig. 29. CASE 2. *When a Cylinder lies upon the Ground oblique with the Picture.*

This alſo may be done with the greateſt Eaſe, by finding the Appearance of two geometrical Squares. Thus, let A be the Corner of the Square for the neareſt End of the Cylinder, AB its Diameter, and AC its given Length; and let H be the vaniſhing Point of the End, and L the vaniſhing Point of the Sides.----Cut off AE equal to AB, and from the Points AE draw Perpendiculars, and compleat the Square a; then draw its Diagonals, &c.

and

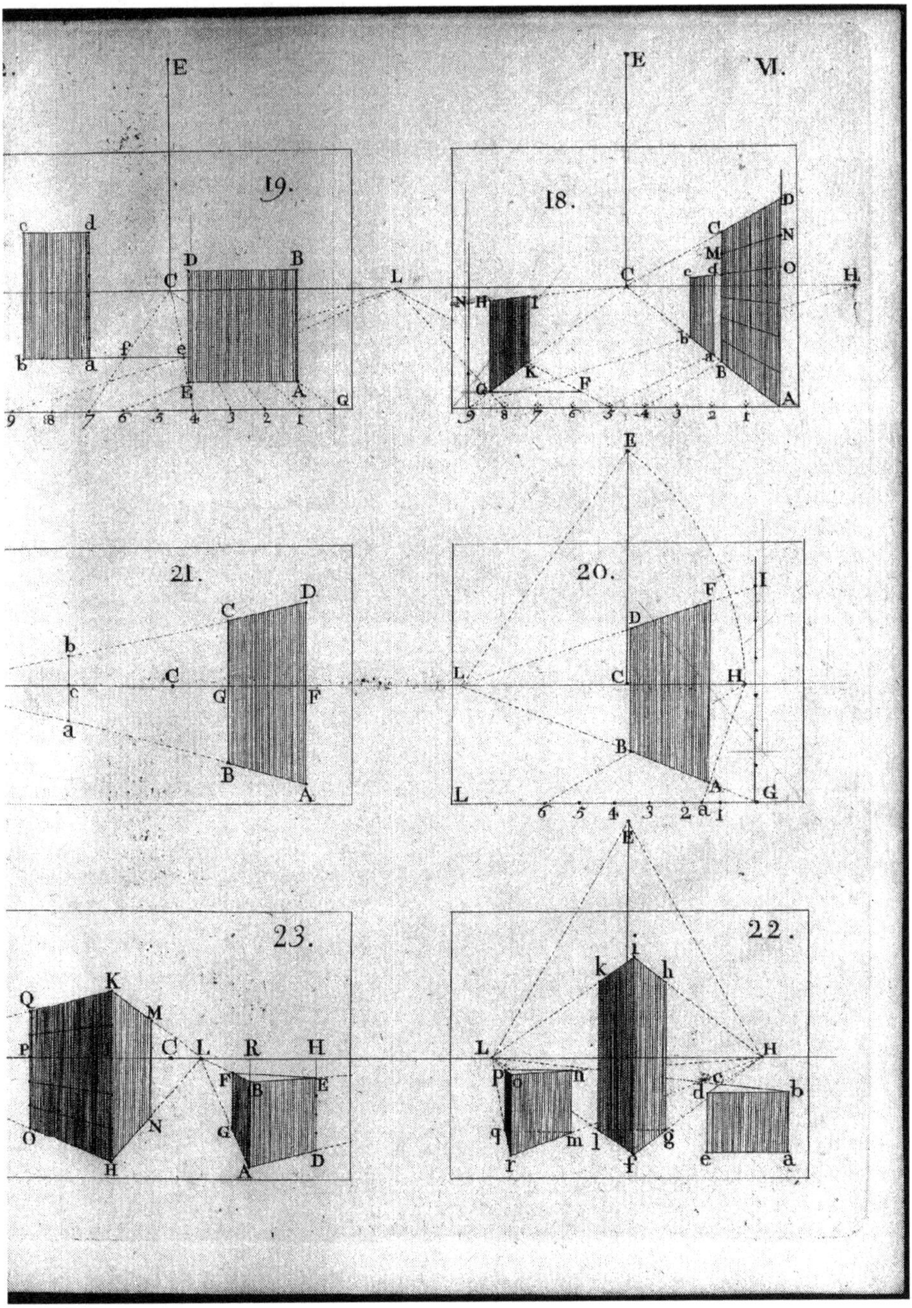
VI.
18.
19.
20.
21.
22.
23.

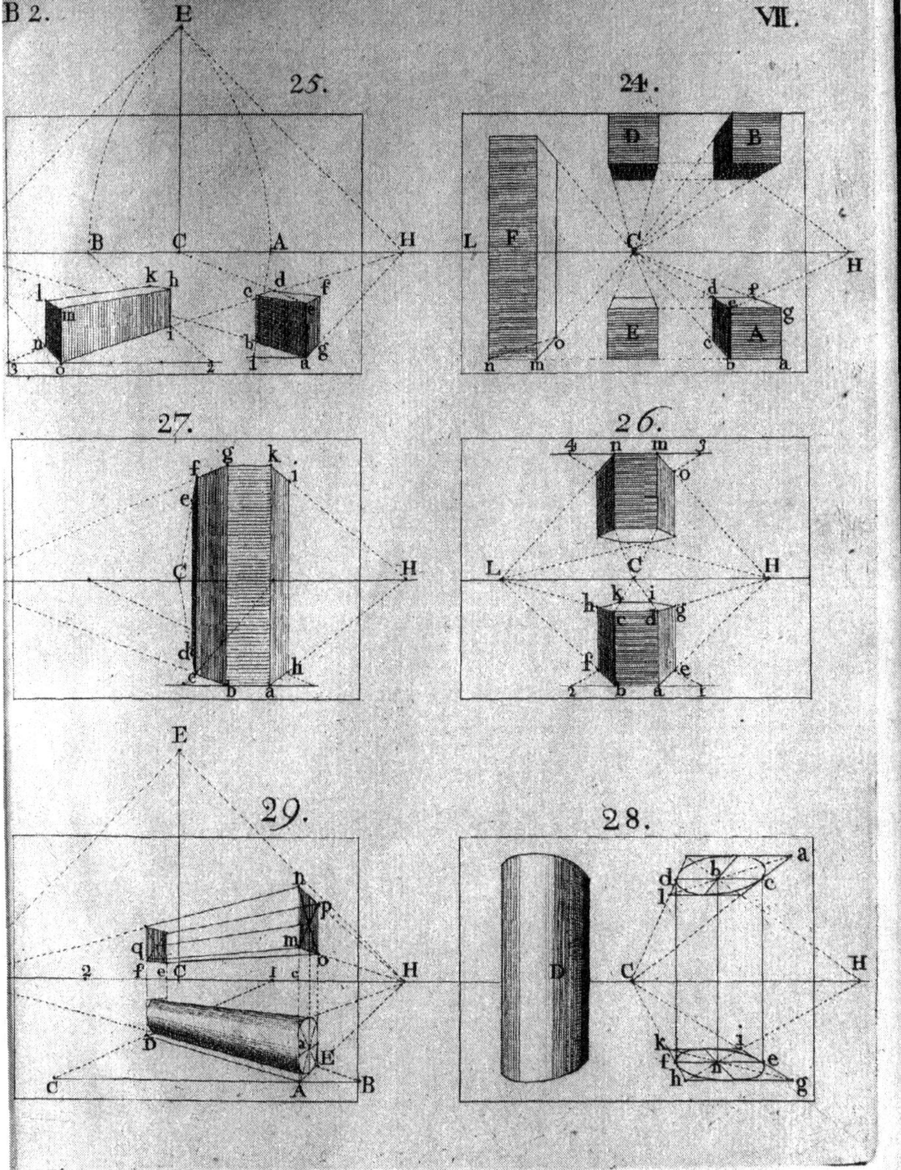

25. 24. 27. 26. 29. 28.

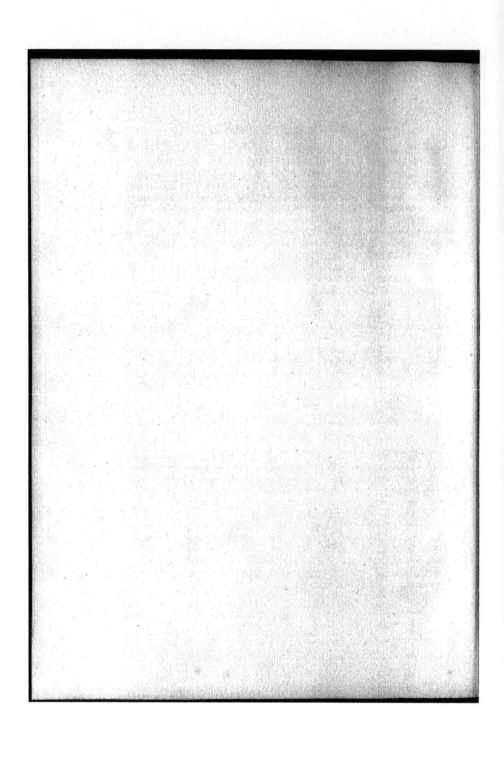

and then the Appearance of the Circle, as in the Figure. And for the Length, cut off AD equal to AC, and from the Point D, make another Square for the fartheſt End, in which draw the Appearance of another Circle; then draw Lines from the Extremities of the Circle a, to L, which will cut the Circle in the Square at D, and thereby compleat the Repreſentation as required.

If there ſhould not be Room enough for the whole Draught below the horizontal Line, it may be done above it, as in the Figure, taking great Care to make them both at the ſame Diſtance from it.—Thus, c n is equal to c A.

From hence it appears, that this Figure is determined after the ſame Manner as the oblong Piece of Wood, Fig. 25; only, one is ſquare and the other circular.

Theſe Examples are ſufficient to ſhew the whole Practice of Perſpective, ſo far as it relates to Objects which lie flat upon the Ground, or are perpendicular to it: For, as I obſerved before, the immediate Objects of Perſpective, are a Triangle, a Square, and a Circle; and therefore were we to multiply Objects to infinity, they would be compounded of ſome or all theſe put together; and conſequently, what has been ſaid already, is ſufficient for our Purpoſe.

SECT. IV.

Of OBJECTS *which are inclined to the* GROUND, *ſuch as Pediments, Roofs of Houſes, and the like.*

THIS Part of Perſpective, neither the *Jeſuit*, nor *Pozzo*, nor many others, ſeem to have had the leaſt Knowledge of; for they have confined themſelves wholly to the horizontal Line, without conſidering any other vaniſhing Line; and therefore, when they have ſhewn how to find the Appearances of inclined Objects, they did it by means of Plans, Elevations, &c. which is not only a tedious, but an uncertain Method. But, Dr. TAYLOR has ſhewn us, that inclined Objects have their proper vaniſhing Lines and Points, as well as thoſe Objects which lie flat upon the Ground, or are perpendicular to it; and that the Method for determining the Appearance of Objects in either Caſe, is exactly the ſame. Which we are now going to demonſtrate.

I. To

Fig. 30. I. *To find the Representation of a Square, by means of its Diagonals only, when it is situated like* GHIK, *Fig.* 18.

METHOD 1. *Let* ab *be the lower Edge.*

Continue ab to its vanishing Point C, and through C, draw EV perpendicular to HL, which will be the vanishing Line of the proposed Plane; then make CⒸ equal to the Distance of the Eye, and draw AB parallel to the horizontal Line, upon which make the Square ABCD of any convenient Bigness, and draw its Diagonals AC, BD; then from Ⓒ, draw ⒸE and ⒸV parallel to the Diagonals AC, BD; and where they cut the vanishing Line EV, will be the vanishing Points sought: Thus, E is the vanishing Point of the Diagonal ac, and V is the vanishing Point of the Diagonal bd.

METHOD 2. *By making a given Angle at the Eye.*

The Angle of a Square is a right Angle, and contains 90 Degrees, the half of which is 45 Degrees; therefore, at Ⓒ, with the horizontal Line, make two Angles, CⒸE and CⒸV, each equal to 45 Degrees, then draw ⒸE, ⒸV, cutting the vanishing Line in E and V; which will be the vanishing Points, as before.

METHOD 3. *By the Distance of the Eye only.*

Through the vanishing Point C, draw the vanishing Line EV, and make CE, CV, each equal to the Distance CE of the Eye, which gives the vanishing Points proposed.

From hence then it appears, that Planes which are perpendicular to the Picture, and to the Ground also, will have their vanishing Lines pass through the Center of the Picture, perpendicular to the horizontal Line; and that all the oblique Lines which can be drawn within those Squares, will vanish into this Line, for the same Reason that all the oblique Lines which can be drawn within a Square that lies upon the Ground, will vanish into the horizontal Line. And from hence also we may conceive, why Roofs, Pediments, *&c.* will have their proper vanishing Points as well as any other Objects. For let abe be the End of a Roof or Pediment, then is E the vanishing Point of the Side ae which is next the Eye, and V is the vanishing Point of the other Side be; and if Lines are drawn through E and V, parallel to the horizontal Line, then these Lines will be the vanishing Lines of the Sides of the Roof, for the same Reason that EV is the vanishing Line of its Ends: As is evident from the next Figure.

II. *To*

II. *To find the vanishing Lines and vanishing Points of a Roof, when the End of the Building is situated like* abcd *in the last Figure.* Fig. 31.

Draw the vanishing Line IJ, as before taught, and make C𝕮 equal to the Distance of the Picture.----Parallel to the horizontal Line, (or if you please upon the horizontal Line) draw AB, upon which, draw the End of the Roof, as ABC; then from 𝕮, draw 𝕮V, 𝕮L, parallel to AC, BC, cutting the vanishing Line in V and L; then are V and L the vanishing Points of the inclined Edges ac, bc. Again, through V and L draw 𝖀𝕷 and vl parallel to the horizontal Line, and then will 𝖀𝕷 be the vanishing Line of the inclined Side aecd, and vl will be the vanishing Line of the inclined Side bcd.

Now in order to find any vanishing Point upon either of the vanishing Lines 𝖀𝕷, or vl, we must proceed exactly in the same manner as in finding any vanishing Point upon the horizontal Line; namely, by setting off the Distance of the vanishing Line, and then drawing Lines from thence parallel to any original Lines whose vanishing Points are required. Thus, let it be required to find the vanishing Points of the Diagonals of a Square, whose Sides vanish into the Center V, of the vanishing Line 𝖀𝕷; like ab, dc, Figure 32.---Make VI equal to V𝕮, and LJ equal to L𝕮; then at I and J, with the Lines VI, LJ, make Angles of 45 Degrees each, as in the Figure, and draw the Lines I𝖀, I𝕷, Jv and Jl; which will give the vanishing Points proposed.---Or it may be done by making 𝖀V, 𝕷V, &c. equal to the Distance V𝕮, which comes to the same Thing. For suppose the Picture removed into the Place of the 32d Figure, where 𝖀𝕷 is the vanishing Line of the Square abfg, and 𝖀 and 𝕷 the vanishing Points of its Diagonals; and let ab be one Edge of the Square, which stands upon the Ground.---From a and b draw Lines to V, which is the vanishing Point of the Sides ae, bd; and then from b draw a Line to 𝖀, and from a, draw a Line to 𝕷, cutting aV and bV in f and g; finally, draw gf; and then will abfg be the Representation of a Square inclined to the Ground, like the Line AC, Fig. 31. And in like Manner, if another Square was required, as fged, it may be found by repeating the last Operation; that is, by means of the Diagonals, as is evident by inspecting the Figure: Or any Number of Squares may be found by the same Method. From whence it is manifest, that the Representation of any inclined Object may very easily be determined, and made of any given Proportion. Fig. 32.

And

And what has been said about the inclined Side a b c d, is equally applicable to the opposite inclined Side; since the only Difference consists in working below the horizontal Line, instead of above it: For v l is its vanishing Line, and v and l the vanishing Points of the Diagonals, *&c.*---I have added the Figure A, which represents, as it were, the Frame-work of the other; and will serve to explain the Thing more fully.

The principal Difficulty in determining the Representation of any inclined Planes, lies in finding the Center and Distance of their peculiar vanishing Lines; therefore, before we proceed any further, we will give some general Rules for that Purpose, as is moreover explained by the 50th Figure.

1. *To find the Center of a vanishing Line.*

Fig. 34. Let 𝔙L be a vanishing Line given.---From C the Center of the Picture, draw C H perpendicular to the vanishing Line 𝔙 L, and then is H the Center of that vanishing Line. Again, let 𝔙𝔏 be a vanishing Line given.---From C the Center of the Picture, draw CO perpendicular to 𝔙𝔏, and then is O the Center of that vanishing Line.

2. *To find the Distance of a vanishing Line.*

Continue the Perpendicular C H, at pleasure, towards 𝔈; and from the Center of the vanishing Line draw H E to the Eye; then is H E the Distance of the vanishing Line 𝔙 L; therefore, set off H𝔈 equal to the Distance HE, and then is 𝔈 the Distance to be work'd with. Again, for the vanishing Line 𝔙𝔏---Continue the Perpendicular CO towards I, at pleasure, and from O set off O J upon the vanishing Line, equal to CE, the real Distance of the Eye, and draw C J; then is C J the Distance of the vanishing Line 𝔙𝔏; and by making OI equal to C J, we shall have I for the Point of Distance of the vanishing Line 𝔙𝔏. From hence then it will appear, that C is the Center of the horizontal Line in the 30th Figure, and it is also the Center of the vanishing Line E V; that C E is the Distance of the Picture, (that is, of the horizontal Line) and C𝔈 is the Distance of the vanishing Line E V: And because the vanishing Line E V passes through the Center of the Picture, therefore the Distances CE and C𝔈 must be equal. Again, V and L, of the 31st Figure, are the Centers of the vanishing Lines 𝔙𝔏 and v l; and V I, L J, are their Distances, and so on. Thus much is sufficient for our present Purpose; but in the

50th

50th Figure I have given one general Rule, not only for determining the Center and Distance of each vanishing Line, but for finding the vanishing Line of any Plane, let its Inclination be what it will: All which should be well remembered.

Having determined the Center and Distance of any vanishing Line, we are then to proceed with our Work in the very same Manner as in drawing the Representations of Planes that lie flat upon the Ground; and, by turning the Figures, we may conceive every vanishing Line to be a horizontal Line, &c.

III. *To find the Representation of a Square* a b c d, *by the vanishing Points of its Diagonals, when it stands perpendicular to the Ground but oblique with the Picture, like* ABDF, *Fig.* 20. Fig. 33.

METHOD 1. *By drawing out a Square.*

Let a b, be the under Side given.---Continue a b to its vanishing Point O, and through O, draw I J perpendicular to the horizontal Line; then is I J the vanishing Line of the Square. Again, from E draw E O, which is the Distance of the vanishing Line I J; therefore, set off O𝔈 equal to OE, and parallel to the horizontal Line draw a Line, as AB, at pleasure; upon which, make a Square ABCD, and draw its Diagonals; then from 𝔈 draw Lines parallel to those Diagonals, which will cut the vanishing Line in I and J; and then are I and J the vanishing Points of the Diagonals a c and b d.

METHOD 2.

Make at 𝔈, on each Side of the horizontal Line, an Angle of 45 Degrees, and draw 𝔈I, 𝔈J, which will produce the vanishing Points proposed.

METHOD 3.

Or, the vanishing Points may be determined in this Example by making O I and O J equal to O𝔈.

IV. *Suppose* a b e *to represent the End of a Roof, as before; then the Sides of that Roof will be oblique with the Eye, like* a b d e, *Fig.* 34; *therefore, let us next find the Representation of a Plane situated in this Manner.*

METHOD 1. *Let* a e *be the lower Edge of the Roof, which let us suppose to be a Square that rests upon the Edge* a e. Fig. 34.

Continue the Side a e to its vanishing Point 𝔏, and draw L𝔈; then at E make a right Angle, and draw EH; and then is 𝔏 the vanishing Point of one Side of a Square which lies upon the Ground, and H the vanishing Point of another Side of the same Square; therefore, from the Corner a draw a H, and through H draw UL perpendicular to the horizontal Line; then is H the Center of the vanishing Line UL, and HE its Distance. Again, make HC equal to EH, and make AC parallel to it; then upon AC draw the End of the Roof, (that is, the Angles of its Inclination) and from C draw CU, CL, parallel to AB, CB, which will cut the vanishing Line UL, in the vanishing Points U and L; and so will U be the vanishing Point of the Edges a b, c d, and L will be the vanishing Point of the Edges ae, bd, and L will be the vanishing Point of the Edge c b: And if a Line be drawn from U to L, it will be the vanishing Line of the inclined Face a e b d; from whence it is evident, that after we have found two vanishing Points of any inclined Plane, if a Line be drawn through those Points, it will be the vanishing Line of that Plane. But to compleat the Representation proposed: Find the Center of the vanishing Line U L, and set off its Distance upon the Perpendicular OI; then draw Lines from the vanishing Points U and L, which will make a right Angle at the Eye; then bisect that Angle by the Line ID, which will give D for the vanishing Point of the Diagonal of a Square; by which means the Square aebd may be compleated.

METHOD 2. *By having the Width, as* ac, *of the Roof given.*

Let a c be the Width, or what is generally called *the Span*, of the Roof; and let U and L be the vanishing Points of the Roof. ----From a, draw aU, and through c draw L b, cutting aU in b; then is abc the Representation of one End. Again, from H draw HE, with which, at E, make a right Angle, and draw EL; then is L the vanishing Point of the Side ae which rests upon the Ground; therefore, draw aL and bL; then find the vanishing Point of the Diagonal of a Square, whose vanishing Points are H and L, and from a, draw aD, cutting bL in d; then from U draw a Line through d, which will cut aL in e, and thereby compleat the Representation proposed.

METHOD 3. *By cutting off one Line equal to another Line given.*

From the Corner a draw af parallel to the vanishing Line UL, and make af equal to one Side of the intended Square; then set off UF equal to UI, and draw Ff, cutting aU in b; and then is ab equal to af. Again, from a and b draw

draw a𝔏, b𝔏, and from a draw a g parallel to the horizontal Line, and make it equal to a f; then set off 𝔏G equal to 𝔏E, and draw Gg, cutting a𝔏 in e; then is a c equal to a g, that is, equal to a f; therefore, draw e𝔙, which compleats the Square abed; finally, draw aH and bL, which will finish the whole Figure.

Method 4. *By having the vanishing Line* 𝔙𝔏 *given, at pleasure.*

From the Center of the Picture draw CO perpendicular to the vanishing Line 𝔙𝔏, and set off the Distance of the vanishing Line from O to I, and let a b be one Side given.---Continue a b 'till it cuts the vanishing Line in its proper vanishing Point 𝔙, and from 𝔙 draw 𝔙I; then at I make a right Angle, and draw I𝔏; and then is 𝔏 the vanishing Point of the Sides a e, b d; and by finding the Point D, the Square may be compleated, as before. Again, for the upright End;---Continue the horizontal Line at pleasure, and make 𝔙𝔈 equal to 𝔙I, cutting the horizontal Line continued in 𝔈; then is 𝔈H the Distance of the vanishing Line 𝔙L; by which means the vanishing Point L of the Side b c may be determined;----Or the vanishing Points of any Lines may be found upon 𝔙𝔏, by inscribing a Figure at the Eye, like the Original of our proposed Representation; as the Square I. Now what is said of a Square, will serve for any other Figure; which, it is presumed, is now so evident as to need no farther Explanation; especially, since a little Practice will make all that has been advanced in this Section very easy and familiar.

Here let us observe, that when Objects are parallel to the Ground, they will have their several vanishing Points in the horizontal Line; when they are perpendicular to the Ground, they will vanish into a Line perpendicular to the horizontal Line, like Fig. 30, 31, 32, 33; when they are inclined to the Ground, but have some of their Edges parallel to the Picture, like a b, ed, Fig. 32. they will then vanish into Lines parallel to the horizontal Line; and will be above the horizontal Line when the Plane leans from the Eye, and below the horizontal Line when the Plane leans towards the Eye; but when the inclined Planes are every way oblique with the Picture, the Eye, and the Ground, like Fig. 34, then the vanishing Points of their several inclined Sides will vanish into Lines aslant the horizontal Line, like 𝔙𝔏. Now, these being all the Variety of vanishing Lines which can ever happen in common Practice, it were needless to produce any other Examples of this Kind: But to aſſiſt the Curious in determining the Repreſentations of Regular Solids, * or ſuch-like complicated Bodies, I have added the ſix following Figures; which may be omitted by the Generality of my Readers, as Things more curious than uſeful, and which are not in the leaſt eſſential to common Practice; and therefore, they are now referred to the next Chapter.

Fig. 35. V. *To find the Repreſentation of a Cube that reſts upon one of its Edges* a b.

EXAMPLE I. *When ſome of its Edges, as* a b, c d, f e, *are parallel to the Picture.*

Let a b be one Edge given, which let us ſuppoſe reſts upon the Ground. Now, becauſe the Edges a b, *&c.* are parallel to the Picture, therefore the End a d f g will be perpendicular to the Picture; and conſequently, the vaniſhing Line V L of that End will paſs through the Center of the Picture, and will be perpendicular to the horizontal Line: And if we ſuppoſe the Diagonal a f to be perpendicular to the Ground, then the vaniſhing Point of the other Diagonal dg will be the Center of the Picture, becauſe it is parallel to the Ground. Therefore, through C draw the vaniſhing Line V L, and make C 𝕮 equal to the Diſtance of the Eye; then at 𝕮 make a Square, in ſuch a manner that its Diagonal 1 2 may be parallel to the vaniſhing Line V L; or, which is the ſame thing, make the other Diagonal a Part of the horizontal Line; then draw 𝕮V and 𝕮L parallel to the ſeveral Sides of the Square, which will produce V and L for the vaniſhing Points of thoſe Sides.----This being premiſed, let us now compleat the Repreſentation, from the Side a b, which is given.---Through L, draw v l parallel to the horizontal Line, and make L l equal to the Diſtance L J of the vaniſhing Line v l; then from L draw Lines through a and b, and continue them at pleaſure; and from l, (which is the vaniſhing Point of the Diagonal) draw a Line through b, cutting L d in d; then from d, draw d c parallel to a b, which will compleat the Face a b c d. Again, from a and d draw Lines to V, and from d draw another Line to C, cutting a V in g; and from L

* Regular Solids, are Bodies terminated by regular Planes, and are five in Number, viz. 1. the Tetrahedron; 2. the Hexahedron, or Cube; 3. the Octahedron; 4. the Dodecahedron; and 5. the Icoſahedron: The firſt of which is compoſed of four equal and equilateral Triangles; the ſecond, of ſix geometrical Squares; the third, of eight equal and equilateral Triangles; the fourth, of 12 regular Pentagons; and the fifth, of 20 equal and equilateral Triangles.

draw

draw a Line through g, cutting dV in f; which finishes another Face: Finally, from c draw cV, and from f draw a Line parallel to dc, which will cut cV in e, and thereby compleat the whole Representation.

Again, When the End adfg stands in such a Manner that the Diagonal af is perpendicular to the Ground; in this Case, the Angles at 𝔈, made by the Sides of the Square with the horizontal Line, will be each equal to 45 Degrees; and therefore C is the vanishing Point of the Diagonal of the Square: But if the End be situated like the Square B, then draw a Square, reposing upon one of its Corners on the horizontal Lines, in the same Manner as you suppose the End of the real Cube to be situated upon the Ground; after which, draw Lines from 𝔈, parallel to the Sides of that Square, and then its Diagonals will cut the vanishing Line V L, continued, in the proper vanishing Points of those Lines; thus, F and H are the vanishing Points of the Sides of the Square, and G is the vanishing Point of one of its Diagonals.

EXAMPLE 2. *When the Cube rests upon one Edge* ab, *that is oblique with the Picture.* Fig. 36.

Continue ab to its vanishing Point 𝔏, and from 𝔏 draw a Line to the Eye E, with which make a right Angle; then draw EH, and through H draw 𝔘L perpendicular to the horizontal Line, and then is 𝔘L the vanishing Line of the End adef. Again, let H be the vanishing Point of the Diagonal ed; then, by making H𝔘 and HL equal to the Distance HE, we shall have the vanishing Points of the Edges ad, df, &c. and if from 𝔘 and 𝔏 we draw 𝔘𝔏, L𝔏, we shall have the vanishing Lines of the Faces abcd, cdfg. Again, find the vanishing Point D of the Diagonal bd, and from D draw a Line through b, then from L draw Lines through a and b, and then will Ld cut Dd in d, and thereby give ad for the Edge ad; therefore, from d draw d𝔏, which compleats one Face. In like manner, from a and d draw Lines to 𝔘, and from d draw dH, cutting a𝔘 in e; then from L draw a Line through e, cutting d𝔘 in f; and then we shall have compleated another Face adef: Finally, from f draw a Line to 𝔏, and from c draw a Line to 𝔘, which finishes the whole Figure.

EXAMPLE 3. *When the Cube stands upon one Corner, as* a. Fig. 37.

Let us suppose the Cube to stand in such a manner, that a Line passing through the upper and under Corners will be perpendicular

dicular to the Ground; in which Case, a Plane aceh, that passes through those Corners, will be perpendicular to the Ground also, and consequently, its vanishing Line will be perpendicular to the horizontal Line. And let us, moreover, suppose, that this vanishing Line, as KI, passes through the Center of the Picture.--- Any where, at pleasure, draw a Square z and its Diagonals; then, upon the horizontal Line, draw a Perpendicular AE, at pleasure also; and at the Point A, with the horizontal Line, make an Angle of 54 Degrees, and draw AH; then at A make another Angle CAD of 36 Degrees, and draw AC; and make AH equal to the Diagonal of the Square z, and AC equal to one of its Sides; then draw CE parallel to AH, and EH parallel to AC: So shall we have a Plane ACEH, which may be considered as the original of the Representation aceh; whose longest Side ah is inclined to the Ground at an Angle of 54 Degrees, and whose shortest Side is inclined to the Ground at an Angle of 36 Degrees; which together make a right Angle; that is, one Angle of a Square. Now, having made these necessary Preparations, let a be the Corner upon which it stands.----Set off the Distance of the Eye CE, and draw KI through C; then from E, draw EK parallel to AH, (Fig. X) and EI parallel to AC, (Fig. X) cutting KI in I and K; then are I and K the vanishing Points of the Plane aceh. Again, through K draw 𝔘𝔏 parallel to CE, which will give the vanishing Line of the upper Face cdef; and since K is the vanishing Point of its Diagonal ce, therefore, by making K𝔘, and K𝔏, each equal to the Distance EK, we shall have the vanishing Points of the Sides cf, cd, &c. by which means that Face may be compleated. Then let ce be the Diagonal given.---From c draw c𝔘, c𝔏, and from 𝔘 and 𝔏 draw Lines through e, which will produce the Face proposed. Again, having two vanishing Points 𝔘 and I, of the Face abcd.---Draw 𝔘I, which is its vanishing Line; and by finding the Center O, and its Distance Oℭ, together with its vanishing Point H of the Diagonal bc, the Face abcd may be compleated. The same may be said of the other Face acfg. The Figure K is drawn in such a manner, as to shew all the Faces of a Cube in the above Situation.

Let us now, without any Regard to a particular Situation of the Cube, suppose ab one Edge given, 𝔗 its vanishing Point, and 𝔗I its vanishing Line; and let C be the Center of the Picture, and CE its Distance.---Find the Center and Distance of the vanishing Line 𝔘I, and draw 𝔗ℭ; then, at ℭ make a right Angle, and draw ℭI;

and

and then will I be the vanishing Point of the Edge ac; and by finding the vanishing Point H of the Diagonal bc, the Face abcd may be compleated. For, from the vanishing Point I, draw a Line through the Center of the Picture, and continue it at pleasure, (as IK;) then from C draw a Line perpendicular to IK, and make CE equal to the Distance of the Eye; then draw IE, and at E make a right Angle; then draw EK, cutting IK in K; finally through K draw a Line parallel to CE, which will pass through the vanishing Point 𝔄, and produce the vanishing Line 𝔄𝔏 of the Face cdef. Again, from 𝔏 and I draw 𝔏I, which will give the vanishing Line of the other Side acfg.

I have dwelt the longer upon this last Figure, as it is a very curious Example, and, as it were, opens the Way to the Projection of all the regular Solids.

EXAMPLE 4. *To find the Representation of a regular Tetrahedron, reposing upon one of its Faces.* Fig. 38.

This also may be done easiest by finding a perpendicular Plane which is supposed to pass through the Middle of the Body, as ade.--Now in order to find the Inclination of the Sides of this perpendicular Plane, draw an Equilateral Triangle AGF, and divide the Side GF into two equal Parts, and draw AE; then at E, with the Distance EA, describe an Arc; and at A, with the Distance AG, describe another Arc, cutting the former Arc in D; then draw AD, ED; and then will AD be the Inclination of the Edge ab, and is 55 Degrees; and ED is the Inclination of the Edge ed, and is 70 Degrees. Having thus got the Inclination of the above Edges, the next thing is to find the Representation of the Face abc, the vanishing Points of whose oblique Sides are H, L.----Bisect the Angle HEL, and draw EC; then is C the vanishing Point of a Line that will divide the Side bc into two equal Parts; and therefore C is the vanishing Point of ae, that is, of the Bottom of the perpendicular Plane ade. Again, through C draw 𝔄D perpendicular to the horizontal Line, and continue it at pleasure; and then is 𝔄D the vanishing Line of the Plane ade: Then at E, the Distance of the vanishing Line 𝔄D, make an Angle with the Line CE equal to 55 Degrees, and draw E𝔄; and then is 𝔄 the vanishing Point of the Edge ad. Again, make another Angle at E of 70 Degrees, and draw ED; and then is D the vanishing Point of the Side dc, by which means the Plane ade may be compleated; and by drawing bd, and cd, the whole Figure will be finished.---Or it may be done

done by making the Figure ADE in ſuch a manner that 𝔘E may be parallel to the horizontal Line; for then, by drawing E𝔘, and ED, parallel to AD and DE, the vaniſhing Points 𝔘 and D will be produced.---Or this Figure may be found by having only the Inclination of the Edge ad, which, we obſerved before, was an Angle of 55 Degrees. Thus, make an Angle of 55 Degrees at E, and draw E𝔘; then ſince H is the vaniſhing Point of the Edge ab, and 𝔘 is the vaniſhing Point of the Edge ad, therefore by drawing 𝔘 H, and continuing it at pleaſure, we ſhall have the vaniſhing Line 𝔘𝔏; and by finding the Center and Diſtance of that vaniſhing Line, and making two Angles of 60 Degrees each at ℭ, we ſhall have the vaniſhing Points of all the Edges of the Side abd; and conſequently, by joining dc, the Figure will be compleated.---What is ſaid of the vaniſhing Line 𝔘𝔏, may be ſaid alſo of the other vaniſhing Line 𝔘I.*

Fig. 39. EXAMPLE 5. *To put a Canted Cube † into Perſpective, reſting upon one of its Square Faces.*

Let ac be one Edge of its under Face, A its vaniſhing Point, and H the vaniſhing Point of another Edge of the under Face; that is, let A and H be the vaniſhing Points of a Square that lies flat upon the Ground.---Through H draw FI perpendicular to the horizontal Line, and make Hℭ equal to the Diſtance of the vaniſhing Line FI. Then at ℭ, on each Side of the horizontal Line, make an Angle of 45 Degrees, and draw ℭF, ℭI; then from F and I, draw FA, IA; and then is IA the vaniſhing Line of the Face abcd; therefore, by finding the Center and Diſtance of this vaniſhing Line, and by that means the vaniſhing Point K of the Diagonal bc, the Square abcd may be compleated.----In like manner, it is eaſy to ſhew, that FI is the vaniſhing Line of the Face g; GM the vaniſhing Line of the Face h; 𝔏N the vaniſhing Line of the Face b; BD the vaniſhing Line of the Face f; FA the vaniſhing Line of the Face k; FN the vaniſhing Line of the Face i; H𝔏 the vaniſhing Line of the Face m; and 𝔘N the vaniſhing Line of the Face e.

* Theſe two Examples are ſufficient to point out the Method for determining the Repreſentation of all the regular Solids; for having got the Inclinations of their ſeveral Planes, &c. their peculiar vaniſhing Lines and Points may be found with the greateſt Eaſe.

† A Canted Cube, is a ſolid Body comprehended under 18 Geometrical Squares and eight equal and equilateral Triangles.

EXAMPLE

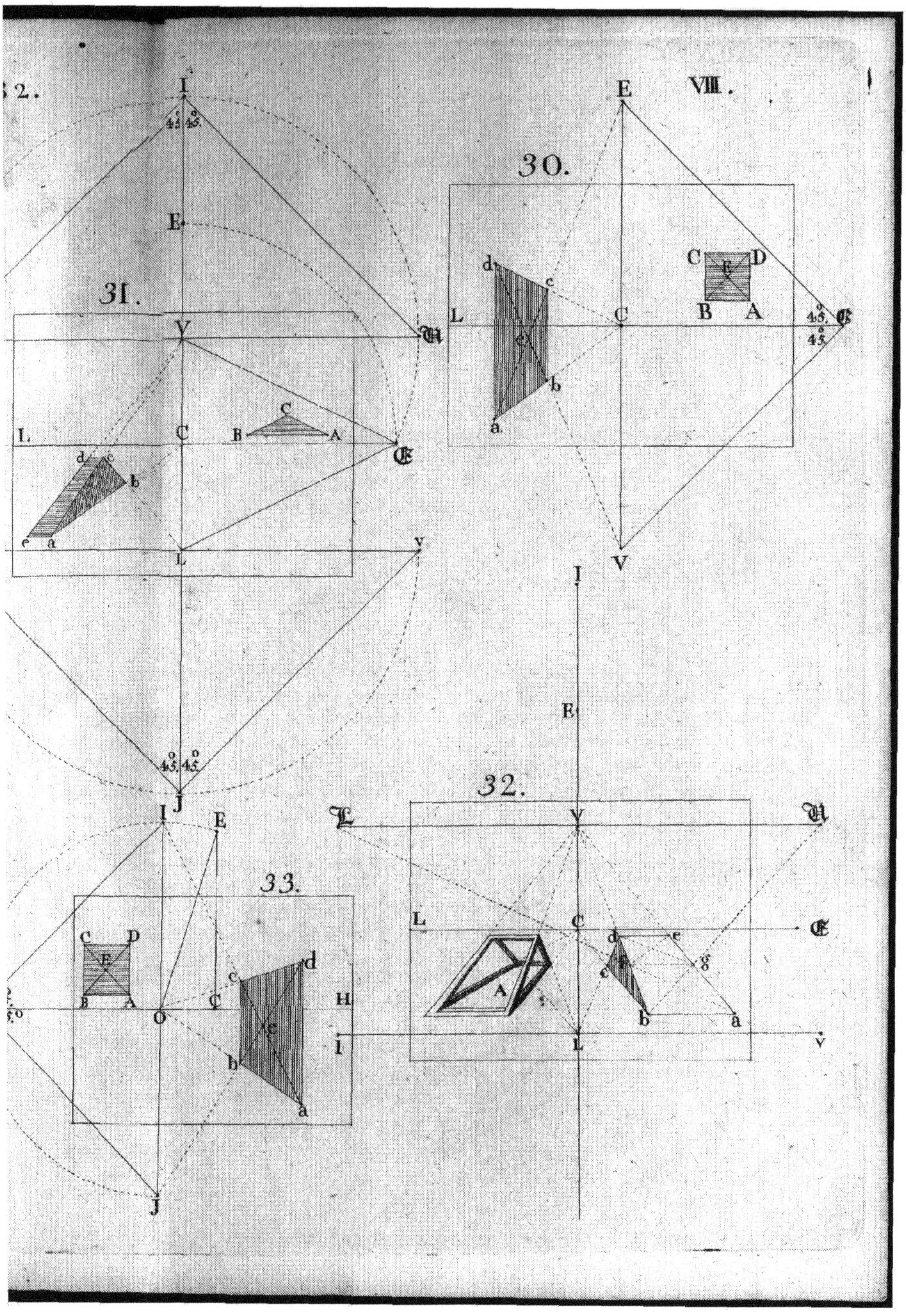
VIII.
30.
31.
32.
33.

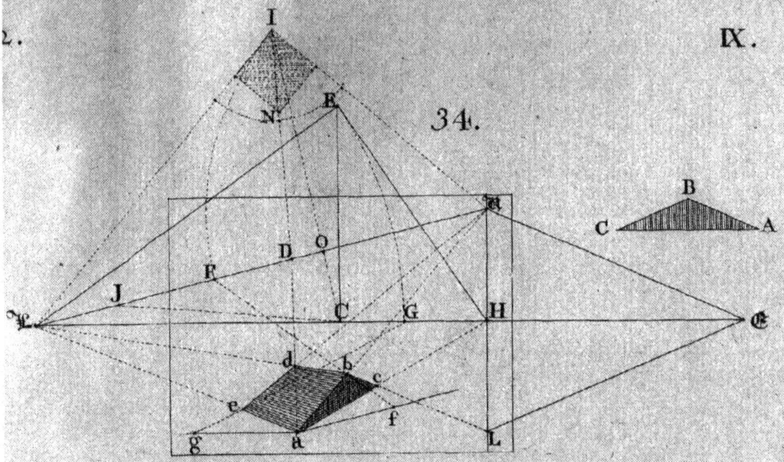
I
N
E
O
D
F
J
C
G
H
d
b
c
e
f
g
a
L
B
C
A

34.

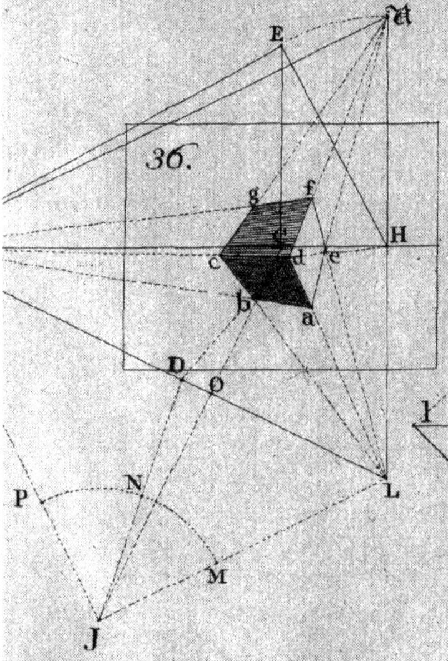
E
g
f
c
d
e
H
b
a
D
O
P
N
M
J
L

36.

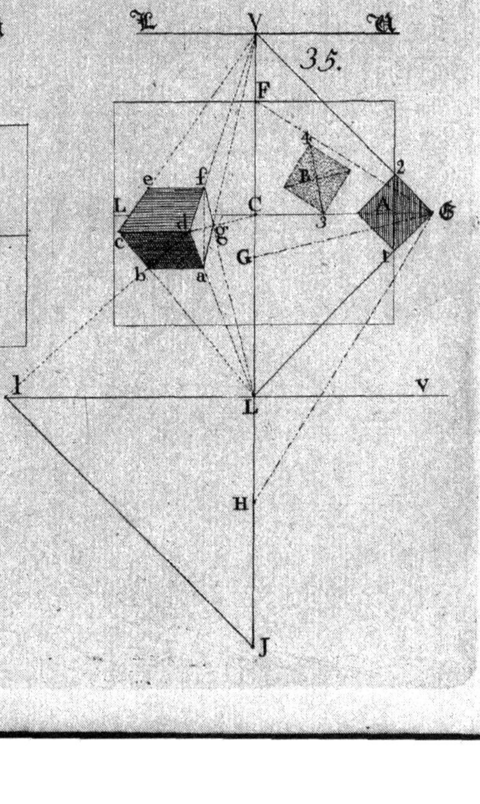
V
F
e
f
L
C
d
g
c
b
a
G
A
B
2
3
1
l
L
V
H
J

35.

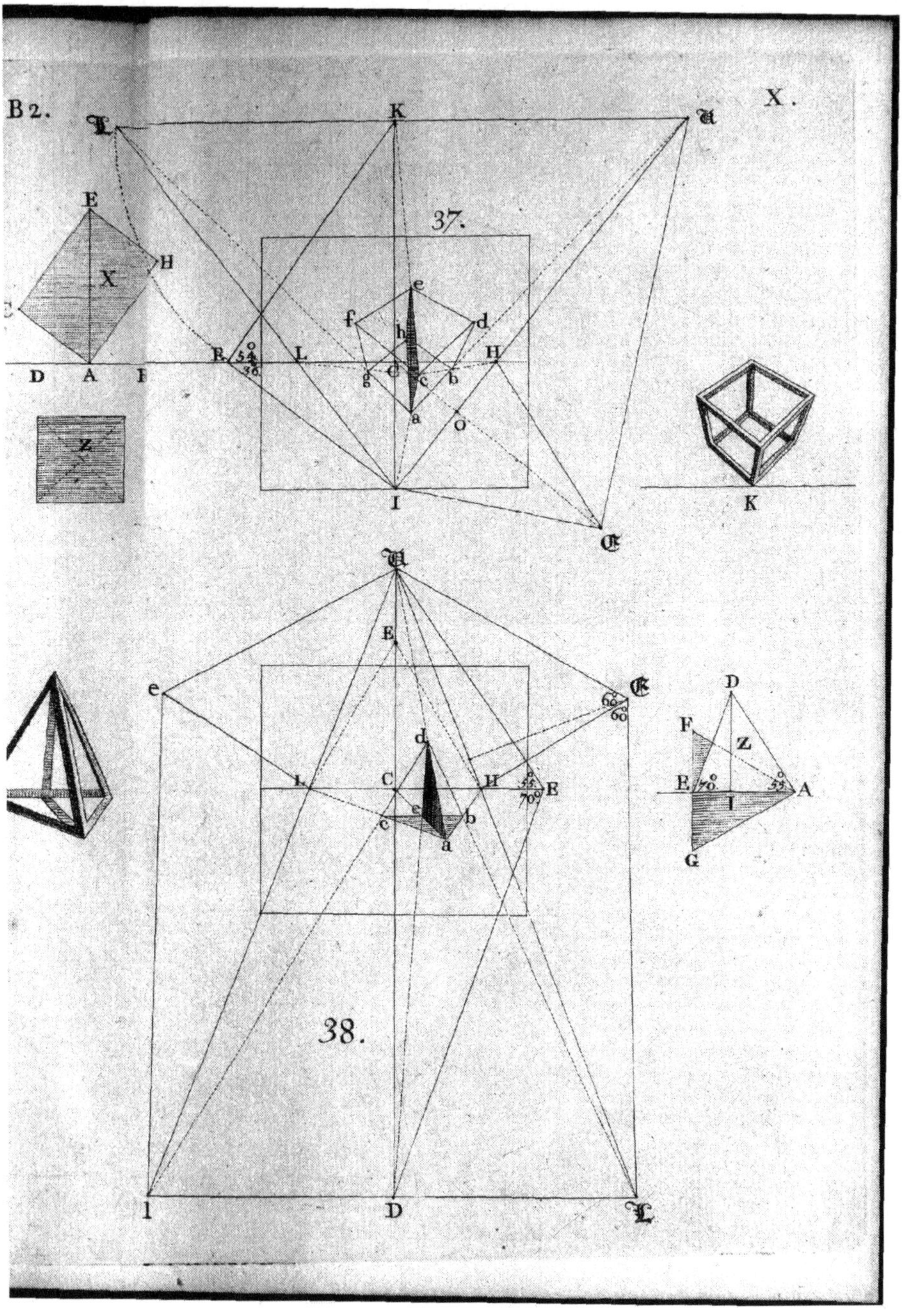
B 2.
X.
37.
38.
X
Z
E
H
D
A
K
I
L
f
d
e
h
g
C
c
b
a
O
Z
F
G
1

39.

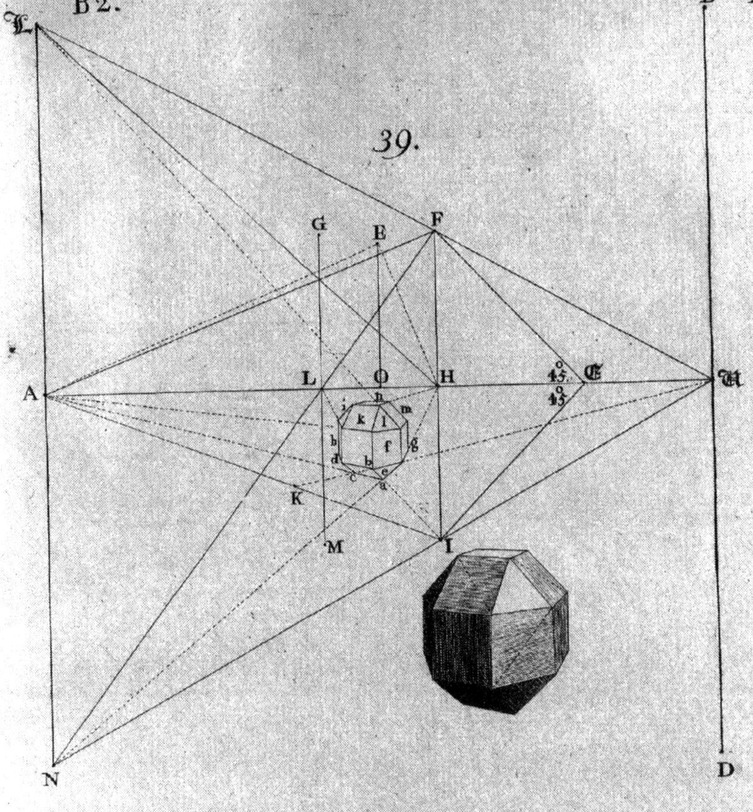

40.

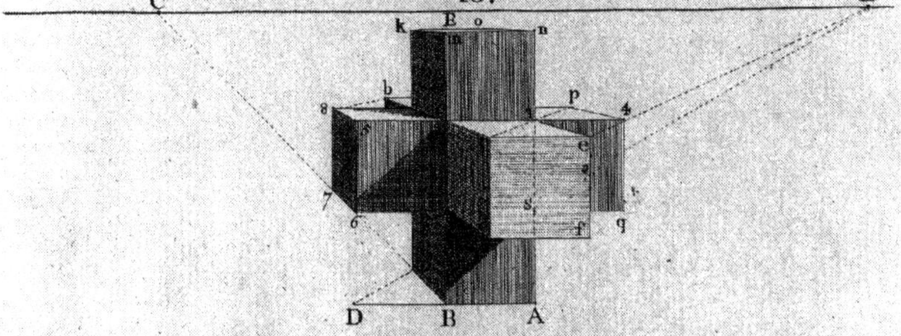

EXAMPLE 6. *To put a double Cross into Perspective.*

Let C be the Center of the Picture, CL the horizontal Line, and LC the Distance of the Eye; and let L be the vanishing Point of the Diagonal of a Square whose Side AB is parallel to the Picture.---Now suppose AB to be the nearest Edge of the Bottom of the Cross,---Continue AB, and make BD equal to it; then from B draw BC, and from D draw DL, cutting BC in a; and from the Points A, B, a, draw the Perpendiculars An, Bm, ak, and make Bm equal to thrice AB; then draw nm parallel to AB, and finish the Top nk; after which, draw 2 3 and s 1 parallel to AB, and continue 2 3 and s 1 on both Sides, at pleasure; then make 3 4 and 2 5 equal to 3 2, and draw 4 q and 5 6 parallel to nA; then from 4, 2, 5, draw Lines to C; and through i draw p 8 parallel to 4 5, and from 6 draw 6 C, then from 8 draw 8 7, parallel to 5 6; which finishes a single Cross. Again, from C draw Lines through 1, 2, 3, at pleasure; and from L draw a Line through 3, cutting cC in c; then draw ce parallel to 3 2, and from e and c draw ef, cd, parallel to 1 2; then from d draw df parallel to ec; finally, from the Corner 8 draw a Line to L, which will cut iC in b, and by that means give the farthest Corner b; from whence the whole Figure may be compleated. Fig. 40.

I have added this last Figure, to shew the vast Ease and Expeditiousness of this Method, preferably to any yet made publick; and I shall have a further Use for it in another Place: However, I will just observe, that there are no more than four Lines in the whole Operation but what are a Part of the Representation itself.

CHAP. III.

The Practice of Perspective abbreviated.

SECT. I.

General Rules, &c.

IN the last Chapter I have given some general Rules, and have explained them by the most useful Examples, so that the whole Practice of Perspective might be deduced therefrom by any one who will consider them with a proper Attention: But lest their Application, in general, should not appear so easy as could be wished, (and to spare the Learner as much Trouble as possible) I shall, in the first Section of this Chapter, collect all the Rules together in their proper Order; and then, in the second Section of this same Chapter, I shall apply them more particularly to common Practice.

Fig. 41. I. *Having one Line* AB *given, whose vanishing Point is out of the Picture, from thence to draw another Line* CD, *which shall tend to the same Point.*

From the Point A draw AC at pleasure, and at any convenient Distance, (the farther the better) draw BD parallel to AC.---Now let AC represent the Corner of any Building, and C the Top of it; and let it be required to draw a Line, as CD, which is supposed parallel to AB.----Make B 6, which is below the horizontal Line, in the same Proportion to 6 D, which is above the horizontal Line, as A 2 is to 2 C; that is, suppose 2 A two equal Parts, and 2 C three equal Parts; then divide the Space 6 B into two equal Parts, and make 6 D equal to three such Parts; and then draw CD, which will, if continued, vanish into the Point E. And by proceeding in the same Ratio, any other Line may be drawn, either above or below the horizontal Line.

1. *When 'tis below the Horizontal Line, to draw a Line, as* 1 5, *which tends to an inaccessible Point* E.

Let AB be the given Line.----Draw A 2, B 6, parallel to each other, and divide them in the same Proportion; thus, let A 2 be divided into two equal Parts, then divide B 6 into two equal Parts also, and a Line, as 1 5, which is drawn through the Points 1, 5, will vanish into E.

2. *When*

2. *When it is above the Horizontal Line, as 4 8.*

Here CD is the Line given, and 'tis required to draw 4 8 in ſuch a manner that it ſhall cut off one-third of the Plane C 2 6 D. Divide 2 C and 6 D each into three Parts, and draw 4 8; which is the Thing propoſed.---Theſe Rules are applied to Practice in the 13th, 21ſt, and 23d Figures.

II. *To make one Line equal to another Line given.*

This may be done by giving a Line, as a c, parallel to the horizontal Line.---For let c H be an indefinite Repreſentation, Part of which is to be cut off equal to a c. From H, ſet off H I equal to H E, and draw a I, which will cut off b c equal to a c.----And ſuppoſe it were required to find the Length of any Line which is in an inclined Plane, then the very ſame Method is to be uſed. Thus, in Fig. 44, let V be the vaniſhing Point of a b, and V L the vaniſhing Line of an inclined Plane, in which a b is ſuppoſed to lye. ---Find the Center C of that vaniſhing Line, and its Diſtance C E; then make V 2 equal to the Diſtance E V of the vaniſhing Point V, and from a, draw a c parallel to the vaniſhing Line V L, and make it equal to the propoſed Length, and then draw 2 c, cutting a V in b; which will give a b equal to a c. Again, to make one Line, d f, equal to another Line c b, which is given. Let H be the vaniſhing Point of c b, and C the vaniſhing Point of d f.---From the Points H and C, deſcribe the Arcs I E, L E; from c draw a c parallel to the horizontal Line; and from I draw a Line through b, cutting a c in a; then is a c equal to c b: For continue a c 'till it cuts C d in d, and make e d equal to a c; then draw e L, which will cut off d f equal to c b. * Fig. 40. Fig. 42.

III. *To cut off a Line in any given Proportion.*

Let a Line be drawn parallel to the horizontal Line, and continued at pleaſure; and let it be required to cut off a c equal to three Feet.---Thro' one End, as a, draw a Line 3 4, cutting the Bottom of the Picture in 4, and the horizontal Line in 3; then ſet off 3 1 equal to the Diſtance 3 E; and from 1 draw a Line through a, cutting the Bottom of the Picture in e; then from e ſet off three Feet upon the Bottom of the Picture, (as e h) and draw h 1, cutting a c in c; ſo will a c be equal to three Feet.---Again, To cut off an oblique Line, as a b, equal to three Feet.---Set off the Diſ- Fig. 43.

* Theſe Methods are applied to practice in ſeveral of the preceding Figures.

tance 3 1, and from e and h draw e 1, h 1, cutting a 3 in a and b; then is a b equal to three Feet.---Or this may be done without taking the whole Distance 3 E: Thus, take half the Distance, as 3 2, and divide the given Line a c in the same Proportion, that is, into two equal Parts, and draw f 2, which will cut off a b equal to a c. After the same Manner, a Line may be divided into any Number of Parts, or be made of any given Length; for by setting the real Proportions upon the Bottom of the Picture, it may serve as a general Scale for regulating the apparent Size of any Perspective Representation: Thus, a b, or a c, may be divided into three Parts each, or three Feet, by dividing e h, and then drawing Lines to 1, in the above Manner.---These Rules are particularly applied to Practice in the 18th, 19th, and 20th Figures.

What is here said in regard to the cutting off Lines in any given Proportion, when those Lines vanish into the horizontal Line, is equally applicable to Lines in all Kinds of inclined Planes. For let VL be a vanishing Line of an inclined Plane, and V the
Fig. 44. vanishing Point of a Line a b in that Plane.---Continue V a to the Bottom of the Picture in B, and from B draw AB parallel to the vanishing Line VL, and continue it at pleasure; then, upon this Line AB set off the several Measures, as if it were the Bottom of the Picture, and consider VL as the horizontal Line, C as the Center of the Picture, and CE as its Distance; and then the Operation will be the same as in the last Figure.---This also is applied to Practice in the 34th Figure.

IV. *Having sketched-in the proposed Size for an Object upon the Picture, to prove whether it be diminished in Proportion to its Distance.*

Fig. 45. Let a b represent the Height of an Object.-----From any Point, as H, in the horizontal Line, draw Lines through the Extremities a and b of the Figure, and from C, where the lowest Line cuts the Bottom of the Picture, draw the Perpendicular C B; then make this Line a Scale, the same as if it was the Bottom of the Picture; and that will shew whether the Figure be in Proportion for the Place it possesses in the Picture, or not: Thus, suppose the Height is 20 Feet; then g f is too much, and c d too little. Thus again, sup-
Fig. 46. pose the Object to be a House, I say, its Height a b may be proportioned to its Distance by the above Rule. Thus, continue the Edge a b upwards at pleasure, and from the vanishing Point C, of the End, draw C b through the Top of the Roof, cutting a b in b; then is a b the whole Height of the House; therefore from a and b draw

draw two Lines parallel to the horizontal Line, and continue them at pleasure; then any where from the Bottom of the Picture draw a Perpendicular, as 1 2, and to any Point 5 in the horizontal Line draw 1 5 cutting 3a in 3, and from 3 draw the Line 3 4 parallel to 1 2, cutting b 4 in 4; finally, from 5 draw a Line through the Point 4, cutting 1 2 in 2; and then is 1 2 the real Height of the House, which being measured by a Scale of Feet, will shew whether the House be in proportion, or not, to its Distance.----This is likewise applied to Practice in a b c d, Fig. 18.

V. *To find the Length of any Representation by Calculation only.*

Let AB be a real Line whose Representation is sought, and CE the Distance of the Eye; which, in this Case, is parallel to AB.----Make B a in the same Proportion to C a, as AB (the real Line) is to CE, the Distance of the Eye: Thus, let AB be two Parts, and CE three Parts (or, if you please, so many Feet;) then divide AC into five equal Parts, and the Representation Ba of BA, will be two of those Parts; that is, as 2 is to 3: For draw AE, which will determine the Representation of AB, as in the 5th Figure. In like Manner, ec is to cC, as 2 is to 3; or, if you please, ec is to the whole Line eC, as 2 is to 5. And so also for any oblique Line, as DF: For Dd is to dL, as DF is to LE. Or this may be determined, without taking the whole Distance, by Analogy. Thus, half the Distance of CE, as C 1, and half the Length of AB, as A 2, will come to the same thing; for draw 2·1, and it will pass through the Point a.---The next Figure is a farther Explanation of the same thing, but by a different Method. Fig. 47.

VI. *To find the Distance of the Picture from having two vanishing Points of a Square given.*

Let VL be the horizontal Line, C the Center of the Picture, and V, L, the vanishing Points of the Square.---Divide VL into two equal Parts, in A, and with the Distance AV describe the Semicircle VEL; then from C draw the Perpendicular CE, cutting the Semi-circle in E; and then is CE the Distance of the Picture. For draw VE, LE, and they will make a right Angle at E. Fig. 49

VII. *To find the vanishing Lines of any inclined Plane, and their proper vanishing Points, together with the Center and Distance of those vanishing Lines.*

1. *When the Plane is inclined to the Ground, but has some of its Sides parallel to the Picture, like* a c d e. *Fig.* 31.

In this Case, the Rules are laid down and fully explained by that Figure.

2. *When*

2. *When the Plane is not only inclined to the Ground, but has all its Sides oblique with the Picture, like* a b d e. *Fig.* 34.

In this Figure alſo the Rules are fully explained. And theſe are all the Rules which are neceſſary in common Practice, as I have obſerved before; nevertheleſs, to aſſiſt the Curious, I have added the following Figure.

Fig. 50. VIII. *Having given one Side of any inclined Plane, at pleaſure, together with its vaniſhing Point, and the vaniſhing Line of that Plane, thence to determine the whole Repreſentation.*

Let VU be a vaniſhing Line given, and ſuppoſe V the vaniſhing Point of one Edge of a Square, (as ae, Fig. 36) and let C be the Center of the Picture, and CE its Diſtance.----From V, the given vaniſhing Point, draw a Line through the Center of the Picture, as VD, and continue it at pleaſure; then from C draw CI perpendicular to VD, and make CI equal to the Diſtance CE, and from V draw VI, then from I draw Ic perpendicular to VI, cutting VD in c; and parallel to IC draw LU, cutting VU in U; then is UL the vaniſhing Line of a Plane perpendicular to that Plane, whoſe vaniſhing Line is VU; that is, VU and LU, in this Figure, are the ſame as 𝔘L and 𝔏L in the 36th Figure, where the Plane a b c d is perpendicular to the Plane a d f e. Again, Suppoſe the Angle which another Plane made with the Plane whoſe vaniſhing Line is VU, was a different Angle (ſuppoſe 60 Degrees) and it was required to find its vaniſhing Line.--- Then, as before, draw a Line VD through the Center C of the Picture, and find the vaniſhing Line LU of a Plane perpendicular to that Plane, whoſe vaniſhing Line is VU; after which, continue cD at pleaſure, and make cD equal to the Diſtance Ic of the vaniſhing Line LU; then draw DU, with which make an Angle at D equal to 60 Degrees, and draw D𝔏; finally, draw V𝔏; and then will V𝔏 be the vaniſhing Line propoſed.---Again, to find the Center and Diſtance of a vaniſhing Line.---From the Center of the Picture, draw a Line perpendicular to any vaniſhing Line, which will give the Center of that vaniſhing Line: Thus, CH and Cc are perpendicular to VU and LU, and therefore H and c are the Centers of thoſe Lines.----Again, for the Diſtance of a vaniſhing Line.----Upon the Perpendicular Cc, and at the Center C, draw another Perpendicular CI, and make CI equal to the real Diſtance CE; then draw Ic, which will be the Diſtance of the vaniſhing Line

Line LU, which being transferred into Cc continued, as cD, will give the proper Distance to be work'd with.

IX. *The following is a Method for finding the Representation of the Plan of any Building, &c. when the Distance to be work'd with is not greater than from the Center to one Corner of the Picture, as* CE. Fig. 51.

Draw CE; perpendicular to which, draw K through C; which consider as the Bottom of the Picture. Under K draw out the real Figure in its proper Situation, as ABC; then from the transposed Place of the Eye, draw Lines parallel to the several Sides of the Figure, which will give H and I for the vanishing Points of those Sides, and which are to be transposed into the horizontal Line, as H and L; after which, draw the Perpendicular CM, and from M set off the several Distances CF, CG, *&c.* upon the Bottom of the Picture; and then, by drawing Lines to the proper vanishing Point of each Line, as in the Figure, the whole Representation may be compleated, exactly in the same Manner as if the original Figure had been drawn out under the Picture.

In the next Place, I shall shew how to determine the Appearance of those Sorts of Objects which most frequently occur in common Practice; for this will explain more fully the Use of the preceding Rules, and at the same Time, will shew the Shortness and Expeditiousness of this Method of Perspective. And as I have by former Examples, so I shall likewise, in the next Section, make use of such Objects as are simple in their Parts, and of the most general Use. To explain my self more fully. A Pedestal, for instance, is but one Part of an Order in Architecture, and the Idea we have of it is, of its being the Base, or Support, of a Column; but by enlarging the Idea of a Pedestal to that of a large square Building, enriched with Mouldings, *&c.* we may then consider it as such a Building; and therefore, we may conceive, that the same Rules by which the Appearance of a Pedestal is determined upon the Picture, will serve for finding the Representation of any Building which is similar to it. In like manner, as to the Situation of Objects which are perpendicular to the Ground, (such as the Walls of Buildings, and the like) they must be either perpendicular to the Picture, parallel to the Picture, or oblique with it; as we have shewn before: And therefore, one Example in each Situation, adapted in a general Manner, will be of much more Service than ten thousand different Schemes by way of Examples; for the one fixes

fixes our Attention to a particular Set of useful and general Ideas, but the other distracts the Mind with Confusion and Obscurity.

The same Arguments will appear equally true, if we apply them to the particular Parts of any Building, such as Columns, Mouldings, and the like. For, first, in regard to Columns; by this Method, we have no Regard to Plans, Elevations, &c. and therefore, it matters not where we begin the Operation, whether at the Top, the Bottom, or at the Middle of it; so that one Rule also in this Case will appear to be universal: And in respect to Mouldings, they must be either plain or curvilinear, either above or below the Eye; and therefore, one Rule in either Case will be sufficient for our Purpose. The same may be said of every other Example in this Section; but what has been said already, will, I hope, be sufficient to explain the Sense of the following Figures, and to silence any Objections which may be made against my not having swell'd my Work with more ornamental Schemes, or, as they are generally called, Curious Examples.

The first Example which I shall produce, is the TUSCAN PEDESTAL, in order to shew how to find the Representation of strait Mouldings, when they are either parallel, perpendicular, or oblique with the Picture, or when they are either above or below the Eye. In the 52d Figure one Side is parallel to the Picture, the other perpendicular to it; and in the 53d Figure, both Sides are oblique with the Picture.

SECT. II.

The foregoing Rules of Perspective more particularly applied to common Practice.

I. *To put a* TUSCAN PEDESTAL *into Perspective.*

1. *When one of its Sides is parallel to the Picture, then the other Side will be perpendicular to it; so that one Rule will do in both Cases.*

Fig. 52. LET AB represent the Bottom of the Plinth in Front.---Now, from this one Line AB, the Appearance of the whole Pedestal may be found: For continue AB at pleasure, and draw a Line IK perpendicular thereto, and make IK equal to the Height of the Pedestal; then, upon IK, draw the Capital and Base in their proper Proportions: This being done, continue Lines from each Moulding,

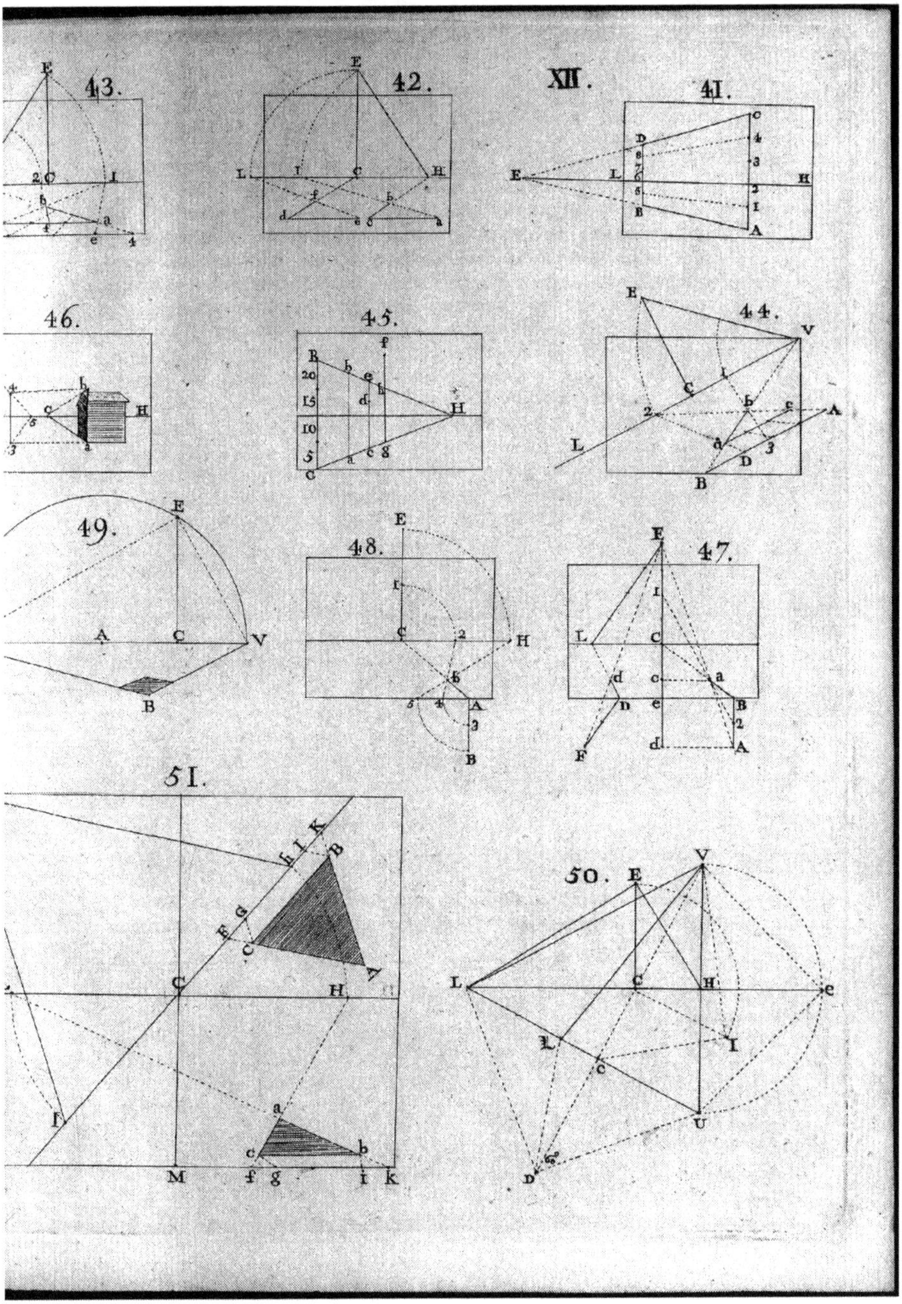
XII.
41.
42.
43.
44.
45.
46.
47.
48.
49.
50.
51.

Moulding, which will form ſeveral Rectangles, and thereby divide the Planes 1 2 3 4, 5 6 7 8, into a Sort of Net-Work; then, by putting theſe Planes into Perſpective (as in the Figure) we ſhall have ſufficient Guides for drawing all the Mouldings. But to be more particular in the Operation.----Make AD equal to AB, and cut off AE equal to AD; from whence the Plinth may be compleated.---In like Manner, for the Die.---Draw the Diagonals upon the Top of the Plinth, and any where upon the Edge hg, ſet off the Projection of the Plinth, as 1 9; then draw one Line from 1 to C, and another Line from 9 to L, which will give the Projection 1 2; then, if you draw a Line through 2 parallel to hg, it will cut the Diagonals ah, bg, and give the Corners of the Front Side; and if you draw a Line from b to C, it will cut the Diagonal dc, and give the further Corners; therefore, by drawing Perpendiculars from a, b, c, we ſhall have all the Edges of the Die which can appear in this Situation.---As to the Height of the Die, or the Height of the ſeveral Mouldings, they may be found by drawing a Perpendicular from the neareſt Corner of the Repreſentation, as BH, and transferring thereon the ſeveral Heights from IK, as in the Figure; then by drawing Lines from the ſeveral Points upon BH (which meaſures the Height of each Moulding) to the vaniſhing Point of the Diagonal ah, we ſhall have thoſe Heights tranſferred unto the Edge am of the Die; thus ai and km are the Heights of the Baſe and Cornice; ſo that by finding the Appearance of the Planes 1 2 3 4, 5 6 7 8, and drawing the Mouldings therein, and by drawing the triangular Planes at the Corners, we may finiſh the whole Repreſentation with the utmoſt Eaſe and Expedition.

But before we begin to draw out any Object in Perſpective, we muſt firſt conſider, whether the Whole, or only a Part of it, is to appear; and muſt ſketch out the Size we intend it ſhall be of, or, at leaſt, give one Line for its greateſt Dimenſion. Thus, if the whole Pedeſtal is to appear, then give AB, which is neareſt the Eye, and call it the utmoſt Length of the Plinth: But if only the Top is to appear, then give HO, and call it the utmoſt Extent of the Cornice; then, by cutting off Or equal to OM, that is, equal to OH, we ſhall have the Depth Or of the Cornice, *&c.* from whence, and with the Aſſiſtance of the Plane 5 6 7 8, (which is found exactly in the ſame Manner as the Plane 1 2 3 4) we may compleat the whole that is wanted.

Now, in order to do all this, it is neceſſary that the Artiſt ſhould (as was obſerved before) be able to apply the preceding Rules with the greateſt Readineſs; particularly That which teaches how to cut off one Line equal to another Line given.

2. *When both Sides are oblique with the Picture.*

Fig. 53. In this Figure, let A be the neareſt Corner of the Plinth, AC, AB, the Length of two Sides AG, AF, and Ak the Height of the whole Pedeſtal properly divided; (that is, like BH in the laſt Figure.)---Cut off AF, AG, equal to AB, AC, and draw the Plinth and the Diagonals upon the upper Square; then draw 1 b parallel to AB, and make it equal to the Projection of the Plinth; then cut off 1 c equal to 1 b, and from c draw Lines to H, and from 1 draw a Line to C, (the vaniſhing Point of the Diagonal 1 2) which cutting each other in 2, will give the Edge 2 7; and by drawing Lines from 2 to their proper vaniſhing Points L and H, they will cut the Diagonal kg, and thereby give the other Corners of the Die, as in the Figure.----For the Height of the Mouldings; draw Lines from 4 and 5 to C, which will cut 2 7 in the Points required; by which means the triangular Planes a i k, f b g, *&c.* may be found, and from thence the Mouldings may be compleated.

Here alſo, if we want only the upper Part, we may begin at the Point 8, making 8E, 8D, each equal to the Length of the Cap, *&c.* then, by finding the Plane 5 6 7 8, as in the former Caſe, we ſhall have ſufficient Guides for compleating the Figure.

Here let us obſerve, that when the Pedeſtal has one Side parallel to the Picture, then the Plane 1 2 3 4, (Fig. 52) which is a Guide for the Moulding, may be begun any where upon the Edge a b: But when it is oblique with the Picture, then we muſt begin from the neareſt Corner, as a; and by attending to the Figures, we may conceive, that in the firſt Caſe, the Mouldings in the Directing Plane, are like the Ends of Mouldings cut off ſquare; but in the latter Caſe, they are like Mouldings cut off at what is called the Mitre Joint. And from hence we may alſo obſerve, that all the Difficulty in putting Mouldings into Perſpective, lies in finding the little Planes 1 2 3 4, *&c.* and therefore the Reader ſhould conſider them attentively before he proceeds any farther.

II. *Of*

II. *Of* CIRCULAR MOULDINGS, *&c.*

The Method for determining the Appearance of Circular Mouldings, is much the ſame as that for finding the Repreſentation of ſtraight Mouldings, *viz.* by imagining a Plane to paſs through the Mouldings in a perpendicular Manner, and then putting that Plane into Perſpective: As in the two laſt Figures.

1. *To put a* TUSCAN BASE *into Perſpective.*

Give one Line for the Width of the Plinth, and draw out the proper Projection of the Mouldings, and the Plane ABCD; then cut off the oblique Side equal to the Front, and compleat the Plinth; after which, draw the Diameters and the Diagonals upon the Top of the Plinth, as in the Figure; and then draw the Repreſentation of a Circle for the Seat of the lower Torus. Again, for the Bottom of the Shaft of the Column; from the Center H of the Column, draw the Perpendicular HL, and from a, where the Diameter ae cuts the Plinth, draw ad parallel to H; then make ad equal to the Height of the Mouldings AD, and from d draw a Line to C, which will cut HL in I; then will I be the Center of the Square for the Bottom of the Column: Therefore, upon the upper Edge of the Plinth, and from the Point a, make a 1 equal to the whole Projection of the Mouldings; then cut off ab equal to a 1, and draw bc parallel to ad, which will give the little Plane for the Mouldings; within which draw the Mouldings; and then we ſhall perceive that c is the Middle of the neareſt Edge of the upper Square: Therefore, through c draw a Line EF parallel to the Edge B 1 of the Plinth; then from H draw a Line through the Center 1, cutting EF in E, and then is cE half the Width of the Square: Therefore make cF equal to cE, and from thence compleat the Square, and within it draw the Repreſentation of the Circle, as in the Figure: Finally, from the Extremity of each Circle draw the two oblique Lines 2, 3, which together with the little Plane for the Mouldings, *&c.* will be ſufficient Guides for compleating the whole Baſe, as was propoſed; which is evident by inſpecting the Figures 57 and 59. Fig. 54.

As for making Columns, *&c.* of any given Proportion, or at any Diſtance; the Rule for cutting of a Line in any given Proportion, in the 43d Figure, is ſufficient for that Purpoſe.

2. *To put a* TUSCAN CAPITAL *into Perspective.*

Fig. 55. Let K be the Center of the Square for the Bottom of the Capital.---Through K draw a Line AB parallel to the horizontal Line at pleasure, and from f and e of the Base, draw Lines parallel to the Axis HI of the Column, cutting the above Line in E and F; then is EF the Diameter of the Column: Therefore diminish it in its proper Proportion, as 3 4; then is 3 4 the Diameter of the Neck of the Column: Therefore with the Line 3 4 draw the Appearance of a Square, and in that Square draw the Representation of a Circle as before directed; so shall we have a Guide for the under Part of the Capital. Again, make KI equal to KF, (that is, equal to Half the Diameter of the Column) and through I draw GH parallel to AB, then make IG, IH, each equal to KA, or KB, (that is, equal to Half the Diameter of the Top of the Abacus) and then with the Line GH draw the Appearance of another Square, which will represent the Top of the Abacus: Finally, from C draw a Line through I, cutting the Edge 5 6 in a, and from a set off a 1 for the Projection of the Capital, and draw the little Plane abcd for the Mouldings, as before: From whence the remaining Part of the Capital may be compleated, as in the 56th and 59th Figures*.

I shall just mention a Method for finding the Point where the Diagonal of a Square will be cut by a Circle inscribed in that Square; which may be of use in this and some other Cases. It is
Fig. 54. this: Divide the Edge BG into seven equal Parts; then set one Part from each Corner, as B4, G5, and draw Lines to C, which will cut the Diagonals in the Points required. I do not say, this is mathematically exact, but, I presume, it is near enough for the intended Purpose.

These are the most simple, as well as the most general Methods I can think of for mix'd Mouldings; and I believe any Person who is but tolerably skilled in Drawing, will find them sufficient for his Purpose, upon all Occasions.

3. *To find the Representation of a* CORINTHIAN CAPITAL.

Fig. 62. Let AB be the Diameter of the under Part of the Capital, and let ca be the Center, or Axis, of the Capital, properly divided for the Height of its Leaves, Volutes, and Abacus.---From the Line

* In this Case the Projection of the Capital, (according to Mr. *Gibbs*, from whose Book I have taken my Proportions) is one sixth Part of its Length, and the Projections of any other Mouldings may be determined in the same easy Manner by a Scale and Compasses.

AB,

AB, which is given, find the Appearance of a Square, in which, draw the Diameters and Diagonals, and then the Repreſentation of the Circle; which will determine the Places for the Stalks of the great Leaves, as repreſented by the Dots: Again, through o draw b d parallel to AB, and make ob, od, each equal to half the under Part of the Abacus; with which Line bd, draw the Appearance of another Square, and divide it like the Plan 1 2 3 4, Fig. Z. of the under Part of the Abacus, and then draw the Repreſentation of it, as in the Figure: Again, through a, draw another Line parallel to bd, and make it equal to the upper Part of the Abacus; then, by finding the Repreſentation of the Square a b c d, Fig. Z, we may draw the Appearance of the upper Part of the Abacus, and from thence compleat the Abacus, as in the 60th Figure: Finally, find the Middle of each Face of the Abacus, as n, e, and draw Lines n 1, *&c.* to the correſponding Points at the Bottom of the Capital; then find the Height of the Leaves by drawing Lines from C through the Dots in c a, 'till they cut 1 n in 2 and 3; after which draw the Baſket; then, by a nice Eye, compleat the Capital; beginning as is exemplified in the 60th Figure.—The Lines drawn from the Corners of the upper and under Square, will ſerve as Guides to prevent our giving the Leaves too much Projection. In Fig. 61, the Capital is compleated, and the Figures X and Z are added to explain the Thing more fully; one of which is the Plan, and the other Half the Profile of a Capital.

Here it is neceſſary to take Notice, that upon Account of bringing the Diſtance of the Picture within the Compaſs of each Plate, and to make the Figures as large as poſſible, ſome of them have not that agreeable Shape which could be wiſhed; but if the Reader will chooſe a greater Diſtance, and follow theſe Rules, he will find every Objection of this kind, that may ariſe, immediately vaniſh.

III. *Of* Columns *parallel and oblique with the Eye.*

1. *Let it be required to find the Appearance of two Columns in Front, and let* a b *be the Diameter of the under Part of the Plinth, and* c *the Center of the Column.* Fig. 63.

Continue a b at pleaſure, and any where upon it, as at A, draw a Line AB perpendicular to Ab; upon which Line ſet the ſeveral Heights for the Baſe, Capital, Entablature, *&c.* then from c, the Center of the Column, draw a Line c d parallel to AB, and

and from the ſeveral Diviſions upon AB, draw Lines parallel to the horizontal Line, which will cut cd, and give the Heights of the Baſe, Capital, and Entablature. Now, having got the ſeveral Heights, we are to conſider cd as the Axis of the Column, (that is, a Line which paſſes through the Middle of it) and then at every Dot make a Square, equal to the Diameter of that Part of the Column, *&c.* which that Dot ſtands for: Thus ab is the under Part of the Plinth, and by means of H, and the Diagonal 12, we may compleat the firſt Square. So alſo, r is the Square for the Bottom of the Shaft, p for where the Column begins to diminiſh, t for the Top of the Shaft, and v for the Top of the Abacus; and therefore, having got theſe ſeveral Squares, we ſhall have ſufficient Guides for compleating a Column of any Order. Again, for the other parallel Column ex.---From c to e, and upon the Line AB continued, ſet off the Diſtance which the Center of one Column is from the other, and draw ex; upon which, ſet off the ſeveral Heights, as before, from the Line AB, and then find the ſeveral Squares, as before directed.

2. *For oblique Columns.*

Upon AB continued, ſet off the Diſtance which the Centers of thoſe Columns are from the Center of the Corner Column, and draw a Line from e to C; then cut off em, en, equal to ef, eg, and from the oblique Sides of the Square e, draw Lines to C; from whence the other Squares m and n may be compleated, as before.---For their Heights,--Draw mo and nq, parallel to ex, and from x draw xC, which will give their ſeveral Heights.

Now, if we would put an Entablature over the Columns; then the Height of the Architrave, Freeze, and Cornice, may be drawn from their reſpective Diviſions, upon the Line AB; and the Appearance of the Mouldings peculiar to each Part, may be found by the Rules already laid down for that Purpoſe. Or, they may be found thus,--Let agbf, in the Figure Z, repreſent the upper Part of the Capital x belonging to the corner Column; and we want to find the Corner of its Entablature; that is, the Corner of the lower Facia, or Freeze:--Set off the Projection of the Capital from n to e, and draw a Line to C, which will cut the Diagonal ab, and give the Corner of the Facia; ſo that by drawing the Line l from the Dot in the Diagonal, we ſhall have the Corner propoſed. In like Manner the Projection of the Cornice may be found. Continue 70 (which meaſures its Height) at pleaſure, and make

oh

o h equal to the real Projection of the Cornice; then through h draw a Line from C, and from H draw a Line through o; and where it cuts C h continued in i, will be the Corner of the Cornice, *&c.*

From hence then it is evident, that any Number of Columns may be drawn with the greatest Ease and Expedition, let their Situations be what they will; and from hence also we may observe, that any Part of a Column may be immediately produced upon the Picture in the very Place in which it is intended, without drawing out the Whole, or any other Part than that which is really to appear.

Here it may not be improper to take Notice of what we have observed in Chap. VI. Book I. concerning the Representations of parallel Columns, which, we observed, would grow bigger and bigger the further they are removed from the Center of the Picture; and to point out a Method to be practised by those who are satisfied with the Reasons upon that Head; and by that Means, to give all the Columns an agreeable Shape. It is this :----First find Fig. 63. the Representation of that Column which is nearest the Center of the Picture, as e x; then set off the Distance for the Centers of the other Columns, and draw the Squares for the Plinth, Capital, *&c.* and then, upon each Side of the Axis, set off at the Bottom of each Column Half the Diameter of the corner Column, and at the Top of the Column set off Half the Width of the Neck of the corner Column: Finally, draw Lines from thence, so as to diminish the Column in a proper Manner; and thereby we may make all the Columns that are parallel to the Eye of the same Bigness. As to the great Projection of their several Bases, they will not look at all preposterous, if they are done by any one who has but a tolerable Eye for Drawing, and is careful in taking a proper Distance for the Eye.

IV. *Of* STAIRS *parallel and oblique.*

1. *For* PARALLEL STAIRS.

Let AB be the Length of one Step, B 1 its Height, B 4 its Fig. 64. Depth, C the Center of the Picture, and CH the Distance of the Picture.---Find the first Step by the Height B 1, and its Depth B 4; then make 4 O equal to 4 B, and 1 D equal to 1 B; by which means the upper Step may be found. Now, by continuing B O, and BD, and by dividing them properly, any Number of Stairs may be determined. Or, if only those above the Eye are to be seen, then

then begin with the Line a b c, and proceed in the aforesaid Manner.

2. *For* OBLIQUE STAIRS.

Fig. 65. Let AB be the Length, BO the Depth of two Steps, BD the Height of two Steps, and C the Center of the Picture.---By means of the Points H, L, cut off B a, B F, *&c.* equal to B A, BO, *&c.* then by making BD equal to the Height of the Steps, they may be compleated, as in the Figure: And after the same Manner the Stair above the Eye is to be found.

V. *Of an* ARCH *and* PEDIMENT.

1. *For the* ARCH.

Fig. 66. Let A be the Corner of the Arch.---Set the several Divisions for the Width and Center of the Arch upon A B, and for its Height upon the Edge A 1, and draw Lines to C; by which means the parallelogram c d e f may be found, which will be a Guide for drawing the Arch.

2. *For the* PEDIMENT.

Let a b D be the Pitch of the Pediment, and C D the Distance of the Picture.---Find the vanishing Points V and L, and draw Lines from thence through the Top and Bottom of the Cornice; which will intersect each other, and give the Representation of the Pediment.

VI. *Of* HOUSES *parallel and oblique.*

1. *For* PARALLEL HOUSES.

Fig. 67. Let A B, and B F, be the Length and Depth of the House, BD the Height of the Walls, and C the Center of the Picture.---Draw the vanishing Line V L, and find the vanishing Points V, L, of the Roof; then draw V L parallel to the horizontal Line, which will be the vanishing Line of that Part of the Roof which fronts the Eye. And the Roof which covers the Pediment b d e is found by drawing the perpendicular a b, and, from the Extremities thereof, Lines to C and V, which will give a Triangle a b c, whose Side c b is the Top of the Roof.---Or the Height of the Roof 3 4 D, may be found by continuing BE, and making D E equal to the proposed Height.

2. *For* HOUSES *that are* OBLIQUE.

Fig. 68. In this Figure A B is the Depth, and A C the Length of the House, V I is the vanishing Line of the End, and V, I, are the vanishing

nishing Points of the Roof; the vanishing Line of the Pediment, *&c.* is v l, and its vanishing Points v and l; the Length of the Roof over the Pediment is found by means of the Triangle a b c, as before.

VII. *To put the Inside of a Room into Perspective.*

Let ADFE be a Picture upon which the Inside of a Room is to be drawn.---Here C is the Center of the Picture, and AB the Length of the Room.---Set off the several Divisions from A to B, and cut off the several Spaces upon A 1 equal to those upon AD; then set off the Heights upon AE, and draw Lines to C; which will be sufficient for our Purpose. Fig. 69.

If any Representation of this Kind is to be drawn upon a Wall, so as to make a Deception like the Continuance of a Room, Care must be taken to choose a proper Distance, and to make the Height of the horizontal Line exactly equal to the Height of the Eye, *viz.* about five Feet six Inches. If the Wall be too large for any Distance that can be taken within the Room, then some other Subject must be painted upon it, such as will admit of its being divided into Frames, Compartments, or the like: And the same may be said in regard to Cielings; for, in either Case, if the Distance be an improper one, all the Representations will have a bad Effect.

These Examples are the most general I can think of; and I flatter myself, that they will be found sufficient to answer every Design which can be proposed in common Practice: But if there should appear any Difficulty in applying the aforesaid Rules upon some extraordinary Occasions (as when the Design consists of many Parts, or when it happens that any of the vanishing Points are out of the Picture) then the best Way will be to draw out the whole Design, by Way of Model, in a small Compass, upon Paper, and from thence, by a proper Scale, or by Net-Work, to transfer the whole unto the real Picture; for then the most distant vanishing Points may be very easily come at. Or in many Cases, the real Picture may either be laid flat upon a Floor; or else have Rules made to fix upon the back Part of the straining Frame by Screws, or some such Contrivance, whereby, and with the Assistance of small Twine fixed upon Pins at each vanishing Point, we may produce almost every Representation which can be desired.

The three following Figures I have not only given as Examples in Perſpective, but have attempted to diſpoſe each Object in ſuch a Manner as to produce agreeable Shapes, Effect, *&c.*---The firſt repreſents a Variety of Figures tending to various vaniſhing Points in the horizontal Line, below the horizontal Line and above it; amongſt which, are the five regular Solids; and the whole together, contains all the Rules and Principles of Perſpective. The next Figure is a View of *Framlingham* Caſtle in *Suffolk*, a Place of great Antiquity, and formerly the Seat of the *Howards*, *Mowbrays*, *&c.* which is produced in this Place as an Example of a Building that tends to ſeveral vaniſhing Points upon the horizontal Line only: And the laſt Figure is an Example of a Landſkip, by a very great Genius in that Way.

52.

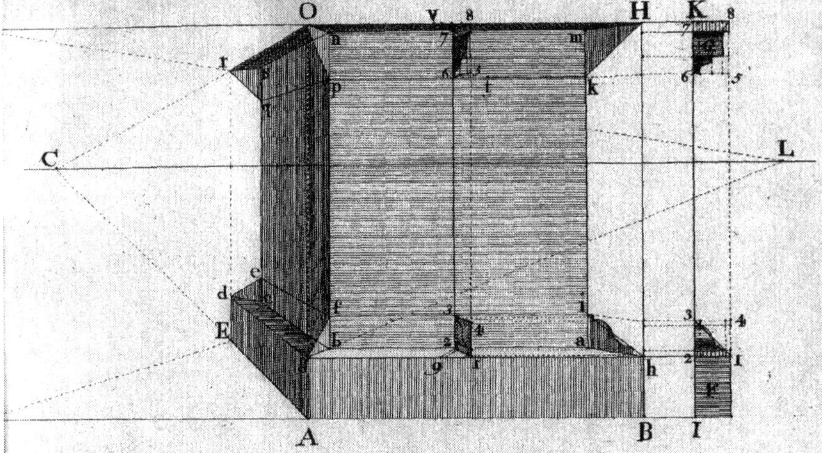

53.

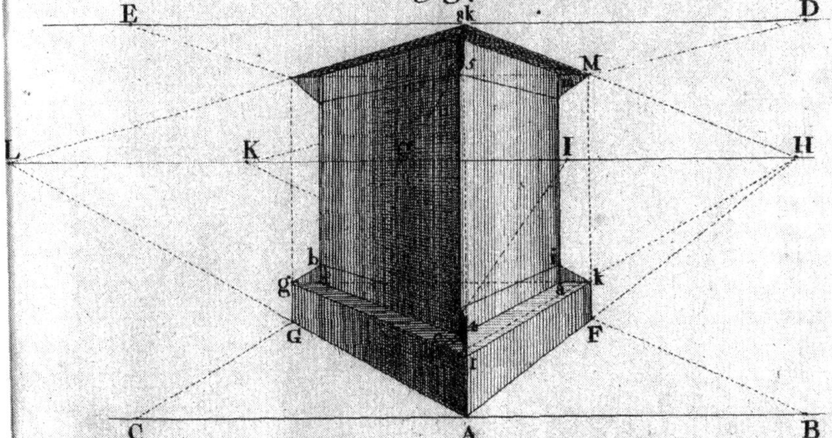

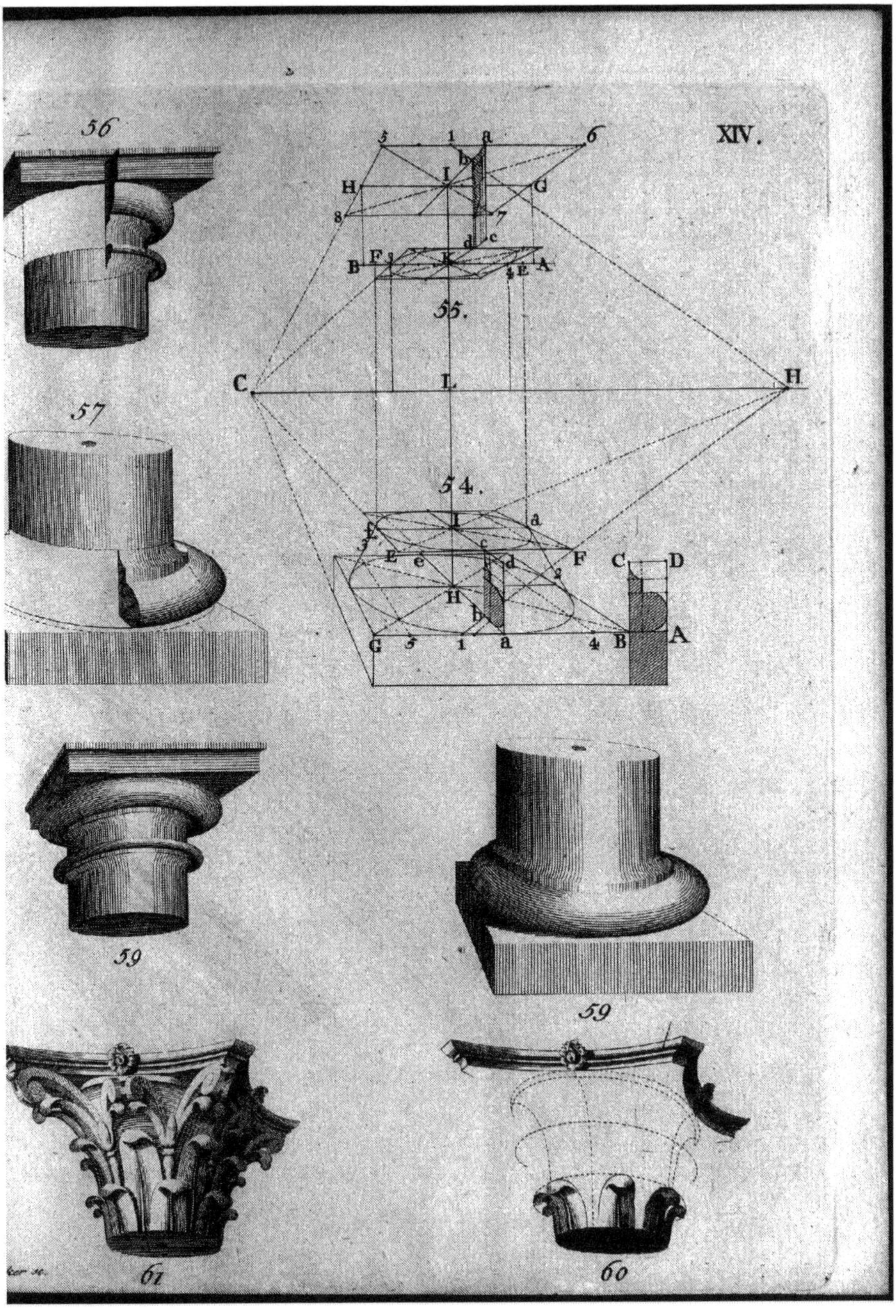
XIV.
56
57
55.
54.
59
59
61
60
5 1 a 6
b I H G 8 7
d c B F K E A
C L H
f I a E e c d F C D
H b A
G 5 1 a 4 B

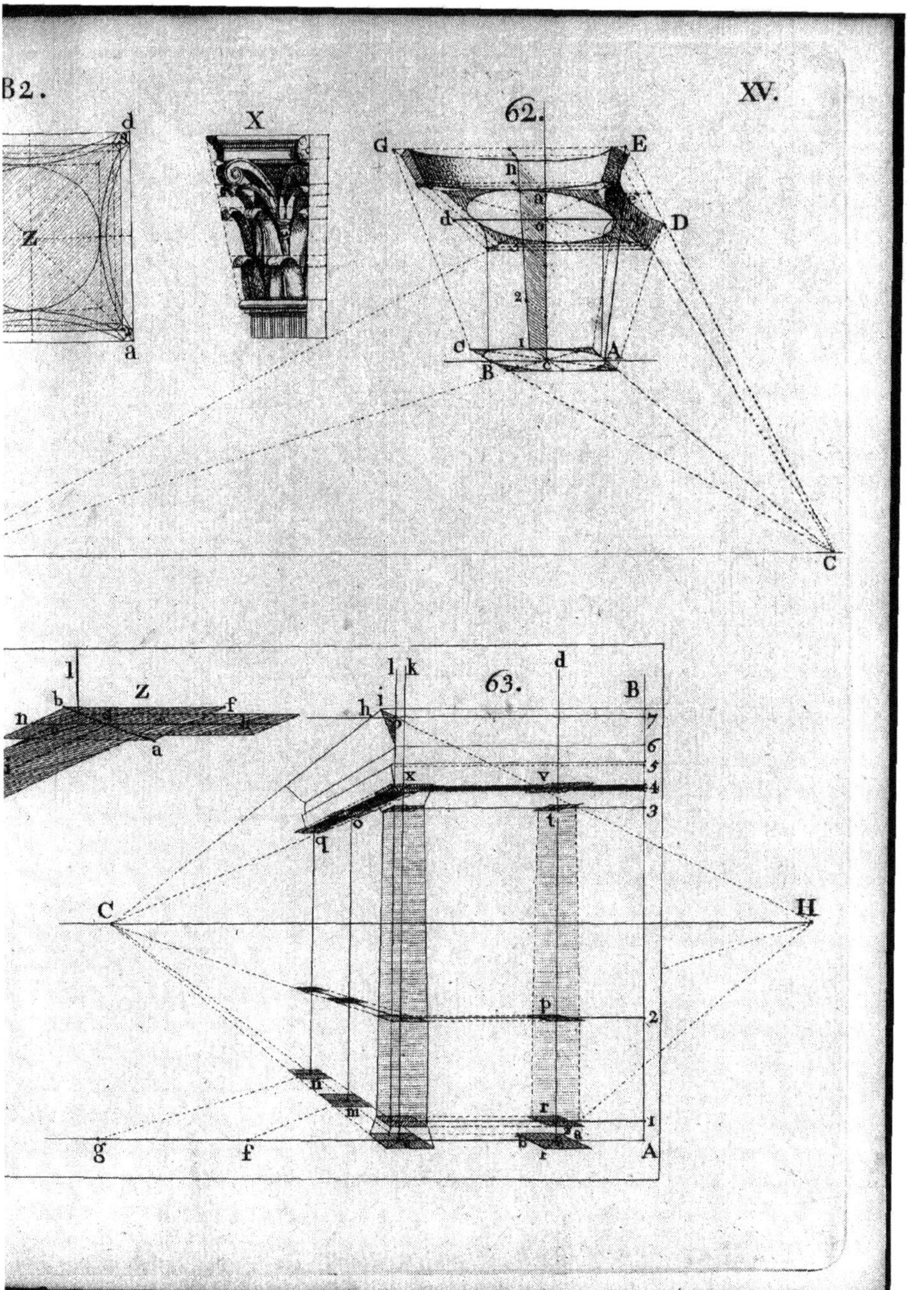

B2.
XV.
X
62.
63.

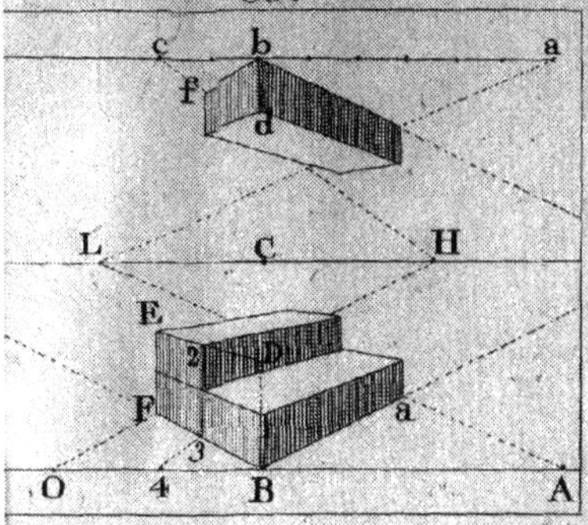

65.

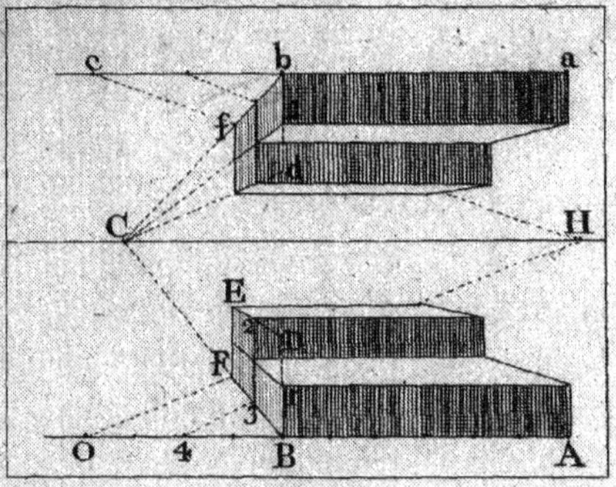

64.

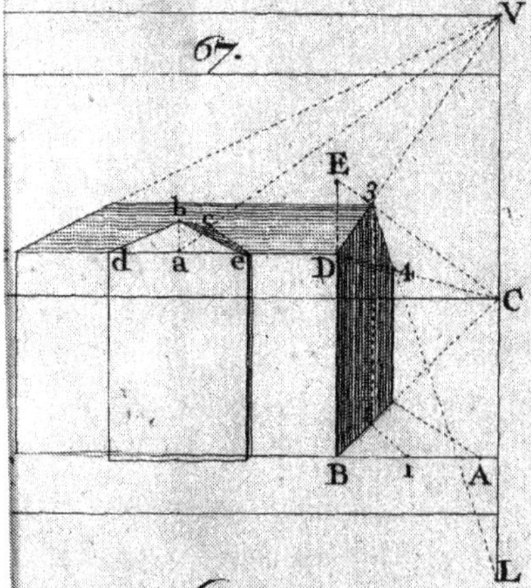

67.

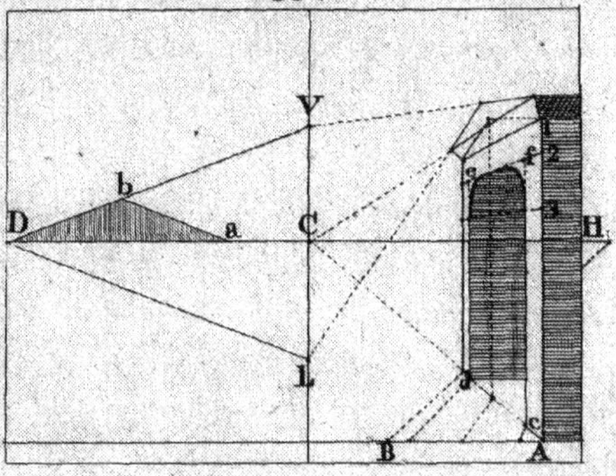

66.

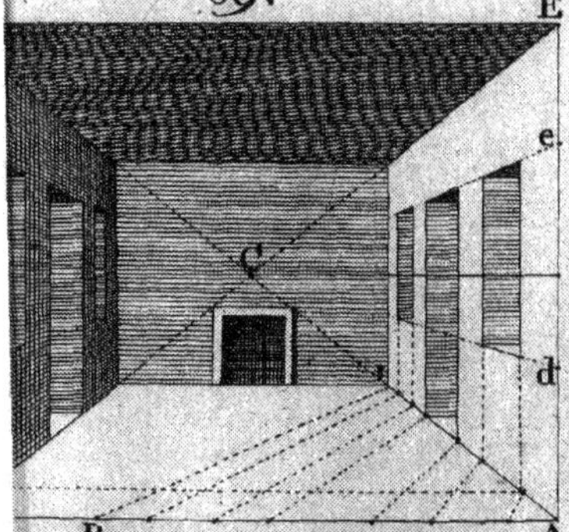

69.

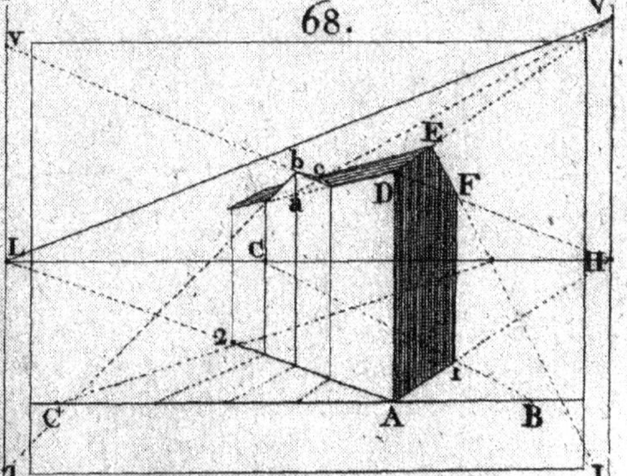

68.

B. 2. XVII Fig. 70.

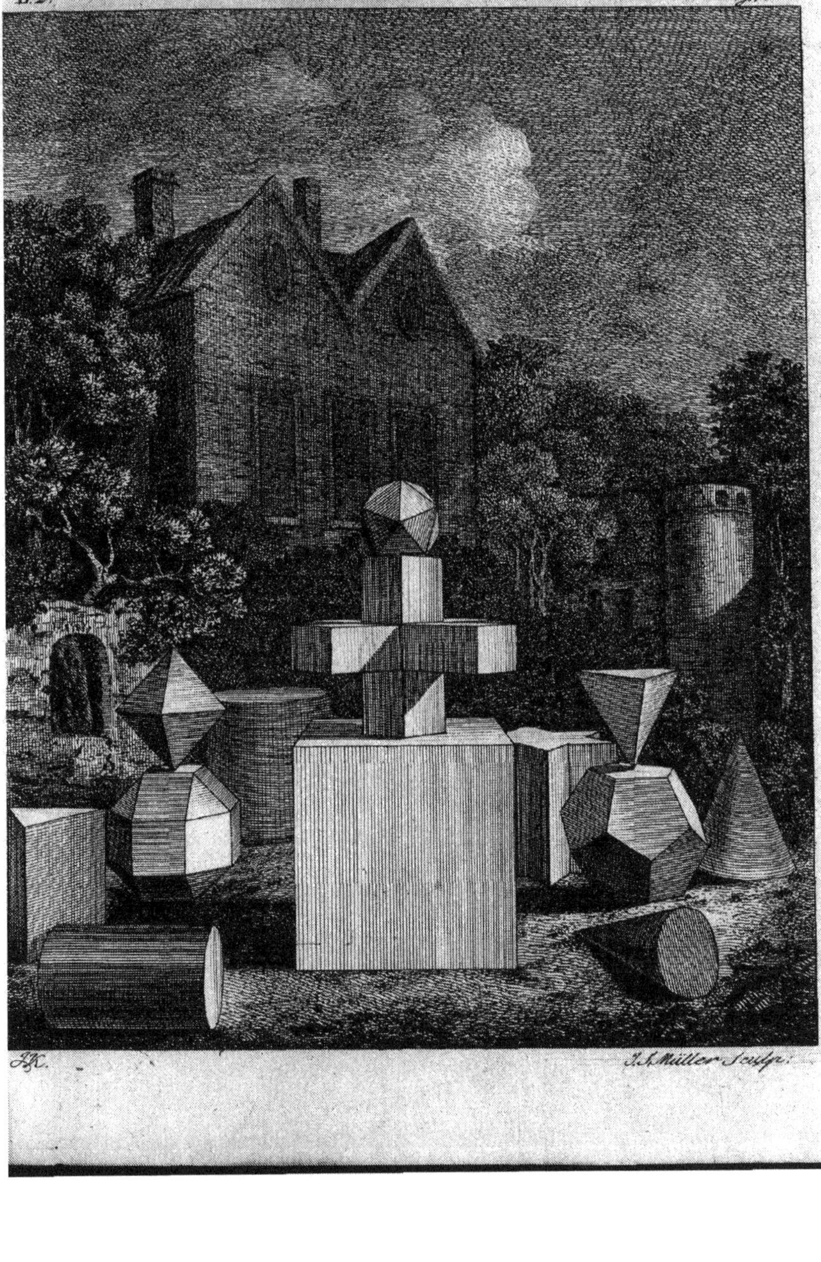

J.K. J. S. Müller Sculp.

B. 2. 71 XVIII.

TK: delin. J. Wood sculp.

72

T. Gainsborough fecit aqua forte J. Wood perfecit.

CHAP. IV.

Of the PARALLEL PICTURE, *such as Cielings, or the like; or what is usually called,* Horizontal Perspective.

THIS Kind of Perspective is extremely easy, because little more is required to be known than what has been already taught in Sect. II. Chap. II. of this Book; *viz.* How to find the Appearance of Objects which are supposed to lie upon the Ground. For most Objects which are drawn upon Cielings, are supposed to be perpendicular to them; and therefore, the Rules for determining the Representations of Objects in this Manner, are exactly the same as those for determining the Representations of Objects which lie flat upon the Ground, in the perpendicular Picture; and consequently, the Rules which serve in one Case, will serve in the other also.

The first Things to be considered in these and the like Representations, are, the Distance of the Eye, and the Center of the Picture.---As to the Distance of the Eye, that is unalterable, because the Picture is fixed; therefore, if the Cieling be so large, or so low, as to subtend too great an Angle at the Eye; that is, if the longest Dimensions of the Cieling be much greater than the Distance at which the Spectator is to look at it; then, in this Case, the Cieling should be divided into Compartments, which may serve as Frames for the intended perspective Representations: And we must be always careful, when we take the Height of any Cieling from the Floor, to deduct the Height of the Spectator's Eye therefrom, which is usually about 5 Feet 6 Inches. And in regard to the Center of the Picture, the general (and, I believe, the best) Method has been, to fix it in the Middle of the Picture, unless any Thing prevents the Eye from seeing it conveniently from that Place; because then there will be a Uniformity of the Parts, which will agree with each other, and be more likely to deceive the Eye.

And it is to be observed, that in these Kinds of fixed, or immoveable Pictures, the Spectator should always fix his Eye directly against the Center of the Picture; for otherwise the Representations will not have their desired Effect.

Now, in order to draw any Piece of Perspective upon a Cieling, the best Way seems to be this, *viz.* Take the Dimension of the Cieling, and make an exact Calculation of the Distance and Height of the Eye; then draw out the intended Design upon a large Piece of Paper, by Way of Model, and from thence transfer it unto Canvas, with the Addition of Colouring, Effect, &c. and finally, from thence draw it upon the Cieling, by Net-Work.

1. *To draw upon a Cieling a Deception, which, viewed from a proper Point, shall appear like the Sides of the Room continued upwards.*

Fig. 73. 74. Let ABFD be a Cieling drawn upon Paper to a certain Scale; and let E be the Eye, EC its Distance, and C the Center of the Picture. Now, let it be required to make the Cieling appear as if the Sides of the Room were continued upwards equal to the Length AB.---Through the Center of the Picture draw E 1, E 2, parallel to AB, which may be considered as the horizontal Line; then draw Lines from the Corners A, B, F, D, to the Center C, and make CE 1 equal to CE; by which means A a may be cut off equal to the given Length AB, and consequently, from thence all the Representations may be compleated, as in the Figures: Thus, a b being drawn parallel to AB, gives the Side ABab, and a d being drawn parallel to AD, compleats the Side ADad, &c.--- In the 73d Figure, the Center lies out of the Middle of the Picture; but in the 74th Figure, the Eye is directly in the Middle.

Here we may observe, that if Lines are drawn thro' the Center of the Picture parallel to the Sides of a Room, then those Lines may be considered as so many horizontal Lines, and may be made use of accordingly. Thus, E 1 CE 2 will serve as a horizontal, or vanishing Line, for all Objects which can lie upon the Planes ABab, DFdf; and ECE 3 will serve as a horizontal Line for any Objects which can lie upon the Planes ADad, BFbf.---By turning the Figures we may conceive this very clearly; but in the next Figure it is more fully explained.

In this Figure I shall shew how to find the Representation of such Objects only as may occur in common Practice, such as Columns, Pilasters, Arches, and Windows. And first of Columns.

2. *To find the Appearance of* TWO CYLINDERS *upon a Cieling.*

Fig. 75. Let the Circles H, I, represent the Ends of two Cylinders, and let E 2 CE 4 be the vanishing Line of the Plane ABab, CE 3 the Distance, and C the Center of the Picture.---About each Circle H, I,

H, I, describe a Square, and make CE4 equal to CE3; then draw a Line from each Corner of the Square to C; and then, by means of the Point E4, a Parallelopiped may be made of any Length, which will be a Guide for compleating the Cylinder; as is shewn in Figure 29 of this Book. Now, by the same Method, the Appearance of Columns may be determined, with this Difference only, that three Squares must be found as Guides instead of two; that is, one for the Bottom of the Column, another where it begins to diminish, and the Third at the Neck of the Column.

3. *To find the Representation of* TWO PILASTERS.

Let F and G be the Ends of the Pilasters.---From each Corner draw Lines to C, and, by means of the Point E2, cut off each Pilaster to its proper Length.

4. *To determine the Appearance of a* SQUARE OBJECT *which lies oblique with the Picture.*

Let 5 be one Corner, 57 the given Length, and E2, E4, the vanishing Points of the Sides.----From the Corner 5 draw Lines to the above vanishing Points, and cut off 56 equal to 57; from whence the Figure may be compleated.

On the opposite Side DEde, I have finished these Representations with Shadows, *&c.*

5. *To put an* ARCH *into Perspective.*

Let KM be the Width of the Arch, Mh the Height to where the Arch springs, and hi the Height of the circular Part; and let E1CE3 be the vanishing Line, CE2 the Distance of the Picture, and C its Center.---From K and M draw Lines to C, and cut off Mn, no, equal to Mk, hi, then draw the Parallelogram nopq, which will be a Guide for drawing the Arch. Again, for the Depth of the Opening,---From K draw a Perpendicular to DA, and make it equal to the proposed Depth; and from its Extremity z draw a Line to C; then from q draw a Line parallel to Kz, which will cut Cz, and thereby give the proper Depth; do the same on the other Side; then draw the bottom Curve for the other Side of the Arch, parallel to the upper Curve, as in the Figure; and so will the Representation be compleated.

6. To

6. *To find the Appearance of a* Window, *the Top of which we will suppose to be even with the Top of the Arch, and to be two Diameters in Height.*

Set off the real Width L f, and its Height L g, and from the Points L, f, g, draw Lines to C; then continue the Line o p to r, which will give the Top r s, and from E 1 draw a Line through the Corner r, cutting g t in w; then from w, draw w v parallel to r t, which compleats the Window r s o x. The Depth is found in the same Manner as the Depth of the Arch, *viz.* by the Perpendicular L.

On the opposite Side to this also, are the above Figures wholly compleated.

7. *To put a* Cornice *into Perspective.*

Draw out the Projection, *&c.* of the Cornice, about which de-
Fig. 76. scribe the Plane A B C D; then put that Plane into Perspective, as F G H I; from whence all the Mouldings may be determined, as in the Figure.

8. *To put a* Base *and* Capital *into Perspective.*

Fig. 77. For the Base,----Altho' nothing more than the Plinth can in general be seen by the Eye, yet I have here given a Method for determining the whole Projection.---Let AB be the Diameter of the Plinth, and B F the Height of the Base; make a Square with A B, and from B draw a Line to C, and cut off B D equal to B F, and from D draw D C parallel to A B, and with D C make another Square; then divide A B into eight equal Parts, and one of those Parts (according to *Gibbs*) is the Projection of the Mouldings: Therefore, make B 1 equal to one of those Parts, and from 1 draw a Line to C, cutting the Edge of the farthest Square in 3; then from 3 draw a Line parallel to C D, and set off the Distance 3 D upon the other three Sides of the parallel Square; then, by drawing Lines through those Points, we shall have a Square equal to the Diameter of the Column; and from these two Squares the whole Appearance is to be compleated.----The Figure G represents it as finished.

9. *To put a* Capital *into Perspective.*

Let AB be the Diameter of the Bottom of the Capital, 1 2 the Diameter of the Abacus, 1 3 the Height of the Capital, and B 2 the Projection of the Capital.----Set off B b equal to B 2, and make the

the Square abcd; then draw 1C, 2C, and cut off 1D equal to 1 3; then draw DF parallel to AB, and with DF make a Square; finally, from the Corner of one Square draw Lines to the corresponding Corners of the other, as in K; then shall we have sufficient Guides for compleating the Capital.

10. *To put the* HUMAN FIGURE *into Perspective.*

Having made a Design of the Figure, describe the Frame about it, as ABCD, and then reticulate it in a proper Manner; after which, put that Frame and the Reticulation into Perspective, as abcd, which will give all the Foreshortnings, as in the Figure. Fig. 77

I am very sensible, that 'tis impossible to give Rules for putting the Human Figure correctly into Perspective, and that the greatest Part must be left to the Judgment of the Artist; yet the above Hint may be of some Service in designing Figures for the above Purposes. So likewise, as to the Size of Figures which are to be seen at a considerable Distance; I know of no Rules by which they can be correctly determined; and therefore, in such Cases, the best Way is, to sketch out several Figures of different Sizes upon the intended Picture; then, by surveying them from the Point of View, the Eye will immediately inform the Artist which is of a proper Proportion.

In Book I. Chap. IV. Sect. 3, we have given some general Rules from Mr. *Hamilton*, for drawing any Perspective Representations upon vaulted Roofs, Domes, or other uneven Surfaces; and therefore, if the curious Reader would inform himself of that Kind of Perspective, he must refer to those Figures, where this Article is considered at large; which will sufficiently explain the 78th and 79th Figures, since they are those Rules applied to Practice. But as I have said very little upon drawing a Dome, *&c.* upon a flat Cieling, and as the Operation is quite Mechanical, I shall therefore introduce it in this Place.

In order to find the Representation of Domes, *&c.* it is necessary to draw out the Plan, and Half the Elevation, of the Design which we intend to represent, to a proper Scale, upon Paper: Thus, let the 80th Figure be the Section, or Half the Elevation, of the intended Design; and let the two outward Circles,* and the small Squares and Circles within them, represent the Plan of it: From which two Figures we may perceive, that the Design consists of eight Columns upon Pedestals, with an Entablature, in the Corinthian Order; that those Columns are supposed to stand against a per- *Fig. 81.

a perpendicular Wall A e, Fig. 80; and that the Dome is a Semicircle, and begins to ſpring from the Top of the Cornice. Now, having drawn out the Plan and Elevation, as above directed, the Repreſentation of any Deſign may very eaſily be determined in the following Manner.

11. *To draw upon a flat Cieling the Repreſentation of a Dome* *.

Having given the Elevation and Plan, chooſe the Center and Diſtance of the Picture. Thus E C, Fig. 81, is the Diſtance of the Picture, and C is its Center; that is, E C is the Diſtance at which the Eye is to view the Dome when painted, and directly under C is the Point from whence the Eye ſhould be placed to look at the Picture. Now, this Point C being taken out of the Picture, will give a greater Length for the Columns, *&c.* and will prevent ſome Confuſion, which would be occaſioned by placing the Center within the Picture. Theſe neceſſary Points being ſettled, let us next deſcribe the Parallelogram ABCD about the Elevation, Fig. 80, and then draw Lines parallel to AD, from the ſeveral Heights g, f, e, *&c.* as in the Figure: After which, from the Center of the Picture C, (Fig. 81) draw CD perpendicular to EC, and from E draw EA, parallel to CD; then from A draw AD parallel to EC, and continue it beyond D at pleaſure; and then will EA be a Line for the Plan, and AB a Line for the Elevations: Therefore, from the Point A ſet off the ſeveral Meaſures from AD, Fig. 80, which are the Meaſures of the Plan; and from AB of the ſame Figure, ſet off the ſeveral Diſtances, which are the ſeveral Meaſures for the Elevations: Thus Ad, Fig. 81, is the Width of the Plan AD, and AB the Height of the whole Deſign, properly divided for the Height of the ſeveral Members, which may eaſily be conceived by comparing the two Figures 80 and 81. Having proceeded thus far, the next Thing is to put the Elevation into Perſpective, as the 81ſt Figure; where Abcd, *&c.* is the Repreſentation of ABCD, Fig. 81. This is done by drawing Lines from A and d to the vaniſhing Point C, and then drawing other Lines from the ſeveral Diviſions upon AB, which cutting AC in correſponding Points, will give the apparent Depth of each Part;

* This Method for finding the Repreſentation of a Dome upon a flat Cieling, is principally taken from *Andrea Pozzo*'s Firſt Book upon Perſpective, publiſhed by Mr. *John Sturt*, Engraver, in 1707; and therefore, if what I am going to advance upon the Subject ſhould appear not to be ſufficiently clear, the Reader is referred to the above Book.

from

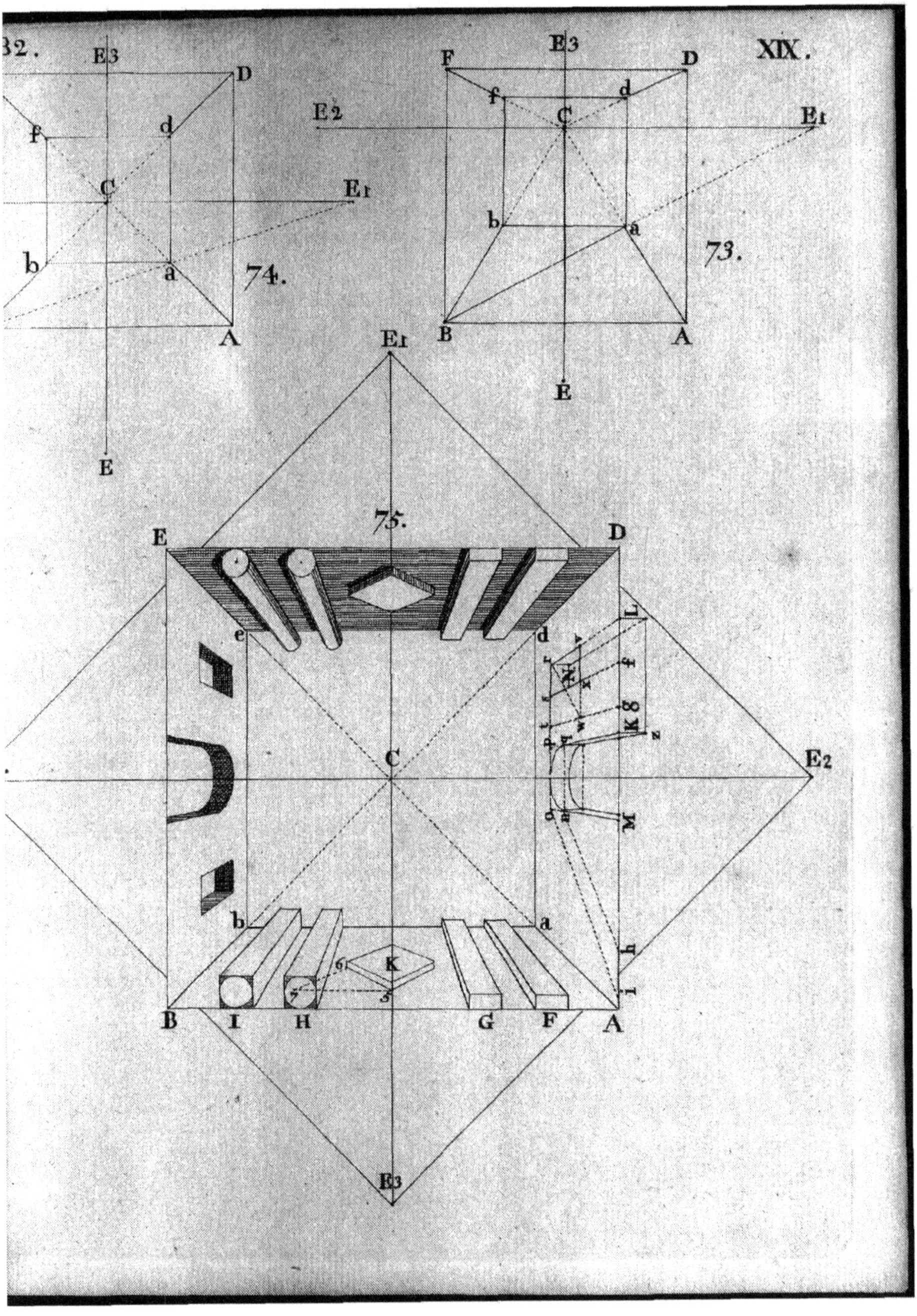
XIX.
74.
73.
75.
E3
E2
E1
E
C
A
B
D
F
a
b
d
f
e
K
I
H
G
L
M

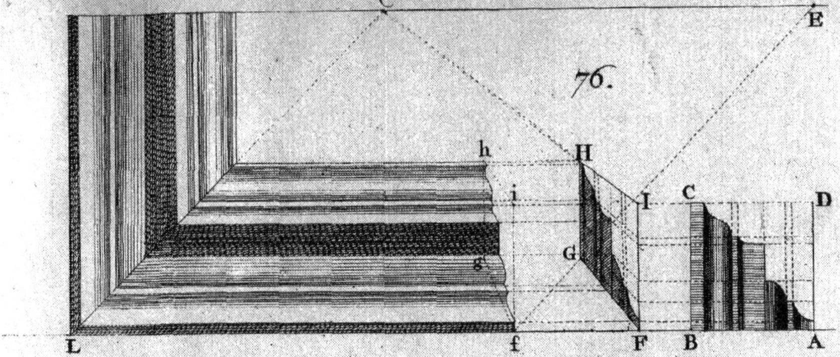
C
E
76.
h
H
i
I
C
D
G
g
L
f
F
B
A

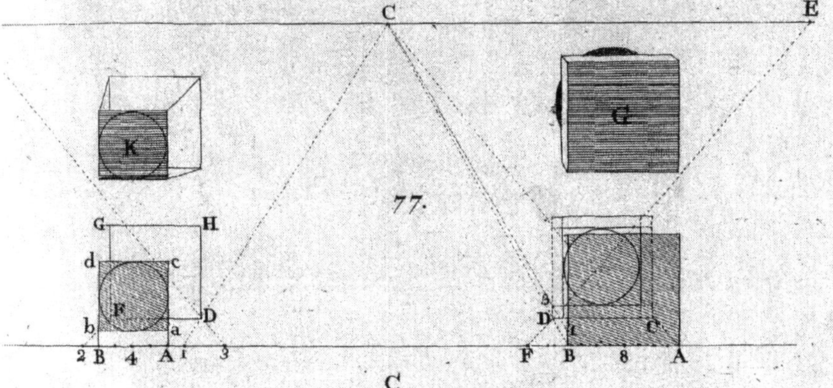
C
E
K
G
77.
G
H
d
c
F
D
b
a
2 B 4 A 1 3
D
C
F B 8 A

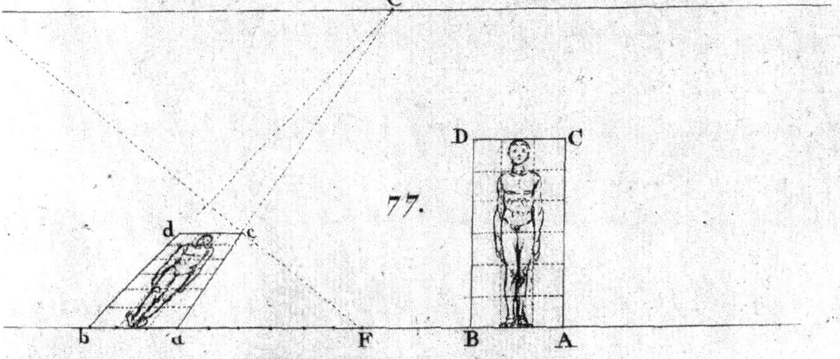
C
D
C
77.
d
c
b
a
F
B
A

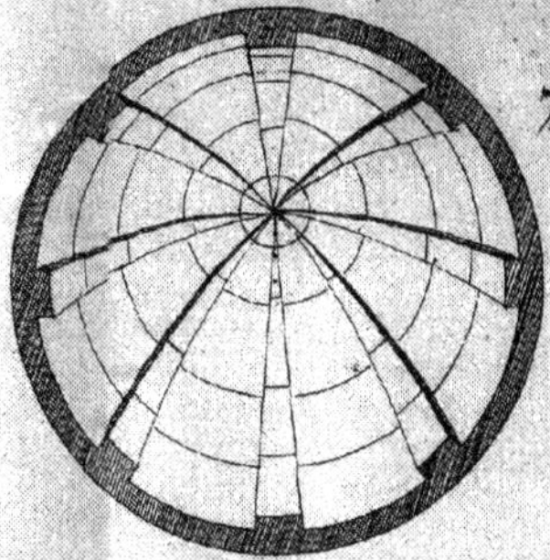

79.

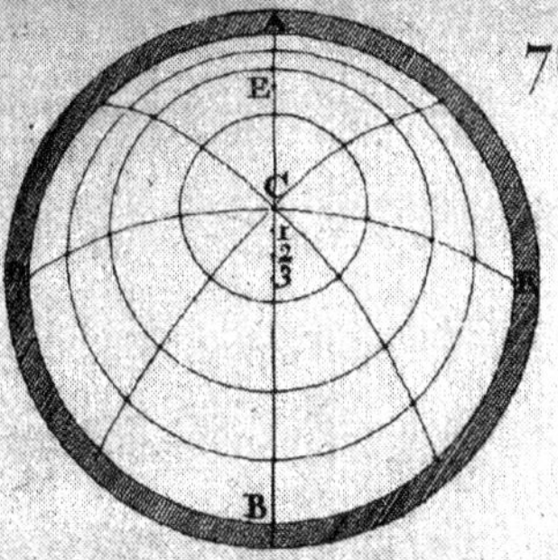

78.

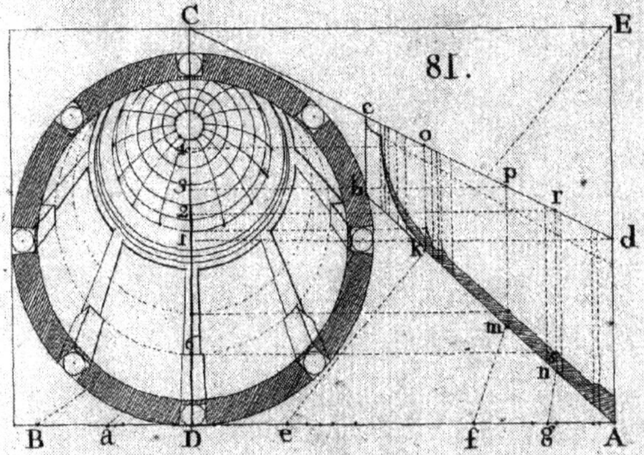

81.

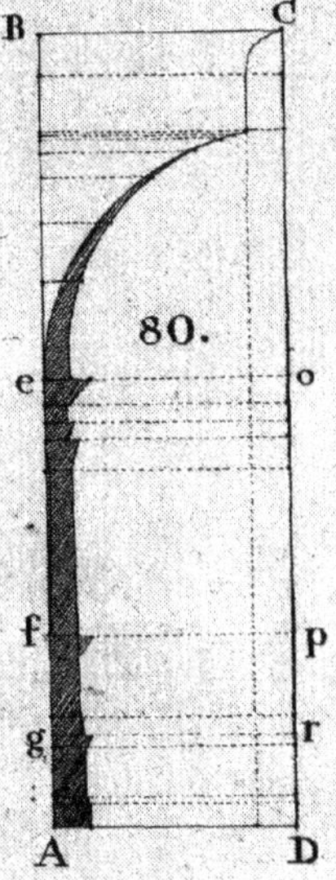

80.

82.

from whence the whole Elevation may be reduced into Perspective, as in the Figure. Having proceeded thus far, the next Thing (and indeed the Principal of all) is, to describe several Circles each from a different Center, and each of a different Diameter; which is done thus: From the several Divisions, as n, m, k, draw Lines parallel to AE, cutting d C in r, p, o; then from d, r, p, o, draw Lines parallel to AB, cutting the Perpendicular CD in 1, 2, 3, 4; then is 1 the Center of the outward Circle, and 1 D (which is equal to A d) is its Radius; therefore, describe the outward Circle, and from the same Center describe the second Circle, and then, within those two Circles, draw the Plan, as in the Figure. Again, for the Height of the Pedestal; draw 5 6, r 2, parallel to AB, cutting CD in 2 and 6; then is 2 the Center, and 2 6 the Radius of that Circle which governs the Heights of the Pedestals. In like Manner, 3 is the Center of the Circle which limits the Length to where each Column begins to diminish, and 4 is the Center of the Circle for the Nose of the Cornice; and so of the rest: All which may be made very familiar by drawing out the Figure. As to the Returns of the Pedestals and Mouldings, they all vanish into the several Centers of those Circles which determine their Heights: Thus 2 is the Center of the Circle for the Height of the Pedestals; and therefore, the oblique Sides of those Pedestals terminate in that Point. And as to the Ornaments which may be drawn upon the Dome, they also are to be determined in the same Manner; as will be evident by a very little Attention to the Figure, and by applying these Rules to Practice in a larger Scale than this upon the Plate.----The 80th Figure is the Representation more nearly compleated, and between each Column I have introduced a Pannel to fill up the Vacancy, and to give a Hint how to introduce Ornaments proper for this Kind of Representations; for whether Figures, Festoons, or any other kind of carved Ornaments, are intended; by inscribing Squares about each, and by dividing them into smaller Squares, we may reticulate each Cell, which will be sufficient for foreshortning all Kinds of Ornaments.

CHAP. V.

The PERSPECTIVE *of* SHADOWS, *&c.*

SECT. I.

THIS Part of Perspective has been very little attended to by most Writers upon the Subject, and yet it is very necessary to be known, and very easy to be understood; for it is built upon the same Principles as the Perspective of Objects, and, therefore, is deducible from the same Rules. But I would not be understood to mean, that the Shadow of every particular Object upon the Picture is to be determined in the following Manner; no; my Intention is, only to give some general Principles, in order to explain the Reason and Nature of such Shadows as are necessary in the Arts of Design; by which means the Artist will form a general Idea of the Perspective of Shadows, and will be the better qualified to dispose them in a Picture.

SHADOWS are either projected by the Sun, or else by a Candle, Torch, or some such luminous Point. But since those produced by a Candle, *&c.* are but seldom wanted, I shall therefore principally have regard to such Shadows only as are projected by the Sun: Which may be reduced under the following Heads.

1. When the Light comes in parallel with the Picture.
2. When the Light comes from behind the Picture towards the Spectator.
3. When the Light comes from before the Picture.

In the first Case, the Shadows will be parallel to the Bottom of the Picture; but in the second and third Cases, since the Light comes in oblique with the Picture; therefore, both the Rays of Light, and the Shadows projected by them, will have their proper vanishing Points; and consequently the Shadows produced thereby will be oblique with the Bottom of the Picture. The vanishing Point of the Rays of Light will be either above the horizontal Line or below it; and those Points will always be in Lines drawn perpendicular to the horizontal Line *: And we may moreover observe, that when the Light comes from behind the Picture, then the vanishing Point of the Rays of Light will be above the horizon-

* See the Additions upon this Head in the Appendix, p. 1.

tal

tal Line; but when the Light comes from before the Picture, then the vanishing Point of the Rays of Light will be below the horizontal Line: All which is exemplified in the following Figures. For in Figure 83, the Light is supposed parallel to the Picture; therefore the Shadows are parallel: In Figure 84, the Light is supposed to come from behind the Picture, and S is taken at pleasure for the vanishing Point of the Shadow of the perpendicular Sides, and L for the vanishing Point of the Rays of Light: In the 85th Figure, the Light is supposed to come from before the Picture; and here S is the vanishing Point of the Shadow, and L the vanishing Point of the Rays of Light; which are both taken at pleasure.

From hence then, and from the following Examples, it will be obvious, that after having drawn out any Perspective Representation, the Shadow of it may be very easily determined upon the Picture; therefore let us now apply what has been said to Practice.

CASE I. *When the Light comes in parallel to the Picture.*

To find the Shadows of the Objects A *and* B, *which are supposed to be cast upon the Ground.* Fig. 83.

Through all the Corners of the Bottoms of the Objects draw Lines parallel to the horizontal Line, and through every Corner of the Top of the Objects draw Lines parallel to each other for the Rays of Light; and their Intersections with the lowest parallel Lines will determine the Appearance of the Shadows, as in the Figure: Thus a is the Shadow of A, and b of B.

From hence we may observe, that since EB is considered as a Ray of Light, therefore EBD is its Angle of Inclination with the Ground; or, in other Words, with the Plane of the Horizon. And we may also observe, that in Proportion as this Angle of Inclination of the Rays is greater or less, the Shadows will be longer or shorter; which accounts for the Reason why the Shadows of Objects are longer in a Morning and Evening, than when the Sun is at any considerable Height above the Horizon: All which may be clearly apprehended by attending to the Figure; or by drawing out other Figures, and then giving different Inclinations to the Rays of Light.

Case 2. *When the Light comes in from behind the Picture.*

Fig. 84. *To find the Shadows of the Objects* A *and* a, *which are supposed to be cast upon the Ground.*

Take S at pleasure in the horizontal Line, for the vanishing Point of the Shadows which the perpendicular Edges cast upon the Ground (for as the Shadow lies upon the Ground, it must vanish into the horizontal Line;) and from this Point S, draw a Line SL perpendicular to the horizontal Line: Then will SL be the vanishing Line of the Rays of Light, and, consequently, somewhere in this Line will be the vanishing Point of those Rays. Now, in this Case, the vanishing Point of the Rays is above the horizontal Line; therefore, take L at pleasure for that vanishing Point, and from thence draw Lines thro' all the upper Corners of the Figures; then from the vanishing Point S of the Shadow, draw Lines through all the Bottom Corners; and their Sections with each other will be sufficient Guides for compleating the Shadows, as in the Figure: Thus, L 3 being drawn through 1, and S 3 being drawn through 2, will give the Point 3 for the Shadow of the Point 1, and 2 3 for the Shadow of the Edge 1 2, &c.

Here let us observe, that in order to determine any Shadow, nothing more is required than to find the Places of a certain Number of Points upon the Picture, which Points are to represent the Shadows of all the upper Corners of any given Objects: Thus, 3 is the Shadow of 1, and 4 is the Shadow of A; therefore, draw 3 4, which is the Shadow of the upper Edge 1 A; and so of the rest.

Case 3. *When the Light comes from before the Picture.*

Fig. 85. *To find the Shadow of the Object* A, *which is supposed to be cast upon the Ground.*

Here S is given for the vanishing Point of the Shadow, L S for the vanishing Line of the Rays of Light, and L for their vanishing Point; which, in this Case, is below the horizontal Line.---- From S draw Lines through all the lower Corners of the Object, and from L draw Lines through all the upper Corners of the Object, as in the Figure; and then their several Sections with each other will be sufficient for compleating the Shadow, as before.

From

From these two last Figures also, we may observe, that the farther the vanishing Point of the Rays is taken from the horizontal Line, the shorter will be the Projection of the Shadows; and the contrary, the nearer it is placed to the horizontal Line: That is, the nearer it is to the horizontal Line, the less is the Angle of Inclination which the Rays make with the Ground; and the contrary, the farther it is from it. Again, by inspecting the two last Figures, we may perceive, that when the Light comes from behind the Picture, the Shadows will be cast towards the Bottom of the Picture, and grow wider and wider continually, and the Front of every Object will be in Shadow; but in the last Figure, the Shadows will be cast towards the horizontal Line, and will grow narrower and narrower continually, and the Front of every Object will be enlightened; and therefore, these Kind of Shadows are the most proper for a Picture, and consequently, deserve the most Attention: For which Reason, I shall henceforth suppose the Light to come in this Direction only; and shall now proceed to shew how to determine the Appearance of Shadows as they are projected by different Planes, *&c.*

In the last Figure the front Side is parallel to the Picture, and the Method for finding the Shadow has been shewn already; therefore proceed we to a Figure whose Sides are oblique, though the same Rule is used in both Cases.

To find the Shadow of the Object A, *which is supposed to be cast upon the Ground.* Fig. 86.

From the vanishing Point S of the Shadow, draw Lines thro' the Bottom Corners, and from the vanishing Point L of the Rays of Light, draw Lines thro' the Top Corners, which (as before) will cut each other, and thereby give several Points, as Guides for compleating the Shadow.--If only the Shadow of the Top was required, then the Seats of each Corner must be found upon the Picture; and from thence the Appearance of the Shadow may be determined: Thus 2 is the Seat of 1, and 3 is its Shadow; and a is the Shadow compleated.

To find the Shadow of an oblique Object, which is supposed to be cast upon the Ground.

Here A is the oblique Side, S the vanishing Point of the Shadow, and L the vanishing Point of the Rays of Light.--From d draw dS, and from a draw aL; then will dc be the Shadow of the Perpendicular da; therefore by drawing bc, the Shadow will be compleated. Fig. 87.

To

To find the Shadows of Objects when cast upon different Planes.

Fig. 88. 1. *To find the Shadow of a perpendicular Object* A, *when it is cast upon a Plane inclined to the Ground, but has some of its Edges, as* 1 2, *parallel to the Picture.*

From the lower Corners of the Object A draw Lines to S, and from the upper Corners draw Lines to L, which would determine the Shadow of A, upon the Ground; but this Shadow being cut by the Bottom 1 2 of the inclined Plane, therefore Part of the Shadow will be cast upon it. Now, to find this Shadow, from b, (where the Line which is drawn from the lowest Corner of the Object A cuts the Edge 2n) draw bc perpendicular to the horizontal Line, cutting the inclined Edge 2e, in c; then from b and c draw Lines parallel to the horizontal Line, and from a (where ba cuts the Line drawn from the other Corner of the Object A to S) draw ad, which compleats the Parallelogram abcd; finally, from where the Edge 1 2 cuts the Ground Shadow, draw Lines through c and d, which will cut the Lines drawn from the upper Corners of A to L, and thereby determine the Length of the Shadow upon the inclined Face of the Object, as in the Figure.

2. *To find the Representation of a Shadow when it is cast by an inclined Object upon a perpendicular Plane* enrs.

From n and e draw Lines to S and L, which will give m for the Shadow of e, and 2mn for the whole Shadow of the Side 2ne; but since 2m is cut by the Edge nr of the Plane enrs, therefore, Part of the Shadow will be cast upon it; which Shadow is determined by drawing a Line from o (where 2m is cut by nr) to e; thus, noe is the Shadow which is cast upon the perpendicular Plane, and 2on is the Shadow that is cast upon the Ground.

Fig. 89. 3. *To find the Shadow of a perpendicular Object* A, *when it is cast upon a Plane* B, *that is every Way oblique with the Picture, but is nevertheless situated in such a Manner as to have the vanishing Line* LP, *of the perpendicular Side* abc, *pass through the vanishing Point of the Shadow.*

From the upper and under Corners of A, draw Lines to S and L, as before; then, from where the Ground Shadow is cut by the Edge a 1, draw Lines to the vanishing Point P of the oblique Side B; which will cut the Lines drawn from the upper Corners of A, and thereby determine the Length of the Shadow.

4. *To*

4. *To find the Projection of the Shadow of a perpendicular Object* A, *when it is cast upon an inclined Plane that is every Way oblique with the Picture.* Fig. 90.

Draw Lines from the upper and under Corners of A, to S and L, then, from where 3 S cuts the lowest Edge 1 a of the farther Side of the inclined Object, draw a b perpendicular to the horizontal Line, and continue the inclined Edge 1 b 'till it cuts a b; then through a and b, draw Lines from the vanishing Point of the Edge 1 2, which will cut 4 S in c; then, from c draw c d parallel to a b, which will compleat the perpendicular Plane a b c d; finally, from where the Ground Shadow is cut by 1 2, draw Lines to b and d, which will cut 5 L and 6 L, and thereby give the Depth of the Shadow, as in the Figure.

Here let us take Notice, that as the Shadows of all Objects that are cast upon the Ground will vanish into the horizontal Line, so, for the very same Reason, the vanishing Points of all Shadows which are cast upon any inclined, or other Plane, will be somewhere in the vanishing Line of that Plane, as was observed in Figure 89.

The 91st Figure is an Example of the Shadow of a cylindrical Object A, cast both upon the Ground and the Object B; and of the square Object C, which is cast upon the Ground and the Object D; which, it is presumed, wants no Explanation.

Before I conclude with the Shadows projected by the Sun, I shall just observe, that altho' I have taken the vanishing Points of the Shadows always within the Picture, for the Conveniency of Room in each Plate; yet, it is to be observed, that, in general, the farther it is taken from the Picture the better.*

Of Shadows projected by the Candle, &c. Fig. 92.

In Shadows of this Kind, nothing more is required than to have the Luminous Point, and its Seat upon the Ground; for by drawing Lines from those Points through the upper and under Corners of each particular Object, the Shadow of that Object may be found, as in the former Figures; and only the Shape of the Shadows will be different; that is, they will grow wider and wider continually, the farther they are projected. I have given several Examples in this Figure, and have put every Line and Point that is necessary in each Operation; which, it is presumed, is sufficient for the Purpose.

* Here the Reader is referred again to the Additions upon Shadows in the Appendix.

SECT. II.

HAving ſhewn how to determine the Appearance of Shadows, I might now proceed to the Conſideration of Aerial Perſpective, *&c.* but as that is handled at large in the laſt Chapter of the firſt Book, the Reader is now referred to that: However, by way of Supplement to what is there advanced upon the Subject, I ſhall beg leave to make the following Obſervations. For, ſince various have been the Opinions about the Colour of Shadows, and as various the Methods purſued by Painters and other Artiſts, I ſhall therefore only offer a few Hints taken from Nature, which perhaps may be of Service to the young Tyros in the Arts of Deſign.

By Shadow then, in this Place, I mean the Colour of that Part only of an Object, which is either turned from the Light, or is Fig. 94. wholly in the Shade. Suppoſe, for Inſtance, the Pillar W to be placed near this Side of the Wall b, and ſuppoſe alſo, that the Rays of Light came from the other Side of the Wall; then, it will be evident, that Part of this Object will be enlightened, and Part will be wholly in Shadow. Now, that Part which is wholly in Shadow, is of the ſame Colour as the whole Object would be of were the Sun not to ſhine upon it; or, in other Words, 'tis of the ſame Colour which the whole Object would be of in common Light. From whence I infer, Firſt, (allowing for the different Accidents of the Sun's Light, the Air, *&c.*) that the Shadow of the Pillar W, is the real Colour of that Object in common Light, but being oppoſed to a ſuperior Light, is, in compariſon of that ſuperior Light, a Shadow. Secondly, That therefore the Colour of all Shadows muſt be proportionably lighter or darker, as that Object to which it is a Shadow, is of a lighter or darker Colour. This I have explained in the following Manner. The Objects W, W, I ſuppoſe to be White; the Object Y, to be Yellow; the Object G, Green; the Object R, Red; the Object B, Blue; and the Object B Black.---Here the ſhadowed Parts of each particular Object are made darker and darker, in proportion as the Colours of the ſeveral Objects proceed from White to Black; which is evident by the Figure. Thirdly, Since then the Shadows of all the above Objects are nothing more than the Effects of common Light, compared with the Effects of the ſuperior Brightneſs of the Sun; and ſince Objects are as diſtinctly ſeen by a common uniform Light, as they are in the Sun-ſhine; therefore thoſe Objects which are in Shadow, ſhould be as highly finiſhed, and their Parts as well made out,

out, in the Picture, as the Parts of the neighbouring Objects, which are in the higheſt Light. And fourthly, from hence it follows, that the Shadow of every Object muſt partake of the real Colour of that Object; and therefore, Black can never be the Shadow of White, nor of any other Colour than that of Black.

By thus ranging the Colours in their proper Orders, we may eaſily conceive the Degree of Darkneſs which is peculiar to the Shadow of each Colour. And if any one would moreover ſatisfy himſelf of the Truth of this, let him have a Number of ſquare Pieces of Wood, painted of different Colours; then, by oppoſing one Side to the Light, the Degree of Shadow will be very viſible.

And from hence alſo we may obſerve, that the ſtronger the Light ſhines upon any Object, the darker will be its Shadow; for in Proportion as the Sun ſhines ſtronger or fainter upon an Object, the Oppoſition of the Light and Shadow will be greater or leſs; and conſequently, the more perceptible will be the Shadow. And this accounts for the Blackneſs of Shadows by Candle or Torch-Light; becauſe the violent Oppoſition between real Light and total Darkneſs, together with the Faintneſs of the Reflections from the Smallneſs of the Luminary, muſt produce that Effect.

From theſe Obſervations then it appears, that the Colour and Degree of Darkneſs to each Shadow, is abſolutely neceſſary to be known, and ought to be well underſtood, in order to produce a good Effect in a Picture, or to repreſent any Object as it appears in Nature. It is in this, and in a proper Diſtribution of the Lights and Shadows in a Picture, that the *Chiara Obſcuro* conſiſts; and it is this, and this only, which can give a Clearneſs to any Shadow, whether in a Painting, Print, or Drawing.

I ſhall juſt offer a few Hints for determining the Appearances of the Reflections of Objects in Water, *&c.* and ſo put an End to this Chapter.

The Reflections of Objects in Water, or any other tranſparent Medium, may be conſidered, Firſt, as to their Colour; and, Secondly, as to the Length of their Reflections. As to their Colour, If the Medium be very clear and tranſparent, the Colour of the Reflections is very near the Colour of the Objects; but in a thick or dirty Medium, the Reflection of an Object very ſenſibly changes its Colour, and partakes more and more of the Colour of that Medium in proportion as it is more denſe and muddy, 'till, at last, the Reflection will entirely disappear. And in order to make Water appear transparent (which is done principally by means of Reflections) the Reflections should be as perfect as possible.

To determine the Reflection of any Object in Water.

Fig. 93. Let 1 be an Object standing upon a Hill, and a its Bottom; then continue the Sides of the Object downwards, at pleasure (as the prickt Lines in the Figure) and suppose c is where the even Ground cuts the Bottom of the Hill; then set off cd equal to c1, which will give the Length of the Reflection. Again, for the Object 3, which stands upon the flat Ground; make the Length of the Reflection f equal to that Object. The Object 4 is too far from the Water to be reflected by it; and the Reflections of the Objects o, n, g, which are floating upon the Water, are each equal to the Height of its peculiar Object. So also as to the inclined Object 2; the Reflection of that must have the same Angle of Inclination with the real Object, and be of the same Length, as in the Figure. From which it appears, that all Kinds of Reflections are very easily determined; since nothing more is required, than to set off the perpendicular Height of each Object, downwards, upon the Water, *&c.*

What has been advanced upon Reflections, relates only to a stagnating Medium; that is, a still or smooth Water, or the like; which is the fittest for an Explanation of this Matter, and will be sufficient for giving the Learner a general Idea of Reflections: But when either the Objects, or the Water, or both together, are in Motion, then, though the Reflections will be wavering and uncertain, yet the above Rules will be of great Service in such Cases; and especially, if they are joined to the Study of Nature.

I cannot conclude this Head without the following Quotation from Mr. *Pope's* Second Pastoral; which, to me, seems an inimitable Picture of Nature, and much to our present Purpose.

"A Shepherd's Boy (he seeks no better Name)
"Led forth his Flocks along the silver *Thame*,
"Where dancing Sun-Beams on the Waters play'd,
"And verdant Alders form'd a quiv'ring Shade."

I have

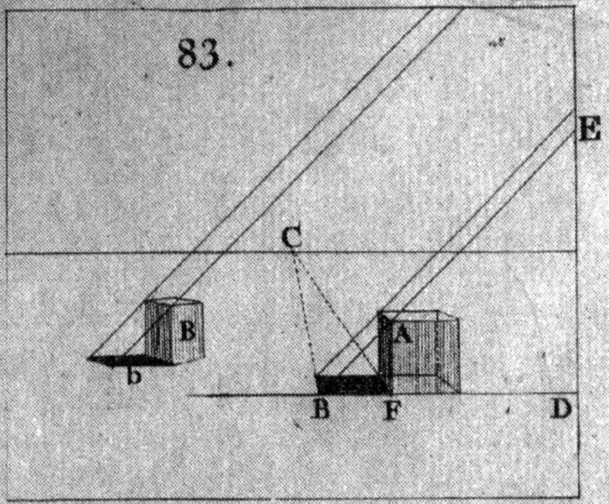
83.
E
C
B
A
b
B
F
D

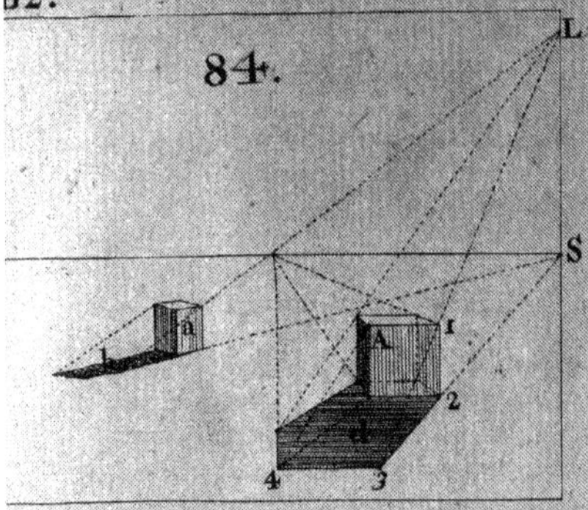
84.
L
S
a
A
1
2
d
4
3

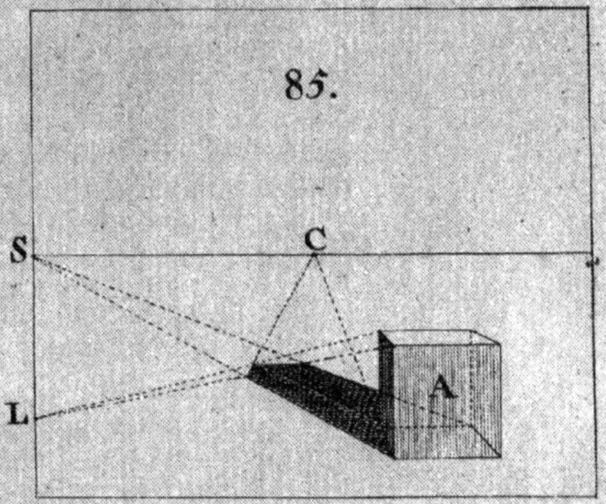
85.
S
C
L
A

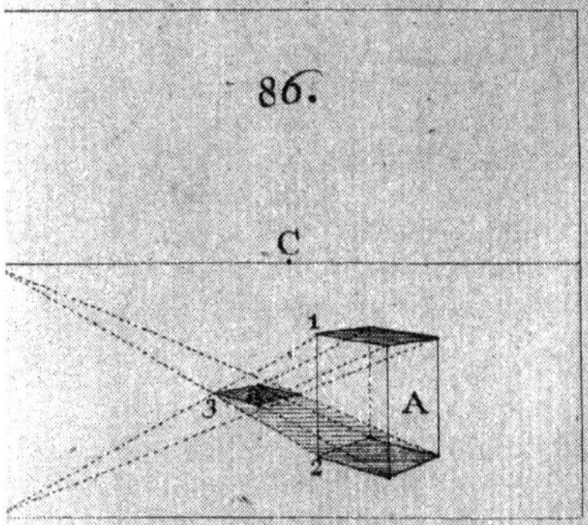
86.
C
1
3
A
2

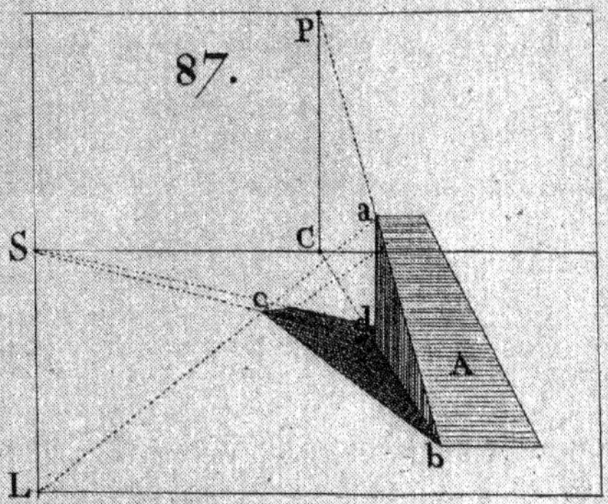
87.
P
a
S
C
c
d
A
b
L

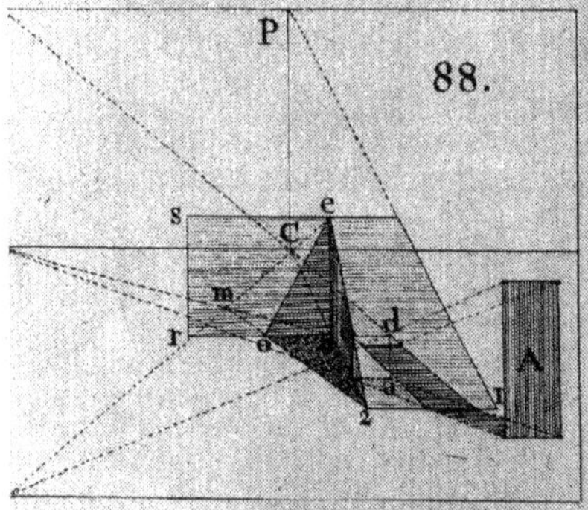
P
88.
s
e
C
m
r
o
d
A
2
1

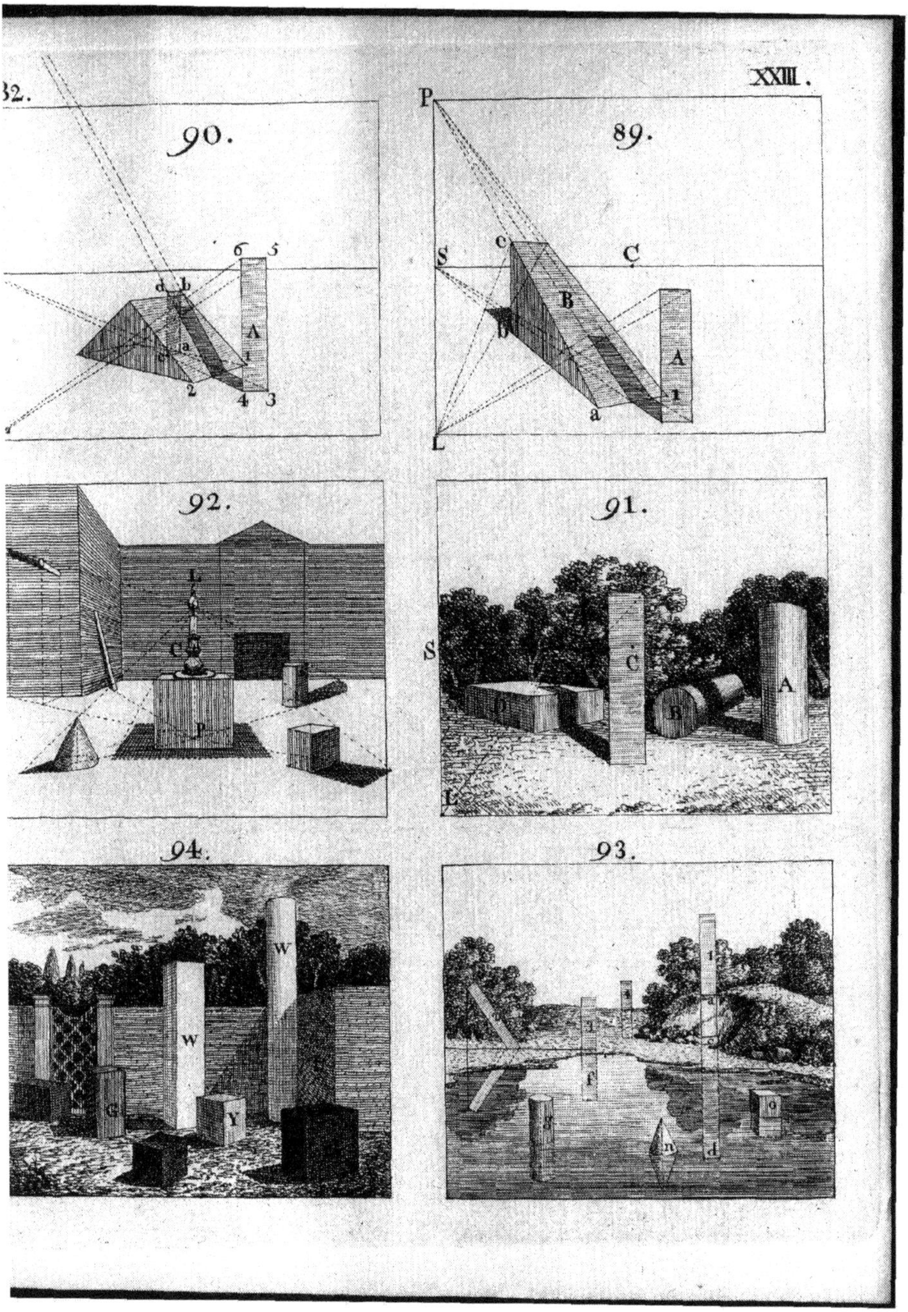

32.
XXIII.
90.
89.
92.
91.
94.
93.
A
B
C
P
S
L
W
W
G
Y

I have now gone through with all I intended to advance upon the Subject of Perſpective, and wiſh the Work may anſwer the Expectations of my worthy Friends and generous Subſcribers; and that the great Pains, Labour, and Expence it hath coſt me, may not prove in vain. I ſay, that here I intended to have put an End to my Subject; but, by the Deſire of ſome particular Friends, I ſhall take a Tranſcript from *Pozzo* and Mr. *Hamilton*, in relation to Scene-Painting; and then ſhall add the different Methods of the moſt conſiderable Authors upon Perſpective; which may either ſerve to divert or inſtruct the Reader; and, at the ſame Time, will ſhew him, which are the preferable Methods, mine, or theirs, either as to Eaſe or Expedition.

CHAP. VI.

Of SCENOGRAPHY; *or* SCENE-PAINTING.

" SCENOGRAPHY is the Art of Painting upon ſeveral " Planes, or Scenes, at different Diſtances, and in various " Poſitions with reſpect to the Eye, in ſuch a Manner that " all thoſe different Scenes, when ſeen from one certain determi- " nate Point, may correſpond with each other, and repreſent one " entire View of the Deſign without Breaks or Confuſion, as if " it were one continued Picture." This is Mr. *Hamilton*'s Explanation of SCENOGRAPHY; who has handled this Subject in a very clear and comprehenſive Manner, both in Theory and Practice; and therefore, what I intend to offer upon it myſelf, ſhall be principally an Abſtract from him. For, ſince 'tis impoſſible for me to treat it in a better Manner than he has done before me, I ſhall therefore refer my Reader to his and *Pozzo*'s * Books, if what I ſhall offer be not ſufficient for his Purpoſe; and in order to be as conciſe as poſſible, I ſhall ſuppoſe him to be acquainted with the Nature and Conſtruction of Theatres in general, and that he only wants to know, how to draw ſuch Repreſentations as are proper for ſuch Places.

The Deſign of Scene-Painting, is not only to decorate the Theatre, but to make that Part of it which lies beyond the Stage, appear much longer than it really is. This is effected by raiſing the Floor to a certain Angle, by ſloping the Cieling, and by raiſing the Scenes in ſuch a Manner, that both Floor, Cieling, and Scenes, ſhall be a Part of a hollow Pyramid, like LlOoNnMm, which, if continued, would meet in the Point T; and after having dimi-
Fig. 95. niſhed each Scene in its due Proportion, then by drawing thereupon the intended Deſign, by the common Rules of Perſpective, ſo that every Scene, when put in its proper Place, ſhall appear as a Part of the general Deſign.

As to the Inclination of the Floor and Cieling, and alſo the Ranging, and the Space between each Scene; theſe, as I obſerved before, I ſhall ſuppoſe my Reader acquainted with, and therefore, ſhall have Regard only to the drawing Perſpective Repreſentations upon Planes ſituated in the above Manner.

* *Andrea Pozzo*, in both his Books upon Perſpective, has alſo been very copious upon the ſame Subject.

Here

Here APFD is that Part of the Theatre which is allotted for the Spectators, KGLM the Proscene, LMON the Curtain, abcd the Aperture in the Curtain through which the Scenery is seen, MLml the Floor upon which the Scenery is placed, PQRS the farther End of the Theatre, E the Eye, EH its Height above the Floor ABDF, h its Seat upon the horizontal Plane efQP, and T the Center of Contraction for the Scenes, Floor, &c. Fig. 95.

Now let ABCD be a Plan of the Theatre, ee the Seat of the Curtain, ML the Opening of the Curtain, bb, &c. the Grooves for the Scenes to slide in, H the Eye, and T the Point of Contraction.---Here the Distance CH of the Eye from the Curtain, is not taken so great as in the last Figure; for, was the Point of Sight placed at one End of the House, then the most ordinary Part of the Company would have the best View of the Scenery; and therefore, about the Middle of that Part of the House which is allotted for the Spectators, is thought the most proper Place for the Eye; as in the Figure. Fig. 96.

And having determined the Plan for the Scenery, and fixed the Point of Sight and Center of Contraction, let us next determine the Height of the Eye, and the Height of the several Scenes.

Let ABCD be a perpendicular Section of the House in the Line OT (Fig. 96.)---Draw Lines perpendicular to HT from the Points H and T, 'till they cut the Line CS of the 97th Figure in the Points h and S; then is h the Seat of the Eye, and S the Seat of the Point of Contraction: Again, continue the parallel Lines through the Seats of the Scenes 'till they cut the Line CS in I, 1, 2, 3, 4, which will give the Distance between each Scene; and from the Point I draw Ie, for the Inclination of the Stage, and continue it beyond T, at pleasure: Then, for the Height of the Eye and Point of Contraction, make Eh in this Figure equal to Eh in Fig. 95 *, and draw ET parallel to CS, cutting IT in T; then is Eh the Height of the Eye, and T the Point of Contraction. Fig. 97.

From hence it is evident, that since the Floor Ie is fixed, the Point of Contraction must be governed by the Height of the Eye. For let xh be the Height of the Eye; draw xe parallel to hS, and then is e the Point of Contraction; and in Proportion as the Height of the Eye is greater or less, the Point of Contraction will be nearer or farther off. By this Method of varying the Height of

* The Reason why Eh is taken for the Height of the Eye, and not EH, is, because efQP is considered as the Ground Plane upon which the Picture is supposed to stand. Fig. 95.

the

the Eye, great Variety of Scenery may be introduced; but how far 'tis allowable to alter the Height of the Eye in Scenes for the same Entertainment, must be left to Experience to decide: However, this we may observe, that it ought never to be above the Middle of the Opening of the Curtain, (that is, above s in Fig. 95) nor much below the Face of an Actor upon the Stage. And in regard to the Point of Contraction; it is not necessary to have it upon the End of the Wall, at t, but it may, and ought in general, to be placed beyond it: For when it is placed at the End of the House, then the Scenes will be too suddenly diminished, and will have a disagreeable Effect, besides other Inconveniencies.

Fig. 97. Again, for the Height of the Scenes.---The Line r s is the perpendicular Section with the Curtain; and the Curtain being considered as a Picture, therefore C is the Center of the Picture; and therefore, upon the Line r s set off the several Distances from s, for the hanging Scenes and Tops of the side Scenes; thus c is for the Tops of the Scenes, and c a for the Widths of the hanging Scenes; therefore from s, c, a, draw Lines to T, which will give the Height of each Scene, *&c.* as in the Figure.

Fig. 96. The Side Scenes are made to project beyond the Line M m, *&c.* which measures the Opening of the Curtain; and they should be brought so forward upon the Stage, that a Line H b, drawn from the Seat of the Eye thro' the Corner of the first Scene a, may meet the succeeding Scene in the Point b, where it is cut by M m: For, by this Means, the Spaces between the Scenes will not be visible to many of the Spectators; but the whole together will appear like one continued Picture. In like Manner, Lines drawn from the Top Corner of each Scene, as b of the Scene f b, to the Eye, will give c a for the Width of the hanging Scenes. (Fig. 97.)

Fig. 96. Again, if Lines are drawn through the Points f, g, h, i, 'till they cut the Line e D, then these Points f, g, h, i, will be the Projections of the Points 1, 2, 3, D upon the Floor of the Stage; and consequently, the oblique Line e i, will, to the Spectators at H, appear to be equal to the Line e D; so that the Back Scene in the Line i k, will appear to be as far from the Eye as the End of the House C D; and, by that means, the Depth of the Theatre will appear to be much greater than it really is.

Having made these necessary Preparations, we will now proceed to shew how to draw the Representations upon each Pair of Scenes, so that the whole, when viewed from a proper Point, shall appear as one continued Picture.

To

To prepare a Pair of Side Scenes for Painting.

Draw aa at pleasure, which call the Line of Interſection that the Scenes make with the Floor of the Stage; then from any Point c, erect the Perpendicular cE, and from the Plan (Fig. 96) take the Diſtances dx, dx, which the Scenes xb, xb, are from HT, and transfer them from c to b; take alſo the Width of each Scene, and transfer it from b to a, as in the Figure; then continue Cc downwards, and make cg equal to f 1, (Fig. 97) and draw fh parallel to aa: Then are ab, da, the Seats of the ſecond Pair of Scenes, and gc their Height from the horizontal Plane efQP, (Fig. 95.) And ſo alſo for the Height of the Scenes;---From a, b, d, a, draw Lines parallel to gE, then take the Height fb of the ſecond Scene, (Fig. 97) and ſet it from b to i; which gives the proper Height. Again, for the horizontal Line and Center of the Picture;---Take 1d (Fig. 97) and ſet it from g to C, and through C, draw HL parallel to aa; then is HL the horizontal Line, and C the Center of the Picture. In like Manner, the Diſtance of the Eye for each Pair of Scenes is to be determined;--Thus Ed (Fig. 97) is the Diſtance of the Eye from the Scene fb; therefore, ſet off CE in this Figure equal to Ed in the 97th Figure: And having got the proper Diſtance of the Eye for one Pair of Scenes, *&c.* we are to proceed with our Work in the very ſame Manner as if it was an upright Picture. And the ſame Methods are to be taken for all the other Side Scenes, the Back Scene, *&c.* taking their Breadths from the Plan, and their Heights from the Elevation: All which may be very eaſily done by drawing a ſmall Model, according to the above Rules, and then transferring the ſeveral Parts unto each Scene, *&c.* Fig. 98.

Or this may be done by conſidering the Curtain as a Picture which is to repreſent the whole Deſign, and upon which are drawn the ſeveral Parts proper for each Scene; then by reticulating the whole, as in the 101ſt Figure, we may transfer the Part peculiar to each Scene, in the ſame Manner as one Picture is copied from another by the common Method of Net-Work: But we muſt take great Care to divide each Scene exactly in the ſame Manner as that Scene is divided by the Reticulation upon the Curtain.

And here it is neceſſary alſo to obſerve, that ſince the Space If, (Fig. 97) which is the Diſtance between the Scenes In and fb, repreſents the whole Space from I to o; therefore, no Part of the Diſtance Io ſhould be drawn upon the Scene fb; but all that comes

comes within that Distance, should be painted upon the Scene In: And so of the rest.

Again, we must take Care to give each Scene such a Projection, that a Line drawn from the Eye through the Edge of one Scene, may cut its succeeding Scene in a proper Manner; as was observed before: For which Purpose we may use the following Method.----
Fig. 99. Set off the several Widths for the Opening of the Curtain, and Width of the Scenes, from the 96th Figure, upon the Line a f, (which I here suppose the Bottom of the Model;) draw also the horizontal Line, *&c.* then, from the Points a, b, c, d, e, f, draw Lines to C, and make a g equal to In (Fig. 97;) then draw g m parallel to a f, and set off the several Divisions g h, h i, *&c.* from g towards m; then draw Lines from all those Points to C, as in the Figure. Thus again, suppose n o the Seat of the first Scene; then draw n p, cutting C k in p; and then is n p the Height of the first Scene. Again, from the Point 2, where the Edge of the first Scene cuts e C, draw 1 2, which will cut C d in 1; then is 1 2 the apparent Breadth of the second Scene: And so of the rest.---In the 100th Figure is a Set of Scenes compleated; where C is the Back Scene, which parts in the Middle; 1, 2, 3, 4, the Side Scenes; and the prickt Lines a b, *&c.* are the Hanging Scenes.

CHAP.

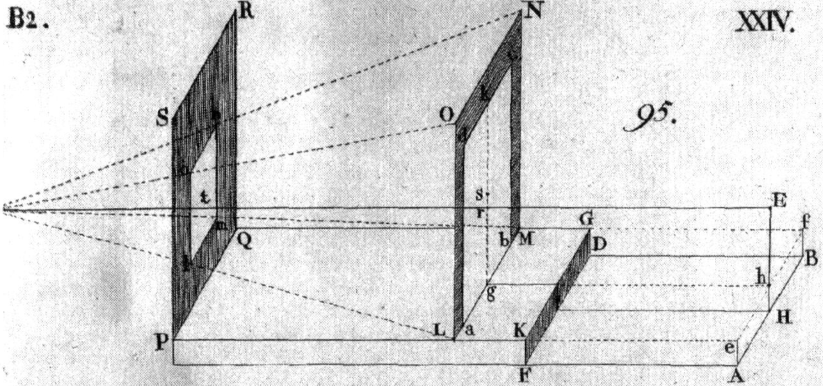
R
N
S
O
k
a
s
t
r
E
f
m
G
Q
b
M
D
B
h
g
H
P
L
a
K
e
F
A

95.

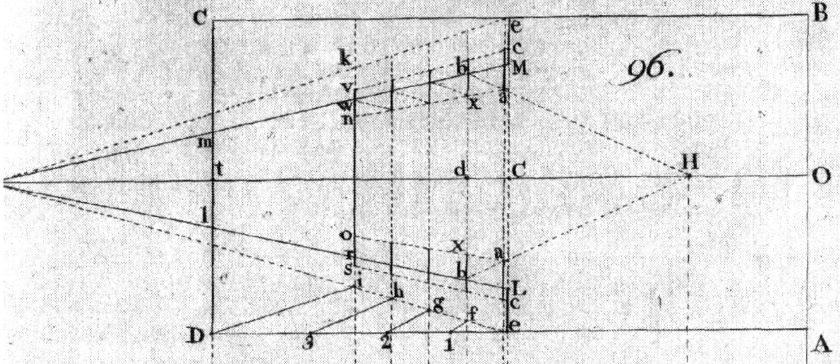
C
e
B
c
k
b
M
v
w
x
a
n
m
t
d
C
H
O
l
o
x
a
r
s
b
i
L
h
g
c
f
D
e
A
3
2
1

96.

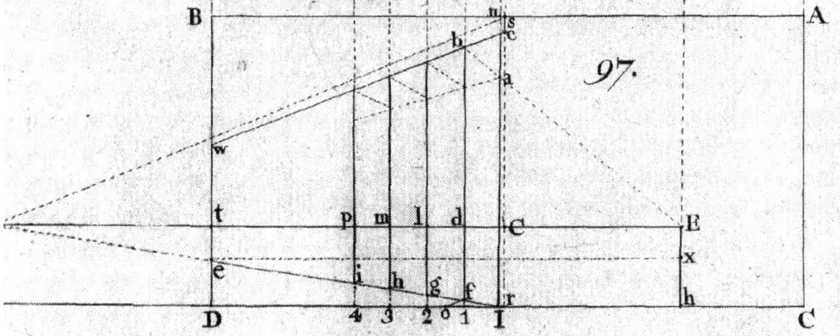
B
n
s
A
c
b
a
w
t
p
m
l
d
C
E
x
e
i
h
g
f
r
h
D
4
3
2
o
1
I
C

97.

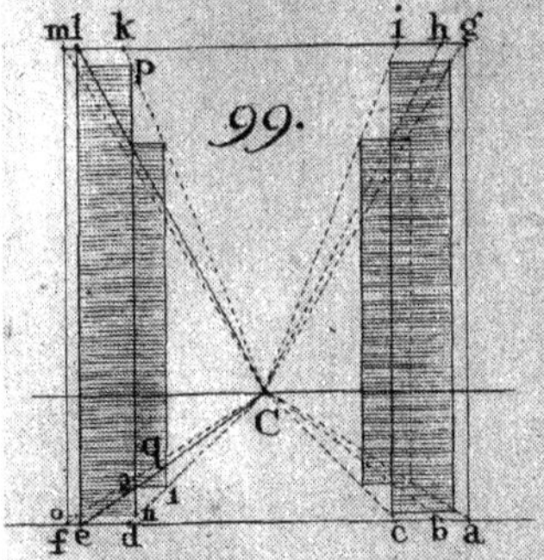
99.
m l k i h g
p q
C
f e d c b a

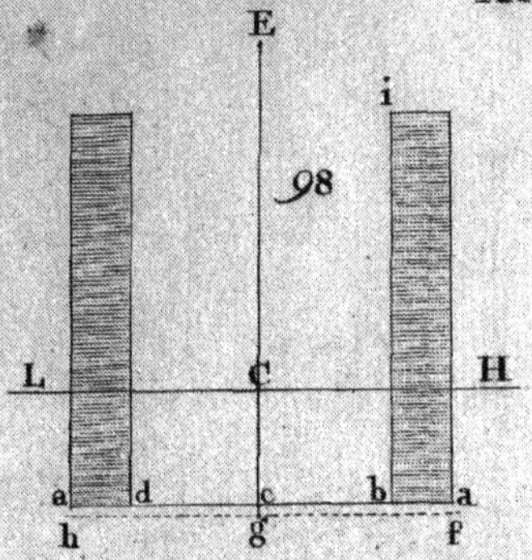
98
E
i
L C H
a d c b a
h g f

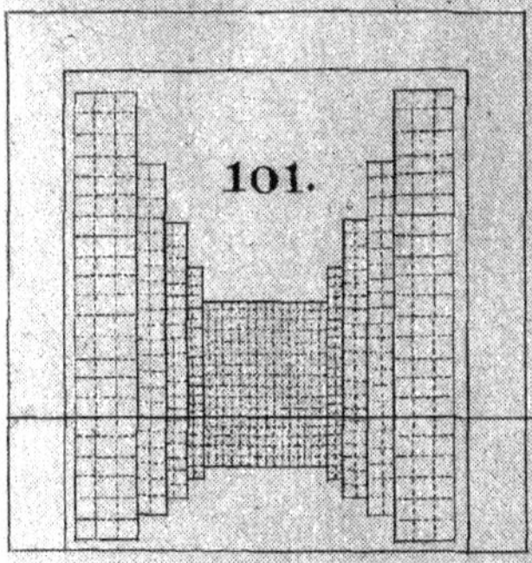
101.

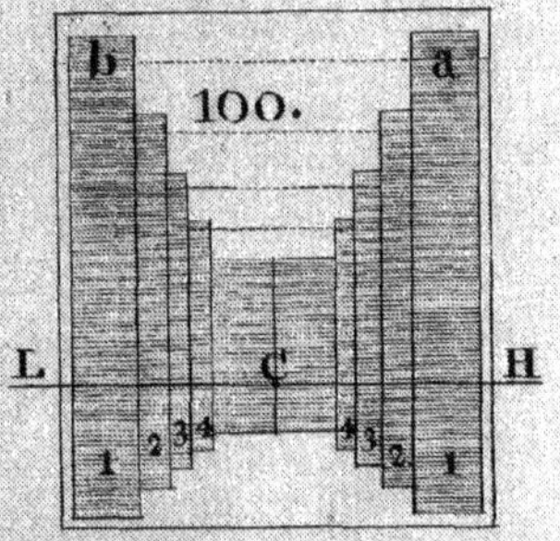
100.
b a
L C H
1 2 3 4 4 3 2 1

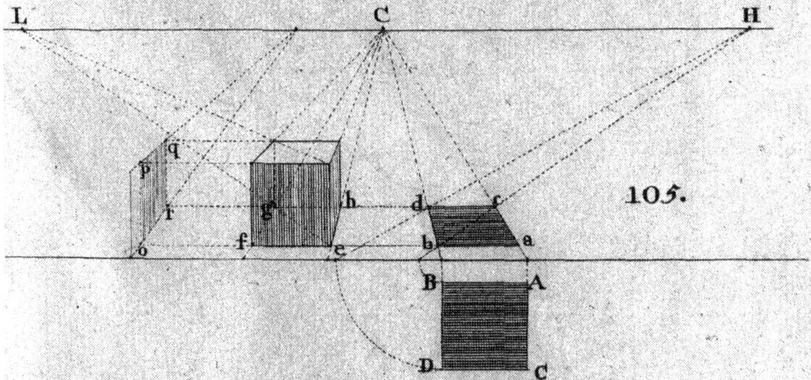
105.
L C H
q p r g h d c
o f e b a
B A
D C

CHAP. VII.

An Abstract of several Methods of Perspective; transcribed from the most eminent Authors.

THE oldest Books which I have met with upon the Subject of Perspective, are, one by VIGNOLA *, and another by MAROLOIS †. And these two Authors seem to me, to have laid the Plan for every System of Perspective (except Dr. *Taylor's* and Mr. *Hamilton's*) since their Times; though few of the Authors who have built upon their Principles, have been so generous as to acknowledge their Obligations to them; but, on the contrary, have set off their Books with pompous Titles, to allure the Public, and to raise in them an Expectation of finding something new and curious. This, though a Practice too common among Authors, is, in my Opinion, an unpardonable Transgression of the Rules of Modesty and Plain dealing; and therefore, to avoid any Imputation of this Kind, I have constantly acknowledged my Obligations to every Author who has lent me any Assistance. It was for this Reason, principally, that I gave my Book the Title of Dr. BROOK TAYLOR'S PERSPECTIVE, &c. But though I must acknowledge my Work to be generally built upon the Principles of that ingenious Author, I hope, I may at the same Time assert, that whoever will compare my Schemes with those that have been before made publick, will find very few but what are intirely of my own Invention.

The following Examples, which are taken from VIGNOLA, MAROLOIS, VREDEMAN FRIESE, the JESUIT, and POZZO, will be sufficient to shew how one Author has copied from another, and the various Methods which have been published. I shall begin with VIGNOLA'S.

* *Vignola* was a famous *Italian* Architect, who flourished in the Beginning of the 15th Century: He wrote a Treatise upon Perspective, which was published in 1644, by *Filippo de Rossi*, with Annotations by *Ignatius Danti*. It was printed in Folio at *Rome*, and is in the *Italian* Language.

† This Work was printed in Folio at the *Hague*, is in *Latin*, and was engraved and published by *Henry Hondius* in 1615; and though tedious in its Operations, is nevertheless a very curious Performance.

I. VIGNOLA's METHOD.

To put a CUBE *into Perspective.*

Fig. 102. Here AC is a perpendicular Section of the Picture, AB is the Bottom of the Picture, and C the Center of the Picture, E the Eye, and ES its Height, D is the Elevation of the Cube, and F its Plan upon the Ground. Now, having settled the above Requisites, draw Lines from every Corner of the Elevation D, to the Eye E, and from the Plan F draw Lines from every Corner to the Seat of the Eye at S; and their several Intersections upon the Line BC, will give the proper Measures for the Height and Depth of the proposed Representation. Thus, from the Points 1, 2, 3, 4, on the Line of Elevation AC, draw Lines parallel to the horizontal Line; then from the Line AB of the Plan, take A b, b a, and set from 1 to a, and take A c, cd, and set from 2 to d; which will give the proper Heights and Depths, as in the Figure. Or, by setting off A 5, 5 6, equal to 7 8, 8 9, and drawing Lines to C, we may get the Depth of the Plan a b c d.

By this Method, we are taught how to make a perspective Scale for any Representation: For having drawn the Elevations and Plans of the proposed Objects, the Line AB may be considered as a Scale for the Plans, and the Line AC as a Scale for the Elevations.

II. MAROLOIS's METHOD.

To put a DOUBLE CROSS *into Perspective.*

Fig. 103. Here ce is the Ground Line, DC the horizontal Line, C the Center of the Picture, and CD the Distance of the Eye.——Draw out the Plan of the Cross, as A, and put it into Perspective, as in the Figure; then, at any convenient Distance c, raise a Perpendicular cd upon the Ground Line, and set the Elevations a, 1, 2, b, upon it; then from c, 3, 4, d, draw Lines to any Point H in the horizontal Line; after which, draw Lines through every Angle of the Plan, parallel to the horizontal Line, which will cut the Line cH, and thereby give the Points by which the Perspective B of the Elevation may be compleated; finally, from every Angle of the Plan draw Lines perpendicular to the horizontal Line, and from every Angle of the Elevation draw Lines parallel to the horizontal Line; and then, their mutual Intersections with each other, will produce the proposed Representation, as in the Figure,——The Reader is desired to compare this with my Method in the 40th Figure.

III. JAN

III. JAN VREDEMAN FRIESE's METHOD. *

To put a CUBE *into Perſpective.*

Make the Bottom BP of the Picture a Scale of Feet, from whence find the Repreſentation of any Number of Geometrical Squares, as in the Figure.——Now let it be required to find the Appearance of a Cube abcd, equal to two Feet in Diameter, and let it be one Foot from the Bottom of the Picture.---Make the Front Face abcd two Squares wide and two Squares high, then give two Squares for the Depth, and from thence compleat the Figure. Fig. 104.

IV. *The* JESUIT's METHOD. †

To put a CUBE *into Perſpective.*

Draw the Plan ABCD, which put into Perſpective, as a b c d; from thence draw another Plan e f g h, then, by *Marolois's* Method, find the Elevation, and from thence compleat the Figure.——— And this ſame Method is taught by *Kircher*, in his Work, entituled, *Ars magna Lucis et Umbræ*, Chap. 3. Fig. 105.

V. ANDREA POZZO's METHODS. ‖

1. *To put a* PARALLELOPIPED *into Perſpective.*

Draw the Elevation A, and from thence the Plan B; then put the Plan into Perſpective, as a g f d; from the Corner a of the Plan, erect the Perpendicular a b, and continue the Top of the Elevation A 'till it cuts a b in c; from whence the Perſpective Elevation may be compleated by *Marolois's* Method: And having got the Depth of one Plan, and the Height of the Elevations, the whole Repreſentation may be compleated by *Vignola*'s Method. Fig. 106.

2. *To put a* PARALLELOPIPED *into Perſpective, which will explain* POZZO*'s other Method.*

Here in Conformity to *Vignola's* Perſpective Scale, AC is the Section of the Picture, AB the Ground Line, D the Eelevation of an Object, and F, H, the Plans of two Objects parallel to the Pic- Fig. 107.

* This Book is a Folio, in *French*, was printed at the *Hague* in 1619. It was corrected by *Marolois*, and engrav'd by *Henry Hondius*.

† This Book is in Quarto, was wrote originally in *French* by a Jeſuit at *Paris*, was tranſlated into *Engliſh* by *E. Chambers*, and was printed at *London* in 1726.

‖ His firſt Book was publiſhed in *Latin* and *Engliſh* by *John Sturt*, Engraver, in 1707; and his ſecond Book was publiſhed by himſelf, in Latin, in 1700; and are both in Folio.

ture; so likewise, E is the Eye, E S its Height, and I is considered as the Seat of the Eye.———From the several Angles of the Elevation draw Lines to the Eye E, and from the several Angles of the Plans draw Lines to I, which will cut BC, and thereby give the Elevations and the Depths of the Plans; from whence the 108th Figure may be compleated. Thus, A 1, A 2, A 3, A4, are each equal to their corresponding Divisions, A 1, A 2, A 3, A 4, upon the Line of Elevation A C, Fig. 107; and 1 o, 1 t, &c. are equal to K o, K t, &c. of the same Figure; and A C is equal to the Height of the Eye S E. But I have put every Line and Point, to explain the Thing the better.

There are several other smaller Treatises upon Perspective, and particularly one by *Bernard Lamy*, entitled, *Perspective made Easy*, which, as it contains some curious Observations upon Painting, &c. is worthy of Notice.

FINIS.

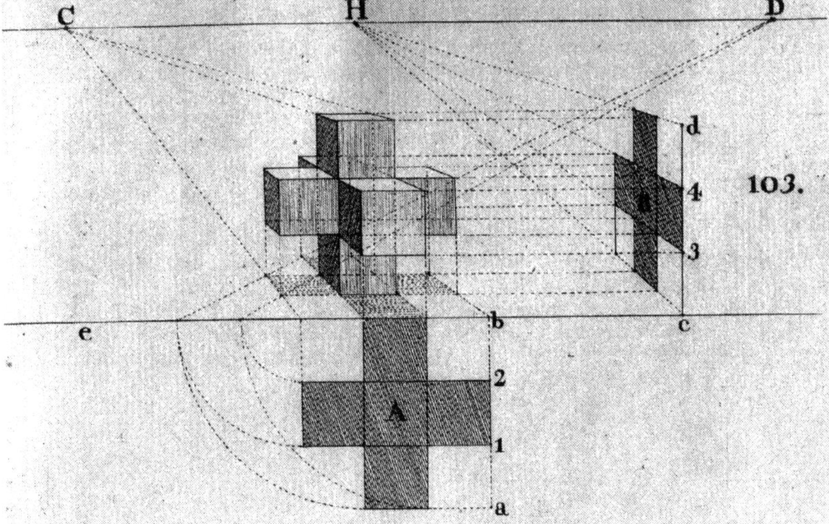

103.

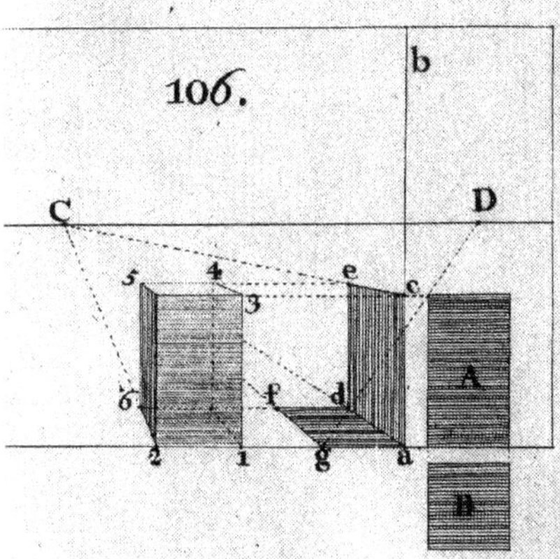

106.

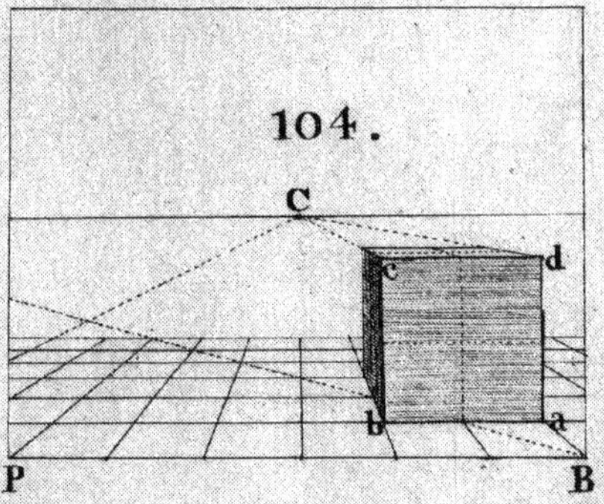

104.

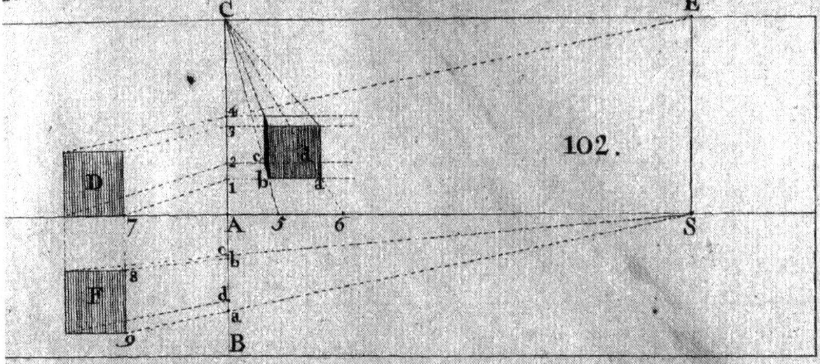
102.
C
E
D
F
A
S
B

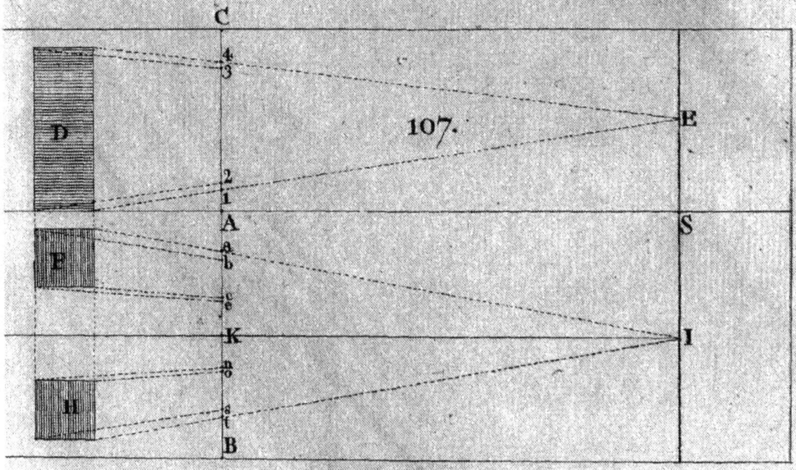
107.
C
D
E
A
S
F
K
I
H
B

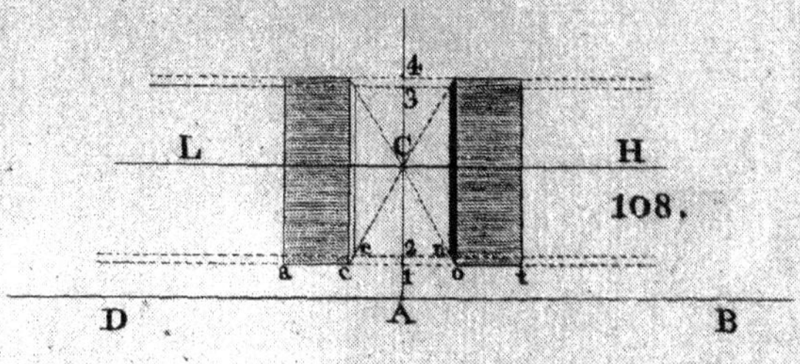
108.
L
C
H
D
A
B

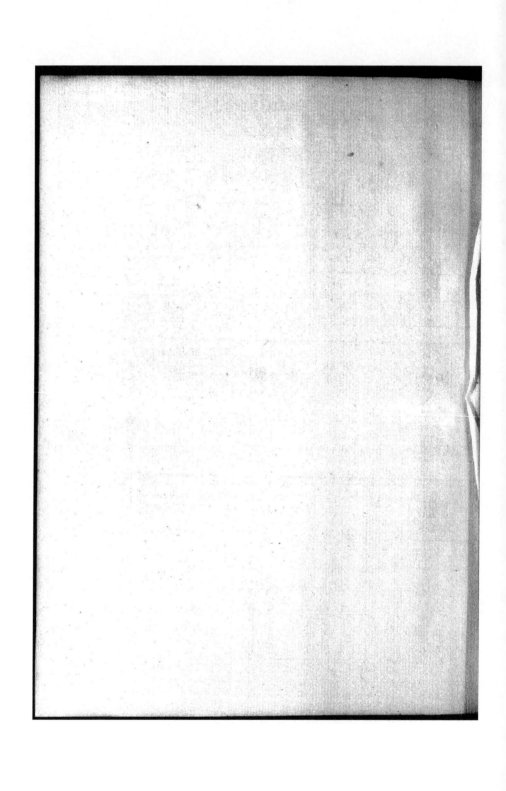

APPENDIX.

THE favourable Reception of the first Impression of this Work had been a sufficient Inducement for publishing a second Edition, if the Number of my Subscribers had not made it absolutely necessary.

When I first engaged in this Undertaking, I much dreaded the Difficulties which presented themselves, both from my own Incapacity, and from the Nature of the Subject: For although I had made Perspective my particular Study for several Years, and was satisfied in my own private Opinion as to the shortness and clearness of the preceeding Method; yet to make it intelligible to others, and useful in general, were Things not to be accomplish'd without much Study, Labour, and Expence. I therefore determined to proceed very cautiously, to view every Article in various Lights, and not to print any thing without having it first approved of by competent Judges.

As this seem'd the most likely Means to prevent my publishing any useless or undigested Figures, so I thought it also a very likely way of avoiding the little ill-natured Criticisms, which are so often made upon the Works of a young Author: And I must confess (with the utmost Gratitude and Thanks) that my Success hath abundantly exceeded my utmost Expectations; for I have been so fortunate as to have the Work approved of in general, and recommended in such a peculiar Manner, by Gentlemen of great Genius and Knowledge, that I now begin to think it secure from public *Censure*, under their kind and powerful Protection.

But it may be necessary to inform my Reader of the Additions which he may expect to find in this Appendix: And, in the first place, I have more largely and more fully considered the Perspective of Shadows; I have also given one Figure to shew why a Down-hill (if merely considered as such) cannot be represented upon the Picture; then I have added another Figure, to explain the nature of what is called a Bird's-eye-view, a sort of Perspective used in drawing Fortifications, and the like. I have also shewn the Use of an Instrument of my own Invention, which may be of Service in Drawing extensive Views, large Buildings, *&c.* and, lastly, I have given the Construction of a small Pocket *Camera Obscura.*——To begin therefore with the Additions to the Perspective of Shadows.

In both the Theory and Practice of Shadows, I have frequently made Use of this Expression, *viz.* "*The vanishing Point of the Shadow;*" which, possibly may require some farther Explanation: Because the Shadows of any Objects which are composed of perpendicular or parallel Planes, will, when put into Perspective, vanish into various Points upon the horizontal Line; and therefore this Article may not seem so very significant, as in fact it is.

By the vanishing Point then of the Shadow, is meant the vanishing Point of such Shadows only, as are suppos'd to be cast upon the Ground Plane (or upon a Plane parallel to it) by the perpendicular Edges of Objects. For since these Species of Shadows will always vanish into the Center of the vanishing Line of the Plane of Rays, therefore this particular vanishing Point will be found to be more useful than any other; as will appear by the following Examples.

And, as I found it necessary to make some considerable Additions to this Part of Perspective, so I have made Choice of such Figures as might contain the most general Rules, and have given some of the most curious and difficult Examples which can be proposed: And that they may be the more clearly comprehended, we will range what we have farther to advance, under the following Heads, *viz.*

I. *When the Shadow is cast upon the Ground, or upon a Plane parallel to it.*

II. *When the Shadow is cast upon a perpendicular Plane,*

III. *When the Shadow is cast upon an oblique Plane.*

CASE I.

When the Shadow is cast upon the Ground, &c.——First, by a perpendicular Object; secondly, by a parallel Object; and thirdly, by an inclined Object.

EXAMPLE I.——*When it is cast by a perpendicular Object.*

Fig. 1. * Here R S is given for the vanishing Line of the Rays of Light, R for the vanishing Point of the Rays, and A B for the perpendicular Object, whose Shadow is sought.

* The Line R S, whether continued or not, will always signify the vanishing Line of the Plane of Rays, and R the vanishing Point of the Rays of Light.

From

From A and B draw A S, and B R, cuting each other in b; then is A b the Shadow of A B. †

Example II.——*When it is caſt by a parallel Object, as the Plane* 1 2 3 4.

Find the Seats of the four Corners upon the Ground, as a, e, n, f; Fig. 8. then from thoſe Seats draw Lines to S, and from 1, 2, 3, 4, draw Lines to R, which will interſect each other, and thereby give the Appearance of the Shadow m.---Now becauſe S and H are the vaniſhing Points of the Plane 1 2 3 4, therefore the Sides of the Shadow will vaniſh into thoſe Points.

Example III.——*When it is caſt by an inclined Object.*

Let 1 2 3 4 be a Pyramid, whoſe Shadow is required.—From Fig. 7. n, the Seat of its Apex or Top 3, draw a Line to S, and from 3 draw a Line to R, cutting n S m m; then from 1 and 2 draw Lines to m, which will compleat the Shadow.---And in the ſame Manner the Shadow of the inclined Edge A B, of the perpendicular Plane A B D, is to be determined.

C A S E II.

When the Shadow is caſt upon a perpendicular Plane.---Firſt, when it is caſt by a perpendicular Object; ſecondly, when it is caſt by a parallel Object, and thirdly, when it is caſt by an inclined Object.

Example I.——*When it is caſt by a perpendicular Object.*

Let ab be an Object perpendicular to the Plane A B C D, and let Fig. 4. it be required to find the Shadow of the Object a b upon this Plane. ---From a and b draw the Perpendiculars a f, b g, and through f, where a f cuts the Bottom AB, draw C g, cutting b g in g; then

† Now that S, the Center of the vaniſhing Line R S, is likewiſe the vaniſhing Point of the Shadow of A B, may be thus demonſtrated.——The Lines A B and R S being parallel, therefore the Plane A B R S will paſs through them both; and ſince the Shadow of A B is caſt upon the Ground, it muſt vaniſh into the horizontal Line: And becauſe R S is the vaniſhing Line of the Plane of Rays which projects the Shadow, the Point S muſt likewiſe be in that Line, and therefore S, the *common Section* of the vaniſhing Line R S, with L S the vaniſhing Line of the Plane upon which the Shadow is caſt, muſt be the vaniſhing Point of the Shadow upon that Plane.——And in the ſame Manner all the foregoing Figures upon this Head may be demonſtrated.

from g draw g S cutting A B in h, and from h draw a Line at pleasure, but parallel to a f, then from b draw a Line to R cutting h e in e; finally, draw a Line from e to a, which will be a Guide for compleating the Shadow, as in the Figure.

EXAMPLE II.——*When it is cast by a parallel Object.*

Fig. 1. Here A B is the Object, and 1 2 3, the Plane upon which the Shadow is cast.---From A draw A S cutting the lower Edge 1 2, in a, and from B draw B R, and from a, draw a g parallel to A B; then will a f be the Shadow proposed: And was the Plane 1 2 3 continued as high as g, then would a g be the Shadow of A B.--- The same may be said of the Shadows a, c, in Figures 2, 3.

EXAMPLE III.——*When it is cast by an inclined Object.*

Fig. 5. In this Figure 1 3 4 5, is an inclined Object, which casts a Shadow upon the Planes A, C.---Find the Shadow of the perpendicular Plane 1 2 3, upon the Ground, which will cut the lower Edge of the Plane A in a; continue 1 a till it cuts the horizontal Line in f; then is f the vanishing Point of the Shadow of the Edge 1 3, therefore from R draw a Line through f, and continue it at pleasure, which will pass through C, (the vanishing Point of the inclined Face 1 3 4 5) then from H, the vanishing Points of the perpendicular Planes A, C, draw H V perpendicular to the horizontal Line, which will cut R V in V, and thereby give V for the vanishing Point of the Shadows a b and c d; therefore from a draw aV, and from b draw b S, from c draw cV, and finally, from 3 draw 3 R, which will give the Point d for the Shadow of the Corner 3.---And in order to find the vanishing Point of the Shadow which is cast upon the Plane G, by the Top 34 of the inclined Plane, continue V S below the horizontal Line, and draw a Line from R parallel to the horizontal Line, which will cut V S in S, and thereby give S for the vanishing Point of that Part of the Shadow; as is evident by the Figure.

CASE III.

When the Shadow is cast upon an inclined Plane.---First, by an Object perpendicular to the Ground; and secondly by an Object inclined to the Ground.

EXAMP.

APPENDIX.

EXAMPLE I. *When it is cast by a perpendicular Object; which will admit of great Variety.*

1st. If the vanishing Point S of the Sides 1 5, 3 4 be the vanishing Point of the Shadow upon the Ground, then will S be also the vanishing Point of the Shadow upon the inclined Plane.—Thus the Shadow c d which is cast by A B upon the inclined Plane will vanish into S. Fig. 1.

2dly. If the vanishing Point S of the Shadow be taken within the vanishing Point H of the Edges 15, 34, then the vanishing Points of the Shadow c d, will be above the horizontal Line; and may always be found in this Manner; *viz,* find the Shadows A a, a c, and continue the vanishing Line R S above the horizontal Line at Pleasure; then from the vanishing Points H, V, of the inclined Plane draw H V, cutting R s in s, and then is s the vanishing Point of c d. Fig. 2.

3dly. If the vanishing Point S of the Shadow be taken without the vanishing Point H of the Edges 15, 34, then the vanishing Point l of the Shadow c d will be below the horizontal Line: And this is found by drawing a Line through the vanishing Points V and H of the Edges 13, 15 of the inclined Plane, till it cuts the vanishing Line R S in l. Fig. 3.

Now the Reason of all this must appear extremely evident, if we consider, first, that however a Shadow is cast upon any Plane, it must vanish into a Point or Points in the vanishing Line of that Plane; because the Boundaries or Out-lines of every Shadow, are considered only as Lines drawn upon a Plane. And secondly, because the vanishing Points of the Sides of any Shadows, and the vanishing Point of the Plane of Rays which projects those Shadows, must always be in the same Plane: But, as we observed before, this will more fully appear by the Figures.

4thly. To find the Shadow of A B C D upon the inclined Plane 1 3 4.---Here V L continued will be the vanishing Line of the inclined Plane: And to find the Shadow cd, first determine the Shadow of A B C D upon the Ground, which will cut the lower Edge of the inclined Plane; then continue R S till it cuts V L in V, and from R draw R L parallel to the horizontal Line which will cut V L in L; and then are L and V the vanishing Points of the Shadow, as in the Fig. 4.

Figure

Figure.——From this Figure we may obſerve, that the Line V L paſſes through the vaniſhing Point H of the Edges 1, 3 4, and therefore the vaniſhing Point V may be found by drawing L V through H.

Fig. 6. 5thly. To determine the Shadow of the Pillar A, when it is caſt upon two inclined Planes.——Here H F and F L are the vaniſhing Lines of the inclined Planes 1 2 4, 2 3 4.——Find the Shadow of the Pillar upon the Ground which will cut the lower Edge of the Plane 1 2 4 in a b; then continue H F till it cuts R S continued in V, and then is V the vaniſhing Point of the Shadow a b c d, and ſo alſo s where the vaniſhing Line F L cuts R V; is the vaniſhing Point of the Shadow c d e f.

EXAMPLE II.——*When the Shadow is caſt by an inclined Line A B, upon an inclined Plane* 1 2 3.

Fig. 7. Having found the Shadow of A B upon the Ground, continue it till it cuts the horizontal Line in s; then from R draw a Line thro' s cutting the vaniſhing Line H V of the Plane 1 2 3, in f, and then is f the vaniſhing Point of the Shadow a b: And if L f be continued it will cut the vaniſhing Line N U in U.

Fig. 8. To find the Shadow of a perpendicular Object when it is caſt upon a Tetrahedron.——Determine the Shadow A b of A B upon the Ground, and draw the Seat a e n f of the Plane 1 2 3 4; then from where the Shadow cuts a f, draw Lines parallel to A B cutting the Edge 1 4, which will be a Guide for drawing the Shadow upon the upper Face, to S. And for the Shadow on the Face 1 4 D, continue the vaniſhing Line H M of 1 4 D, and S R the vaniſhing Line of the Plane of Rays, and their Interſection with each other will be the vaniſhing Point of that Shadow.——As to the Shadows which are caſt upon the Ground by the above Objects, it is preſumed, that they want no farther Explanation.

Theſe are a few of the many Examples which might be produced as a farther Illuſtration of the Perſpective of Shadows; for this Part of Perſpective might be extended to Infinity: However theſe Figures contain ſome of the moſt general Principles that I can think of, and are abundantly ſufficient to ſhew how the Appearances of any Shadows are to be exactly determined, upon all ſorts of Planes, and in the moſt difficult Situations.

A P P E N D I X.

Some Conſiderations upon drawing the Repreſentation of an inclined Plane going from the Eye, or what is uſually called a Down-hill.

To repreſent a Down-hill hath always appeared a Matter of great Difficulty to Painters, and this will ever remain impracticable, ſince, in the Nature of the Thing, it is impoſſible to be done.

For let H L be the horizontal Line, and let F 1, F 2, F 3, F 4, Fig. 9.
and F H, repreſent the ſeveral Angles, or Inclinations of five different Hills: Then we may conceive theſe Hills to be like ſo many inclined Planes. And if they are ſuppoſed to vaniſh into Lines parallel to the horizontal Line, then a a is the vaniſhing Line of the Hill F 2, b b of the Hill F 3, c c of the Hill F 4, d d of the Hill F H, and the horizontal Line H L is the vaniſhing Line of the even Ground F K; for the ſeveral Lines L C, L d, *&c.* are parallel to the original Lines F K, F H, *&c.* From whence we may obſerve that the even Ground (ſuppoſe a Road A B C) will ſeem to riſe upwards, and vaniſh into the horizontal Line H L; and the leaſt inclined Plane will vaniſh below the horivontal Line, but will take up the Space D d upon the Picture; the next inclined Plane will take up the Space Dc, the next D b, and the next D a; and when the Inclination of the Hill is ſo great (as F 1) that its vaniſhing Line will fall below the Bottom of the Picture, then that inclined Plane will totally diſappear, and therefore can have no Place upon the Picture. So that from hence appears the Impoſſibility of repreſenting a Down-hill, (ſingly as ſuch) by the Rules of Perſpective; becauſe, what we actually know to go down-hill in Nature, will, if ever ſo correctly drawn upon the Picture, appear to riſe upwards; which is another ſtrong Inſtance of the Inſufficiency of Perſpective upon ſome particular Occaſions. For in order to repreſent ſuch an inclined Plane, we muſt have Recourſe to Experienee, which will teach us to diſpoſe particular Kinds of Objects in ſuch a Manner, as ſhall convey to the Mind the Idea of a Down-hill; ſuch as ſhewing Part of a Figure, or making the Tops of lofty Objects full below the horizontal Line, *&c. &c.*——As to the Manner of repreſenting Hills when they are ſideways with the Picture, that is ſo very eaſy, as not to be worthy Notice in this Place.

Of

APPENDIX.

Of a Bird's Eye View; and how to put a Fortification, &c. into Perspective.

Although this Part of Perspective is easily deducible from our general Rules, yet I have here added the following Figure, which is sufficient to explain the whole of this Matter. And I have made the Figure very simple, with upright Walls only, and without Bastions, or any the least common Parts of Fortifications.

In drawing the Representations of Fortifications, it is necessary not only to shew one View as seen upon the Ground, but to exhibit also so much of the several Buildings as the Eye can possibly take in at one Time from any Situation. And in order to do this we must suppose the Eye to be removed to a considerable Height above the Ground, and to be placed as it were in the Air, so as to look down into the Building, like a Bird that is flying.

Fig. 10. Suppose therefore M, N, O, to be the Walls of three Fortifications, the lowest (O) of which, is surrounded with a Ditch.——Now to draw these several Representations, we must first choose a proper Height for the horizontal Line, and then proceed exactly in the same Manner, as if we were drawing any Objects by the common Rules; only observing to let the Distance we work with, be somewhat greater than the Space between the Bottom of the Picture and the horizontal Line.——And, if it were required, to draw the Appearance of a Ditch, or the like; then from the Surface of the Ground, as IK, set off I 2 equal to the supposed Depth, and draw a Line to the vanishing Point of the top Edge of the Ditch; and so likewise for the Surface of the Water, which we will suppose to be at the Distance I 1 from the Top of the Ditch. Set this Distance from I to 1, which will be a sufficient Guide for the above Purposes.

It is easy to conceive that the higher the horizontal Line is placed, the more of the Fortification will be seen, and the contrary the lower it is placed.

A Description of an Instrument that may be useful in taking extensive Views, &c.

The Ruler A B is 19 Inches long, and is graduated into 19 equal Parts; upon the upper Edge of it is a doustail Groove to receive the perpendicular Ruler G, which has one End fitted to it, so as to slide very easily; this Ruler is 15 Inches long, and is divided into 15 equal Parts

Parts, and upon the Back-ſide of it (repreſented by F) is a Line drawn exactly in the Middle, and upon this Line is fixed a piece of Barber's Silk, with a little Plummet at the End. The Ruler A B is fixed by two Screws a c, to two pieces of thin Braſs; and theſe pieces of Braſs are fixed at the other Ends by two Screws d e to a ſtronger piece of Braſs b f; this Braſs b f goes cloſe to the Ruler A B, and has a Joint at x which turns upon a Screw; below this Joint is a piece of round Braſs about ſix Inches long, which goes into a Hole made in the Top of the Staff, and may be raiſed higher or lower like a Barber's Block by means of the Screw f; Part of this Staff is C D E, and the whole Length is about 3 Feet, and at the Bottom is, what we call a rank Screw made of Iron and is fixed to the Staff. H I is a Wire 22 Inches long, with a Screw at h to go into the Hole b; the piece of braſs Wire, bent into the Form i k is fixed to the Wire H I by the Screw k; and the Part i goes into the Hole f, in the braſs Piece b f. The ſmall Wire K L. is about 12 Inches long and is flatted at K, at which Place is a little Hole about 1-8th of an Inch in Diameter; this Wire K L is fitted to the Holes l, m, n, o, which are made in the larger Wire H I, and it may be placed higher or lower, by means of a ſmall Screw.——This is a Deſcription of the ſeveral Parts of the Inſtrument; we will next ſhew its Uſe.

Fix a Paper upon a Drawing-board, as in Fig. 12, and divide the Paper length-ways into 19 equal Parts, and Perpendicularly into 15 equal Parts; and in Proportion as you intend the Drawing to be larger or ſmaller, make theſe Diviſions greater or leſs. Then take the Staff and fix it ſtrongly in the Ground, by means of the Screw at the Bottom, and at a convenient Diſtrance from the Proſpect which you intend to take. After this, put the Inſtrument together as in Fig. 13; and fix the Ruler A B, exactly Horizontal by means of the Plummet on the perpendicular Ruler and the Braſs Joint x; then fix the Wire K L. ſo as to have the Eye-hole exactly level with the Horizon, that is equal to the Height of the Eye, and take care alſo to have the greateſt Diſtance of the Eye-hole from the Ruler, equal to the whole Length of the longeſt Ruler A B, and never leſs than the Diſtance h l.——Having thus fixed the Inſtrument, place yourſelf on a Seat, and proceed to make your Drawing in the following Manner.——Look through the Eye-hole, and then move the perpendicular Ruler in the Groove, till you get one Edge exactly againſt ſome principal Object; then will the Parts upon the Ruler ſhew how high the Object is from the Bottom of the Ruler (that is from the Bottom of the

Picture) and you will alſo have its apparent Height; therefore tranſfer this unto the Paper in theſe Squares which correſpond with the Diviſions upon the Rulers. So alſo for the Breadths of Objects; move the perpendicular Ruler ſo as to be even with the Sides of an Object; and the Diviſions upon the lower Ruler will ſhew their apparent Breadths. And after the ſame manner, get the Places and apparent Sizes of as many principal Objects as are neceſſary for aſſiſting you in compleating the whole Drawing; which may be done by this Method with great Exactneſs. —— And having finiſhed the Drawing, the Inſtrument may be taken to Pieces and put into a Box, which may ſerve as a Drawing-board; the Top M may be ſcrewed into the Staff which will ſerve as a Walking-ſtick, and the Stool to ſet on may be made very Portable, ſo that every Part of this Apparatus may be carried by one Perſon with great Eaſe. *

I ſhall juſt Obſerve that the Inſtruments which have been Publiſhed of this Kind, have no Diſtance limited for the Eye hole, which make all the Repreſentations that are drawn by an improper Diſtance moſt egregiouſly Falſe; as is Demonſtrated in what we have ſaid concerning the Diſtance of the Eye in Chap. 6. B, 1. and Chap. 2, B, 2.

The 14th Figure is a ſmall pocket *Camera Obſcura*. The lower Part of this Inſtrument is a ſquare Box, 4 Inches in Diameter with a Looking-glaſs E fixed at an Angle of 45 Degrees. In the Middle of the Side B C is a ſmall Hole 2 Inches in Diameter, in which goes a Tube to Slide 2 Inches long, and in that a Lens for the Object-Glaſs. The Top part F of this Box is a Piece of ground Glaſs to receive the Image from the Looking-glaſs E. But as the Picture will be very ſmall, and conſequently the Object's too much diminiſhed; therefore, on the Top of the Box C D a b, is another Tube G, with a Lens of a large magnifying Power; which being raiſed higher or lower will ſo increaſe the Size of the Picture as to make the whole View very diſtinct. The Fore-part which is left open, may

* But although this Inſtrument is very Simple, and uſeful to any Perſon who is tollerably ſkilled in Drawing; yet I muſt be ſo ingenuous as to acquaint my Readers, that there is another kind of Inſtrument, made by Mr. *Adams*, at *Tycho Brahe's Head*, the corner of *Raquet-Court*, in *Fleet-Street London*: which is ſo conſtructed, that any Perſon, without either the knowledge of Perſpective, or the leaſt Notion of Drawing, may take the Perſpective View of any Building, Proſpect, or Figure, with the greateſt Accuracy. This Inſtrument is newly invented, (but upon a Plan of Sr. *Chriſtopher Wren's*) by a Clergyman in the Country, whoſe Name I am not Commiſſioned to mention; however in Juſtice to ſo ingenious and uſeful a Production, I have taken the Liberty of Recommending it in this Place.

be either made like two Doors to move upon Hinges, or may ſlide in Grooves for that Purpoſe: One of which is abſolutely neceſſary on account of cleaning the Glaſſes &c.——This with the other Inſtrument may be had of the ſame Perſon, mentioned in Page 1 Book I and of Mr. *Adams* in *Fleet-Street*.

FINIS.

A P P E N D I X.

he other side [illegible] from [illegible]
in Greece for one [illegible] which [illegible]
on account of [illegible]
from [illegible]
[illegible]

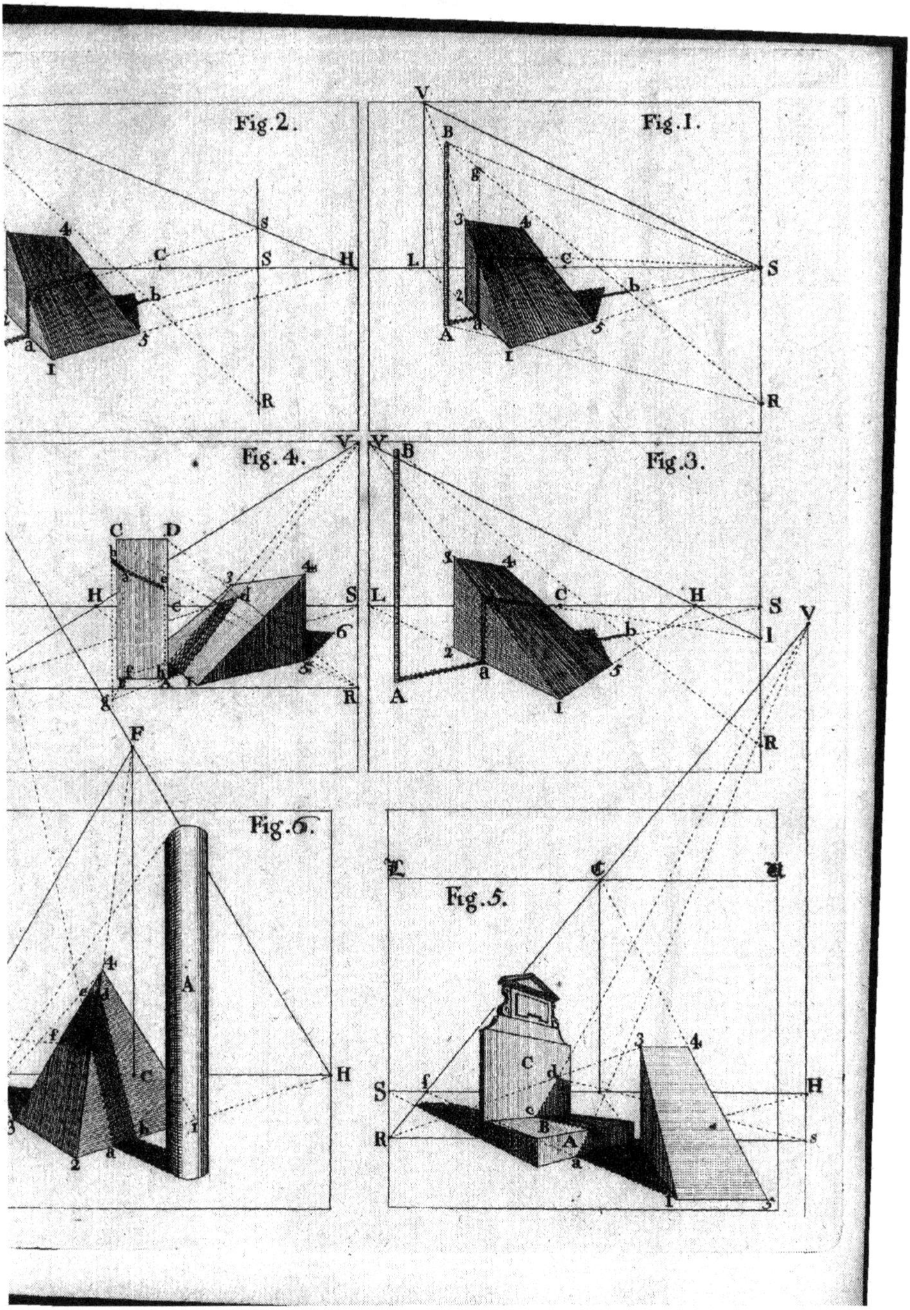
Fig.1.
Fig.2.
Fig.3.
Fig.4.
Fig.5.
Fig.6.

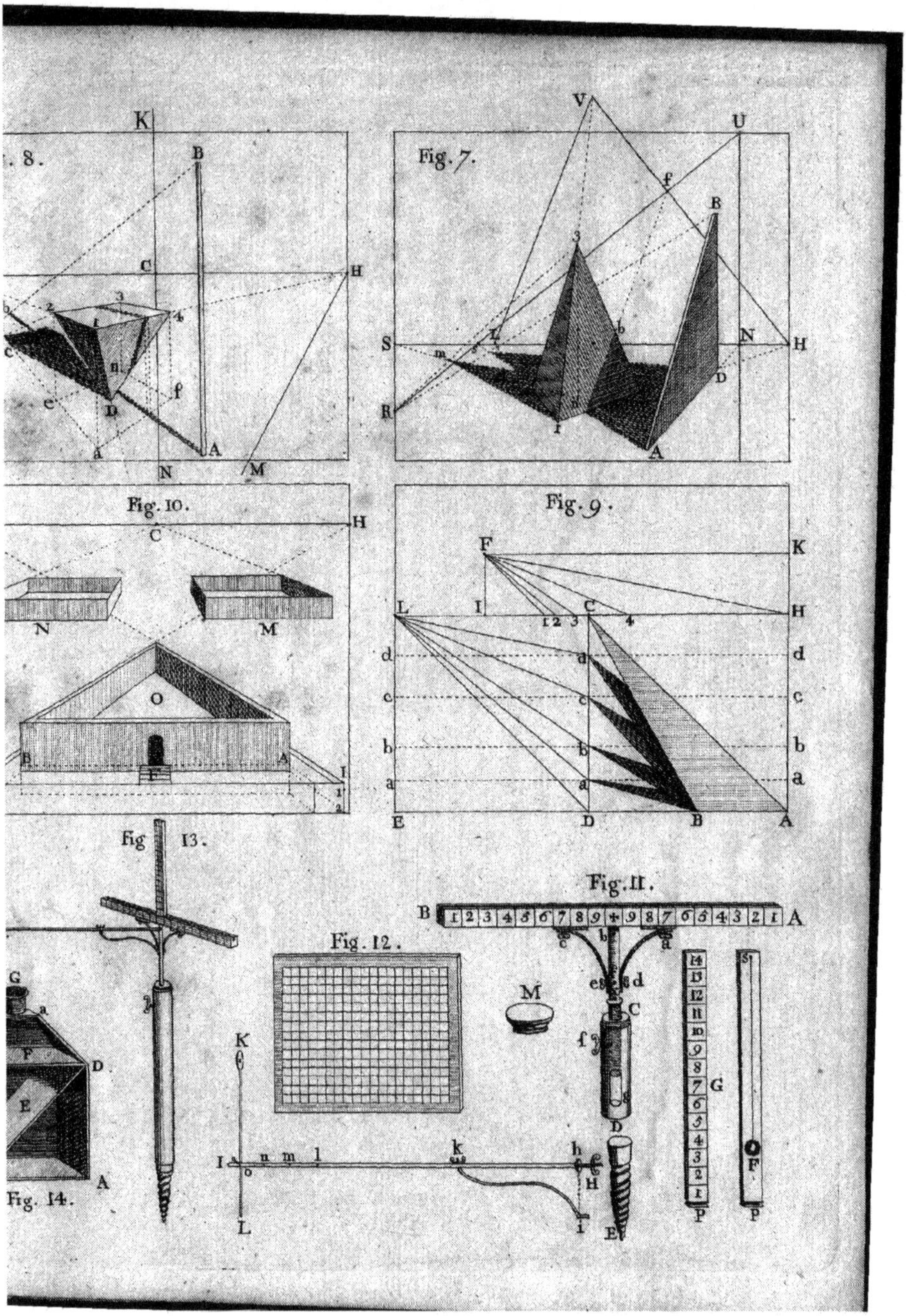
. 8.
Fig. 7.
Fig. 10.
Fig. 9.
Fig 13.
Fig. 11.
Fig. 12.
Fig. 14.

CPSIA information can be obtained
at www.ICGtesting.com
Printed in the USA
BVHW010222130422
634143BV00002B/19

9 781363 047208